Black Girl Civics

A volume in
Adolescence and Education
Ben Kirshner, *Series Editor*

Black Girl Civics

Expanding and Navigating the Boundaries of Civic Engagement

edited by

Ginnie Logan
University of Colorado Boulder

Janiece Mackey
University of Denver

INFORMATION AGE PUBLISHING, INC.
Charlotte, NC • www.infoagepub.com

Library of Congress Cataloging-in-Publication Data

A CIP record for this book is available from the Library of Congress
http://www.loc.gov

ISBN: 978-1-64802-216-6 (Paperback)
       978-1-64802-217-3 (Hardcover)
       978-1-64802-218-0 (E-Book)

CONTENTS

SECTION 1
KINSHIP REFLECTIONS

SECTION 2
TOWARD EDUCATIONAL JUSTICE

SECTION 3
MEDIA INTERSECTIONS

FOREWORD

For a few decades now, government and scholars alike have been interested in how youth engage formally and informally in our nation's political affairs. Of course, some of this interest was innocent and at times not so innocent. Individuals and institutions, including government entities, concern themselves with the study of youth civic engagement for a variety of purposes, including to (a) learn how to entice the next generation into aligning with their particular political stance, (b) understand how to recruit youth into systemic and ethical democratic processes, and/or (c) how to control youth civic unrest, which for some political leaders is possibly the most dangerous and impactful form of a political threat to domestic politics.

Both scholars and governments have historically been interested in Black people's forms of civic engagement for all the reasons mentioned above. Historically, Black youth civic engagement is usually captured as forms of *resistance to oppression* as we see in stories about college-aged students and civil rights movement, the Black Panthers, school desegregation efforts, and the so-called "race riots" of 1967. More recently, scholars have been interested in not only studying historical patterns of Black youth political movements, but also contemporary forms of civic engagement. Yet, race-based agendas inside the academy tend to segregate a gender analysis in scholarly pursuits in efforts to capture a *Black political experience*, and sexism within racial justice community-born movements often render Black girls' forms of leadership and resistance strategies as background noise to larger racial justice narratives.

Black Girl Civics, pages vii–ix
Copyright © 2020 by Information Age Publishing
All rights of reproduction in any form reserved.

The editors of this groundbreaking volume, Ginnie Logan and Janiece Mackey, invite authors to (re)imagine civic engagement from an intersectional perspective. In *Black Girl Civics: Expanding and Navigating the Boundaries of Civic Engagement,* Black girl scholar-activists consider Black girls' civic identities in relation to their race, class, gender, and social locations. The editors offer readers a new understanding of Black girls' ways of navigating political, social, and physical spaces with their conceptualization of *Black Girl Civics.* By centering Black girls and young women in conversations on engaged citizenship from an intersectional perspective, scholars begin to better understand not only Black girls' understanding of themselves as social actors, their families' and communities' roles in fostering their agency, but also the strengths and limitations of U.S. democracy and notions of who or what is a "citizen." Thus, Black girl civics, as evidenced by the collective chapters in this book, offer a more inclusive and comprehensive interpretation of citizenship, civic engagement, girlhood, and youth activism as well as conceptualizations of the idea of civility itself.

Of course, attempts have been made to provide a working definition of youth civic engagement, which many others in this manuscript outline. However, here I will not regurgitate those standardized characterizations for in the midst of Black girl magic, #BlackLivesMatter, #StandWithBlack-Girls, and Black girls rock movements, we deserve our own working definitions that are culturally responsive and gender relevant. As articulated by Jean and McCalla (Chapter 9) in this volume, when contemplating how Black girls come to or perform civic engagement, we must consider "the historical and contemporary forces of oppression that work against Black girls, including but not limited to objectification, criminalization, and sexual violence" (p. 145). The authors presented in the text observe and analyze Black girls' civic performances from a Black feminist and critical race gender lens to put forth a more buoyant depiction of Black girlhood as dynamic and non-stoic.

Living at the intersections of race, class, and gender, in a world that privileges whiteness, wealth, and masculinity, Black girls' ways of *existing, resisting,* and *being in* service to each other and those around them calls for more nuanced and synchronous theoretical and methodological approaches to civic engagement research. BGC offers us a more granular and intersectional language to frame how Black girls engage their families, communities, and schools as social, cultural, and political actors. In this book, Hopes and Watson raises the question in Chapter 3, "What if to be civically engaged meant to be away from the white gaze?"

In response, I ask, "What if to be civically engaged means shifting our interrogations of Black girls' civic engagement away from the White gaze and Western, Eurocentric, elitist paternalistic interpretations of what is good for our communities?" Plainly stated, what might be considered civil or civically good for Black girls, the Black community in general, and other girls of color, especially those youth living and attending school in lower-income and working-class communities, may not always be politically aligned with those doing the investigating. Black girls' civic engagement is unique in that it is synchronously shaped by individuality and collectivism, vulnerability and agency, resilience and resistance, oppression, and (youthful) hope.

Moreover, Black girls' civic engagement is not born in a vacuum; it is born out of interconnectivity with other Black women/mothers and girls/daughters. As Curtis outlines in Chapter 4, BGC is grounded in cultural ethos, planned social action, and Black girls' kinship ties—at once, Black girls' political socialization is embodied and communal! The editors, themselves scholar-activists, have brought forth this text as a call for the co-construction of knowledge with and alongside Black girls and younger women. Throughout the book, readers begin to come closer to understanding the processes by which Black girls express their knowledge of oppression, and how they cultivate extemporaneously theories of freedom. *Black Girl Civics: Expanding and Navigating the Boundaries of Civic Engagement* is another art piece to be added to the mosaic for the writing and liberation of our daughters' bodies and spirits.

—Venus E. Evans-Winters

TOWARDS AN EMERGENT THEORY OF BLACK GIRL CIVICS

An Introduction

Figure I.1 8-year-old Mari Copeny holding a sign saying #Justice for Flint. *Source:* Jacobo, 2016.

> Hello my name is Mari Copeny and I'm 8 years old, I live in Flint, Michigan and I'm more commonly known around town as "Little Miss Flint." I am one of the children that is effected [*sic*] by this water, and I've been doing my best to march in protest and to speak out for all the kids that live here in Flint. (Copeny, as cited in Meyer, 2016, para. 3)

In 2016, Amariyanna "Mari" Copeny wrote a letter to President Barack Obama. She opens her letter by asserting a very particular identity. She tells the president that she is known as "Little Miss Flint," an identity that is connected to her age (little), her gender (miss), and her immediate context (Flint). Mari explains that she is one of the "children that is effected [*sic*] by this water." Her context is not neutral; "this water" is lead-poisoned. While Mari does not explicitly mention race or class in her letter, civil rights investigations have shown that "implicit bias and the history of systemic racism that was built into the foundation of Flint" produced the water crisis (Levengood, 2017, para. 6). The fact that Mari is affected by *this water* means that she is also affected by the racist and classist structures that resulted in poisoned water. So then, race and class become central components of her identity. Little Miss Flint serves as a moniker for an intersectional civic identity that captures Mari's age, her gender, her immediate context, and the nature of her oppression.

What does Little Miss Flint tell us about how African American girls engage in civics? How does Little Miss Flint fall into the long tradition of African American girls who share a legacy of struggle against interlocking structural failures that violate their humanity? We propose that a theoretically contextualized examination of Little Miss Flint can shed light on how some African American girls cultivate their citizen identity in dialectical relationship with their other social identities as they engage in civil society from an age-specific Black feminist standpoint and advance a social justice agenda through social media and other public platforms (Logan, 2018a). Little Miss Flint's story can serve as an introductory case study for an emergent theory of Black girl civics (and the broader goals of this volume).

What does it mean to be a civic actor who is Black, young, and female in the United States? Do African American girls take up the civic mantle in the same way that their male or non-Black peers do? What media, educational, or social platforms do Black girls leverage to gain access to the political arena, and why? How do Black girls negotiate civic identity within the context of their racialized, gendered, and age-specific identities? There are scholars doing powerful work on Black youth and civics, scholars focused on girls and civics, and scholars focused on Black girls in education. However, the intersections of African American girlhood and civics have not received adequate attention.

Black girl civics (BGC) is an emergent conceptual term that attempts to capture the varied, unique, and convergent ways in which African American girls and young women conceive of and express their civic identity as influenced by their race, gender, age, immediate context, and the nature of their oppression. BGC is meant to convey the experiences of African American girls as civic actors (Hyman & Levine, 2008) who utilize their intersectional identity as a point of entry for how they engage the civic landscape.

By African American, we are speaking specifically of the experiences of African-descended Americans who were born in the United States. Given the diasporic nature of African or Black people across the world, we choose to specify on African-descended U.S. born Americans because civic identity is inextricably linked with nationality and the specific history associated with that national identity. This analysis does not purport to simplify or flatten the complex and divergent experiences of African people living in the United States, but rather to hone in on a particular experience characterized by a specific historical context that informs a particular contemporary civic reality. For the sake of simplicity, we use the terms Black and African American interchangeably throughout the rest of this volume.

Theoretically, BGC draws on ideas from Ella Baker and John Dewey about democracy and rests on critical race feminist and age-aware epistemology that acknowledges the endemic nature of race, sex, and age discrimination in the U.S. context. This book begins the journey of understanding and communicating the varied forms of civics in the Black girl experience. *Black Girl Civics: Expanding and Navigating the Boundaries of Civic Engagement* brings together a range of works that grapple with the question of what it means for African American girls to engage in civic identity development and expression. Before we begin, however, let us frame this inquiry, and the volume overall, as an extension of our own lived experiences.

INTRODUCING THE EDITORS

Positionality allows one to ground oneself in how their respective identities influence and/or enhance their teaching, service, and research. This volume was conceived of and edited by two Black female scholars, Ginnie Logan and Janiece Mackey, who have put much of their life's work into enacting BGC. They are both social entrepreneurs who are executive directors and founders of nonprofit organizations working within the communities where they grew up.

Ginnie Logan identifies as a practitioner-activist-researcher who is committed to developing models of praxis that result in emancipatory outcomes for girls, youth of color, and practitioners committed to transformative education. Ginnie serves as the founder and executive director of a nonprofit organization called Big Hair, Bigger Dreams, a girls leadership and financial empowerment organization designed around the experiences of Black girls. Logan first began thinking about the ways that African American girls operate in the civic landscape as compared to males or non-Black youth, as an extension of her community based nonprofit work. However, once entering the academy and studying action civics under the tutelage of Ben Kirshner and other youth voice-focused scholars such as Shelley Zion and Carlos

Hipolito-Delgado, Logan observed that Black girls were often, in practice and in the literature, grouped with other youth of color, particularly as it related to advancing conversations about the centrality and critical importance of youth voice in policy discussions. While African American girls are both youth and of color, Logan's own lived experiences and community-based work lead her to believe that centering the specific narrative of Black girls could potentially lead to insights that otherwise might not be obvious when they are part of larger aggregate groups (Logan, 2017, 2018b).

Janiece Mackey identifies as a race scholar activist committed to racial justice and healing centered engagement (Ginwright, 2018) and sees the nexus of these as necessary ingredients for Black scholars, activists, critical conscious-preneurs, and praxticioners (Mackey, 2015). Janiece is the co-founder and executive director of Young Aspiring Americans for Social and Political Activism (YAASPA), which is purposed to cultivate youth of color in middle school through college to be civically engaged in community and career. Janeice's research and praxis have been grounded in the eclectic of racial identity theories and liberatory epistemologies. Her forthcoming dissertation honors the ways in which Black students navigate the discipline of political science.

As the authors within this book reveal the many ways Black girls and young women enact civics, the editors, have reflected on the ways we have operationalized BGC within our family, schooling, and community spaces. Navigating multiple ecosystems that have endeavored to delegitimize our own efforts to center Blackness and girlhood simultaneously, in this book and/or practitioner work, we desire to humanize, honor, and cherish the activism of Black girls and young women in this volume.

THEORETICAL FRAMING

BGC rests on John Dewey and Ella Baker's definition of democracy wherein all people participate. John Dewey (Boydston, 1980) wrote that democracy is not only a system of government, but also a system of "associated living," in which the "associated life is not a matter of physical juxtaposition, but of genuine intercourse . . . a non-metaphorical sense of community" (as quoted in Saltmarsh, 1996, p. 16). For Dewey, community was about collectivity; he believed that community "broadens the individuals' sense of self, connecting the 'I' to the 'we,' fostering the collective norm that one should forgo self-interest to work for the common good" (Saltmarsh, 1996, p. 16). Dewey's belief that community required interconnectedness and common good formed the foundations of his thinking about democracy. By using a Deweyan democratic frame, we can move past rigid definitions of democracy as limited by institutions of government, which are largely electoral-centered and elite-dominated (Nam, 2016). A Deweyan conception of democracy is participatory and makes room for the widest array of people to participate. This pivot to participatory politics is critical because electorally centered conceptions of democracy exclude large demographics of the American people.

Ella Baker used similar themes of participatory politics in her political organizing work. She practiced and taught a grassroots participatory conception of democracy, advancing the belief that people have the right to participate in their own governance. In fact, for Baker, political power rightfully belonged to the people, and unlike Dewey, she was most concerned with the people most excluded from political power (Mueller, 2004). Her goal was to make power accessible to *all people* (Ransby, 2003). Thus, a Deweyan and Bakerarn conception of democracy provides a far more expansive view of democratic or civic participation that stretches beyond mere voting. Consistent with this lens on participatory democracy, BGC asserts that Black girls are actively and iteratively defining their civic identities as they engage with participatory politics in relation to their everyday lives.

Centering the Black Girl Experience in Civic Expression

The lived experiences of African American girls are impacted by their social access to power and privilege, which is often mediated by their age, race, and gender. At times, their various identities create intersectional (Crenshaw, 1991) experiences, which in turn result in intersectional approaches to civic engagement. BGC, in the tradition of participatory politics, denotes civic choices that are expansive and constantly being negotiated. We acknowledge that racism, sexism, and age segregation are endemic to U.S. society, and therefore assert that civic identity is racialized, gendered, and influenced by the age and environment of the civic actor. Thus, we forsake notions of objectivity and neutrality in civic spaces (Mackey, 2017) as we think about how Black girls engage the civic landscape. Therefore, any analysis of how Black girls do civics, must start with Black girls at the center.

Critical Race Feminist Epistomology

To better understand the positionality that Black girls bring to their civic engagement, BGC is grounded in a critical race feminist epistemology and the work of Black women scholars such as Patricia Hill Collins, Kimberlé Crenshaw, Venus Evans-Winters, Gwendolyn Pough, and so many others. Critical race theory (CRT) feminism is currently the most useful lens for studying, analyzing, critiquing, and celebrating the experiences of African American girls (Evans-Winters & Espirito, 2010).

Within the tradition of CRT feminism, Kimberlé Crewnshaw discusses intersectionality as

> a lens through which you can see where power comes and collides, where it interlocks and intersects. It's not simply that there's a race problem here, a gender problem here, and a class or LBGTQ problem there. Many times [a singular] framework erases what happens to people who are subject to all of these things. (Crenshaw, 2017, n.p.)

When African American women and girls engage in the world, including the civic world, they are engaging from a position where "power comes and collides" because of their position at the nexus of many social locations. This notion of power coming and colliding illustrates the dialectical space in which Black girls and women exist. It is in these dialectical spaces where Black girls simultaneously negotiate the in-between spaces of privilege and disadvantage, of celebration and denigration.

So then, how does one make sense of the dialectical and sometimes contradictory spaces in which African American women and girls exist, particularly as it relates to issues of power? Here we use Patricia Hill Collins theory of Black womens' standpoint. According to Collins, Black women's standpoint is a self-reflexive sense making process and analytical lens that "encompasses theoretical interpretations of Black women's reality by those who live it" (Collins, 1990, p. 386). Therefore, to properly understand the Black woman's or Black girl's experience, we must use their standpoint as the analytical framework. Collins is clear to point out that African American women's experiences are not biologically determined; nor do all Black women have the same experiences. However, a core premise of Black feminist thought asserts that "all African-American women share the common experience of being Black women in a society that denigrates women of African descent" and the commonality of that particular experience does produce "characteristic themes [that] will be prominent in a Black women's standpoint" (Collins, 1990, p. 22). Black women's standpoint provides a useful analytic framework that allows Black women to interpret their lived experiences from their standpoint at the nexus of multiple identities, some of which are celebrated and others of which are denigrated.

Collins (n.d.) goes on to explain that Black women's standpoint overlaps with Black girls' standpoint. She says that "age offers little protection from this legacy of struggle" (para. 12) as she highlights examples of Black girls, who, like Black women, must negotiate experiences where they simultaneously experience racial and gendered oppression. In the same CRT tradition, Venus Evans-Winters, who authored the forward to this volume, utlizes Black feminist epistemologies to analyze the experiences of Black girls. In her book *Teaching Black Girls* (2005), Evans-Winters notes that Black girls develop negotiated identities that are "constructed vis-à-vis their race, class, and gender roles" (p. 174). Evans-Winters illustrates how, because of their intersectional personality and consequential standpoint or analytical frame, Black girls are able to create or engage in resistance behaviors through self-determining practices as they develop resilience to surmount adversity in the face of educational injustice. In short, Black girls, like their adult counterparts, bring a particular analytical frame that emerges as a consequence of their location at the intersection of multiple social locations. And when we read the actions of African American women and girls from a CRT feminist lens, particlarly using their own anatlytical framework, we can get a much clearer understanding of their dialectical negotiation of power.

Black Girlhood Studies

Black girlhood studies is an emerging field where African American women scholars are centralizing and building theories about Black girlhood (Brown, 2009, 2013; Evans-Winters, 2005, 2014; Evans-Winters & Esposito, 2010; Love, 2012). Nicole Ruth Brown (2013) explains that Black girlhood, when viewed as an organizing construct, "makes possible the affirmation of Black girls' lives and, if necessary, their liberation" (p. 1). Black girls' unique existence at the intersection of racism, classism, sexism, *and ageism* position them on an extreme margin and therefore their liberation becomes urgent. Black girlhood scholars argue that theorizing at the margins produces thinking that benefits the whole. In fact, Evans-Winters and Esposito (2010) say that "existence at the margins presents both constraints and possibilities for all educational reform efforts and overall societal transformation. Therefore, research with and on behalf of Black girls benefit the whole of society" (p. 22). In this way, Black girlhood can serve as a site of emancipation and liberation, not only for Black girls, but for others. BGC builds on the tradition of Black girlhood studies, wherein the theory building begins with the experiences of Black girls, as opposed to being rooted in epistemologies of White folks, males, or even Black women. In this way, BGC begins with a Black girl's standpoint and can serve as a site of liberation, not just for Black girls but also for the rest of us. Let us return to Little Miss Flint as an example.

LITTLE MISS FLINT AS CASE STUDY

Little Miss Flint's activism is not limited to the water crisis in Flint. She has leveraged her platform to discuss issues of police brutality and

#BlackLivesMatter; she affirms afro-centric artistic expression, as evidenced by her raising money to take hundreds of students to see *Black Panther* the movie; and she promotes celebratory cultural images of African American girlhood publicly (Espy, 2019; Klein, 2018). Water activism is just one of the varied ways in which Little Miss Flint does civic engagement.

Like her other forms of civic engagement, Little Miss Flint's response to the water crisis is informed by many of her social locations. When she recounts her experience meeting President Obama, her intersectional standpoint becomes obvious:

> [I told him] the water is still bad . . . We didn't get the money [to fix the pipes] approved until December. [We need] new pipes, but they don't care about Flint because some people here are poor and black. They don't care about any poor people that need some help. (Copeny, as cited in Javier, 2018, para. 5)

Mari was not speaking to President Obama devoid of her situated identity and without an analytical frame at play. Instead, she was bringing all of her experiences to bear as she negotiated power in that moment, with one of the most powerful men in the world.

Age Is a Critical Variable in Civics

While CRT feminism and Black women's standpoint theory enable us to center Mari's personhood and analytical frame, there are also limitations to the utility of these theories when applied to youth. The issue of age is often undertreated in Black feminists' analysis. Black feminist theory inequately addresses the issue of age and tends to wholesale transfer theories created around Black women on to the experiences of Black girls. An undertreatment of age has the potential to further marginalize the experiences of Black girls, particularly in the civic arena. When young people enter the civic landscape, age becomes a paramount influence on one's standpoint.

Historically, in the scientific study of youth development, G. Stanley Hall (1904) infamously launched a 100 year dominant narrative that youth was a period of "storm and stress," characterized by upheaval and tumult. Under this umbrella of deficit thinking, youth become a "special category of concern" wherein they were seen as empty vessels and highly susceptible to deviance if not carefully controlled through intervention (Kwon, 2013, p. 29). In the 1990s, a new paradigm of positive youth development emerged, wherein youth were not seen "as problems in need of fixing" by adults but rather as having strengths and potential for positive development, in partnership with adults (Ginwright & Cammarota, 2002; Kwon, 2013; Larson, 2006; Pittman & Flemming, 1991; Wyn & White, 1997). Black girl civics falls into this second tradition of viewing youth as having strengths and untapped potential. Let us use Little Miss Flint as an illuminating example of this asset-based conception of youth.

In her initial letter to the president, Mari informs Obama that she has been doing her best "to march in protest and to speak out." Shining a light on her commitment to "speak out for all the kids that live here in Flint," Mari tells the president that the water crisis is a social injustice, and she is using activism to resist. President Obama wrote back and said, "In America, there is no more important title than citizen. And I am so proud of you for using your voice to speak on behalf of the children of Flint" (Obama, as cited in Meyer, 2016, para. 4). There are several things happening in this exchange. First, Obama is recognizing Mari as an activist. In fact, he discursively stands in solidarity with her when later he says, "Like you I hope to use my voice." Secondly, Obama recognizes her as a "citizen." While Mari never used the word citizen in her letter, Obama's choice to honor Mari with *the most important title in America*, may speak to his sense that young people, even 8-year-olds, are not "future citizens," but rather are civic actors at any age. In normative discussions of civics, colloquially and sometimes in the academic literature, young people are often relegated to the status of pre-citizen or future citizen, because of their isolation from an age-restricted voting process. The future citizen concept tethers citizenship or civic involvement exclusively to voting as opposed to a system of associated living as Dewey had envisioned. But more importantly, this linking of civic access with voting access reifies a host of oppressive assumptions that negatively impact multiple marginalized demographics, such as those marked by felony records, undocumented immigrants, and young people. Therefore, the work of Ella Baker, pushed for a participatory democracy wherein the most marginalized also have access to political power. The uncritical treatment of youth as *future citizens* further consolidates the literal and symbolic privileges of citizenship with those who already maintain privilege in the civic landscape (Alexander, 2010; Flanagan & Levine, 2010; Hart & Atkins, 2002). So when Obama referred to Mari as a citizen, the most important title in America, he discursively challenged a dominant narrative that would have otherwise relegated Mari to the civic margins because of her age.

Lulu Brezzell, Mari's mother, says that Mari has a mind of her own. Brezzell explains that Mari saw "her sister covered in rashes [from the poisoned water]. She saw people getting sick and dying, and she said, 'What can I do to help?'" (Bauer, 2017, para. 10). Brezzell explains that Mari is "very outspoken. And it's like, yes, she's challenging all these people, but at the same time, she's at home challenging me" (Brezzell, as quoted in Ryan, 2019, para. 9). According to Brezzell, Mari not only operates from her own set of ideas but also challenges the thinking of adults in and outside of her home. In fact, when she was 11 years old, Mari publicly critiqued the ageism she experienced. In an interview with *Bright Light* she was asked about the most significant challenges to her activism. She responded "I'm an 11-year old...I am always told to stay in a child's place and to stay in my lane. Making adults realize I am serious is the biggest challenge" (Copeny & Komai, 2019, para. 8). We can see from her own words and the words of her mother that Mari is operating from her unique social location, not only as a person impacted by lead-poisoned water but also as a girl child, a person of color, and a person living amongst poor people. But of all of those social locations, she states that the biggest challenge she confronts is the one connected with her age. Mari says, her biggest challenge is dealing with people who believe she should stay in a child's place. If we use her own standpoint as an analytical frame for making sense of her experience, and by extension the experiences of other Black girls engaged in civics, age may be the biggest limitation to their efficacy and ability to negotiate power.

Ginwright and Cammarota (2002) expand on this conception of youth being well positioned to make sense of and resist their oppression because of their actual proximity to it. Their social justice positive youth development framework advances a premise that youth, particularly youth of color in urban communities, develop the capacity to be politically aware and resist their oppression when they are "subjected to political decisions and economic realities that impose significant constraints" on their lives (p. 87). Accordingly, once "young people see the connection between identity and power relationships, they develop a healthy self-awareness that recognizes how oppression and privilege mark their own struggles and the struggle of others" (p. 89). In this way, Little Miss Flint, as her mother claims, saw what was happening in her home, in her larger community, and in turn developed a critical sense of awareness. In fact, she developed a public civic profile, as Little Miss Flint, by which she continues to advance good work that is mediated by her sense of the world.

By recognizing Little Miss Flint with the title of citizen, Obama not only sets aside ageist notions that marginalize young people's role in civil matters, he also discursively embraced the type of civic engagement she herself has embraced, a civic engagement built on activism and a commitment to justice. Obama says that he is proud of Mari's activism, "I am so proud of you for using your voice to speak on behalf of the children of Flint," but also says, "Like you, I'll use my voice to call for change" (Obama, as cited in Meyer, 2016, para. 5). Therefore, Obama has not only acknowledged Mari's activism (her marching, protesting, and her advancing change) as a form of civic engagement, but also stood in solidarity with her activist civic expression by saying that he too is using his voice to call for change. This seamless discursive interplay between activism, civics, citizenship, and youth is pushing against normative expressions of civics that often relegated youth and activism to the non-civic space.

Why Civics?

If many African American girls, like Mari, engage in activism as their primary form of civic participation, why not have a book called *Black Girl Activist*? Why do we use the term *civics*? In using the word civics, we mean to capture the wide range of meaning making, activities, and forms of participation, where young people speak up and try to influence public discourse or policy, which may include but may not be limited to activism. Black girl civics as a theoretical frame seeks to create room for the myriad of ways that Black girls engage in the public square. As an example of Black girls engaging in diverse forms of civics is 9-year-old Zianna Oliphant who observed a fatal police shooting in North Carolina and made an emotional plea at her city council (Levin, 2016). Another example is Marely Dias, who founded #1000BlackGirlsBooks at age 11 and was featured in Forbes 30 under 30 by age 15. Marley Dias used social innovation and business to address what she felt like was an under-representation of Black girls in youth literature. Another example is when several high school girls enrolled in a Big Hair, Bigger Dreams summer program, collectively volunteered over 60 hours at their local Salvation Army to prepare and serve food, clean the facilities, and organize the clothing bank, so that transient community members could enjoy hot meals, adequate clothing, and clean facilities. A final example occurred when Black girl participants in YAASPA successfully co-hosted a press conference and advocated for 3 years to pass policy via the Regional Transportation District (RTD). They were able to push the RTD Board to vote yes for the Youth Pass program which allowed for a 70% discount to youth riders. In this way, BGC is not limited to activism; it encompasses the many ways in which African American girls enact civics in their daily lives from advancing policy, petitioning city councils, engaging in community service, and innovating enterprising political solutions to social and economic problems.

We know that African American girls move beyond normative expressions of civics, such as voting, to engage in a spectrum of civic and political activity that may include community organizing, engaging political leaders, volunteering, civil disobedience, digital activism, and more (Allen & Light, 2015; Ginwright, 2007; Ginwright & James, 2002; Kirshner, 2015; Logan, Lightfoot, & Contreras, 2017; Westheimer & Kahne, 2004; Youniss & Hart, 2005; Zuckerman, 2014). While these forms of civic engagement are not limited to African American girls exclusively, they help us to understand that Black girls, and many youth of color, tend to move beyond the false dichotomy of the civics and activism binary, and therefore in naming this book *Black Girl Civics*, rather than *Black Girl Activism*, we too are honoring the nuance, complexity, and boundary-pushing ways that Black girls show up in civic spaces.

When we analyze Little Miss Flint as a civic identity, as opposed to limiting it to exclusively an activist identity, we learn that Black girls use a variety of platforms and tactics including social media, protests, marches, dialogging with the president, and artistic expression to advance a better world, not just for themselves but their families, communities, and arguably their nation. We need not simply rely on Little Miss Flint as an example of this emergent concept of BGC; we can also turn to other African American girls, such as Yara Sayeh Shahidi (actress and activist), Chanice Lee (blogger and author of *Young Revolutionary: A Teen's Guide to Activism*), and Niaomi Alder (Mari's best friend and sister in activism) as a few more examples of how Black girls engage in civic practice. BGC begins the work of creating a framework for understanding how African American girls assert their citizen identity and expression in all of its forms. The chapters in this volume continue the work of careful examination of particular case studies, contexts, and phenomenon.

INTRODUCING THE CHAPTERS

Black Girl Civics: Expanding and Navigating the Boundaries of Civic Engagement brings together a range of works that grapple with the question of what it means for African American girls to engage in civic identity development and expression. The chapters collected within this volume openly grapple with and negotiate the ways in which Black girls engage with and navigate the spectrum of civics. This collection of 11 chapters features a range of research from ethnography to empirical inquiry.

Just as we have stated in our positionality framing, we asked authors to do the same within their chapters. We desired to push on the notion that authors should be separate from or have distance from their research. The book is broken into three sections. The first section is titled "Kinship Reflections." We begin the book grounded in the notion of kinship to honor lived experience and ways of being centered in family-oriented ways of knowing. Centering Blackness in kinship, albeit in one's home or even in a classroom, is a depiction of a civic ethos that is often overlooked and invisibilized. The second section, titled "Toward Educational Justice," emphasizes education. In order to problematize a normative lens of education as solely grounded in schooling, we include community organizing as part of this section to push on the ways we have been socialized to digest schooling as the epitome of education. Miseducation is a major component of schooling and thus an intense amount of unlearning is necessary to be rooted in Blackness at the intersections of class and gender. This section includes representations of women who position themselves intentionally in their identities as a model and bridge to Black women and femmes who are seeking to actualize their own formation of BGC. The third section is titled "Media Intersections." The final section grapples with the ways in which Black girls and women are portrayed and displayed in media. Rather than taking a deficit approach or a lens that centers solely on pain, the chapters in this section demonstrate joy and reclamation through the agency of Black girls and women. #Blackgirlmagic is a hue that is honored and further unveils the versatile ways in which BCG is operationalized.

Section 1: Kinship Reflections

In Chapter 1, Kel Hughes demonstrates the sense of moral obligation Black women carry and embody through *other mothering*. She honors the ethic of care that a family of eight imbues as a beautiful daily endeavor through this lens of other mothering. In Chapter 2, Celicia Bell and Jasmine Clayton, a mother and daughter pair, engage in a self-reflective autoethnographic tale of their emergent civic sensibilities. Bell and Clayton weave together their experiences to illustrate their growing sociocritical civic literacy. In Chapter 3, Jeanelle Hope and Vayra Watson reveals the promise of an elective course taught by Black women. Hope and Watson reject normative notions of civics and illustrate the criticality of sisterhood and what they coin as *hood civics,* which centers the ways Black girls create a narrative of their own lives rooted in their experiences. Lastly, Sabrina Curtis extends the conversation in the book concerning the nexus of pedagogy and civics through a public health social action center as her case study. She endeavors to better understand the ways Black girls make meaning of their experiences in the center and found the girls were able to put together social analyses rooted through a racial and gendered lens.

Section 2: Toward Educational Justice

Chapter 5 shifts the dialogue of the book toward education. Charlotte Jacobs walks readers through how Black adolescent girls navigate a predominantly White elite schooling experience. Rather than centering her chapter on Whiteness, she focused on BGC. She highlights th ways student voice was operationalized and how students leveraged their lived experiences in classroom spaces. The agency of Black girls and women are further discussed in Chapter 6 through the lens of #Blackgirlmagic, by Alaina Neal-Jackson. The hashtag is discussed due to the perceptions of what it manifests in the gaze of folks outside the Black female community, but is then tied back to the actions and ways it is utilized by Black girls and women on a daily basis in post-secondary education. Chapter 7 maintains the lens of activism discussed by Tracie Lowe, but takes readers to a higher education school space. Lowe partners with Black women graduate students to learn the ways in which they define activism, how they came into their activism, and how they testify to the ever present need for more structures within higher education to be dedicated to Black women. Lastly, Chapter 8 wraps this section up in a community setting that is pushing for an educational paradigm shift for education and reproductive justice led by youth. Julia Daniel and Annie Thomas discuss the power of participatory action research with Black femmes at the center of leadership development and action. The authors immersed themselves as co-creators of participatory action research study, which entails 4 years of data collection efforts that further highlights the agency and civic abilities of Black femme youth.

Section Three: Media Intersections

The final section takes the book into the realm of media literacy as a form of BGC. Chapter 9 reveals media analyses of Black girls under 18 years of age engaged in civics. With a focus on Solange's album, Cassandra Jean and Dana McCalla highlight four Black girls through speeches, interviews, and community experiences through the thematic messages embedded within Solange's album. Acts that may often be dismissed were honored as ways Black girls contribute to our communities consistently. Chapter 10 acknowledges the power dynamics at play that Black girl activists encounter as they share their stories and perceptions of current events. Cierra Kaler-Jones and Autumn Griffin highlight nontraditional news sources for their data collection to honor and make visible the activism of Black girl activists. The use of sources like *The Root* along with social media are utilized to offer a *clapback* against those who try to delegitimize the activism of Black girls. Lastly, Chapter 11 magnifies the ways in which Black girls and women exhibit prowess through a national study concerning media representation of Black girls and women. Tierra Tanksley humanizes Black women as leaders in activism particularly in social media spaces. She closes the book out with a notion that Black women know how to use their versatility to be an activist, renew a sense of trust concerning the media, and provide a collective space for healing and solidarity.

As the chapter that follow continue the conversation about the myriad of ways Black girls and young women express civics, we hope that this volume begins the conversation of pushing and pulling, dialectically engaging, and seeking to understand from a Black girl's standpoint what it means to be a civic actor who is Black, young, and female in the United States. By honing in on the experiences of Black girl's civic experience and expression, we believe that there will be lessons of liberation and redemption, not just for Black girls but also for the rest of us.

In Solidarity,
Ginnie Logan and **Janiece Mackey**

REFERENCES

Alexander, M. (2010). *The new Jim Crow: Mass incarceration in the age of colorblindness.* New York, NY: New Press.

Allen, D. S., & Light, J. S. (2015). *From voice to influence: Understanding citizenship in a digital age.* Chicago, IL: The University of Chicago Press.

Bauer, M. R. (2017, March 15). *This nine-year-old is still fighting for clean water in Flint, USA.* Retrieved from https://www.vice.com/en_nz/article/jpnvjb/this-nine-year-old-is-still-fighting-for-clean-water-in-flint-usa

Boydston, J. A. (1980). *John Dewey: Democracy and education (1916).* Carbondale: Southern Illinois University.

Brown, R. N. (2009). *Black girlhood celebration: Toward a hip-hop feminist pedagogy* (Vol. 5). Bern, Switzerland: Peter Lang.

Brown, R. N. (2013). *Hear our truths: The creative potential of Black girlhood.* Champaign: University of Illinois Press.

Collins, P. H. (n.d.). *Defining Black feminist thought.* Retrieved from http://www.feministezine.com/feminist/modern/Defining-Black-Feminist-Thought.html

Collins, P. H. (2002). *Black feminist thought: Knowledge, consciousness, and the politics of empowerment.* Abingdon, England: Routledge.

Copeny, M., & Komai, A. (2019, March 11). *"Little Miss Flint" Mari Copeny.* Retrieved from https://brightlitemag.com/2019/03/little-miss-flint-mari-copeny/

Crenshaw, K. (1991). Mapping the margins: Intersectionality, identity politics, and violence against women of color. *Stanford Law Review, 43*(6), 1241–1299. https://www.doi.org/10.2307/1229039

Crenshaw, K. (2017, June 8). *Kimberlé Crenshaw on intersectionality, more than two decades later.* Retrieved from https://www.law.columbia.edu/pt-br/news/2017/06/kimberle-crenshaw-intersectionality

Espy, J. (2019, December 25). *As Little Miss Flint, Amariyanna 'Mari' Copeny continues to shine a light on the water crisis.* Retrieved from https://www.metrotimes.com/detroit/as-little-miss-flint-amariyanna-mari-copeny-continues-to-shine-a-light-on-the-water-crisis/Content?oid=23423416

Evans-Winters, V. E. (2005). *Teaching Black girls: Resiliency in urban classrooms* (Vol. 279). Bern, Switzerland: Peter Lang.

Evans-Winters, V. E. (2014). Are Black girls not gifted? Race, gender, and resilience. *Interdisciplinary Journal of Teaching and Learning, 4*(1), 22–30.

Evans-Winters, V. E., & Esposito, J. (2010). Other people's daughters: Critical race feminism and Black girls' education. *Educational Foundations, 24*(1–2), 11–24.

Flanagan, C., & Levine, P. (2010). Civic engagement and the transition to adulthood. *The Future of Children, 20*(1), 159–179.

Ginwright, S. A. (2018). *The future of healing: Shifting from trauma informed care to healing centered engagement.* Retrieved from https://medium.com/@ginwright/the-future-of-healing-shifting-from-trauma-informed-care-to-healing-centered-engagement-634f557ce69c

Ginwright, S., & Cammarota, J. (2002). New terrain in youth development: The promise of a social justice approach. *Social Justice, 29*(4), 82–95.

Ginwright, S., & James, T. (2002). From assets to agents of change: Social justice, organizing, and youth development. *New Directions for Youth Development, 2002*(96), 27–46.

Hall, G. S. (1904). *Adolescence: Its psychology and its relations to physiology, anthropology, sociology, sex, crime, religion, and education.* New York, NY: D. Appleton. https://doi.org/10.1176/ajp.61.2.375

Hart, D., & Atkins, R. (2002). Civic development in urban youth. *Applied Developmental Science, 6*(4), 227–236.

Hyman, J. B., & Levine, P. (2008). Civic engagement and the disadvantaged: Challenges, opportunities and recommendations (CIRCLE Working Paper #63). Medford, MA: Center for Information and Research on Civic Learning and Engagement.

Jacobo, J. (2016). *President Obama to meet with "Little Miss Flint" before he addresses water crisis.* Retrieved from https://abcnews.go.com/US/miss-flint-meet-obama-addresses-water-crisis/story?id=38851663.PhotobyJakeMay/TheFlintJournal-MLive.com via AP.

Javier, C. (2018, July 9). *'They don't care about any poor people': Little Miss Flint talks about her city's water crisis.* Retrieved from https://splinternews.com/they-dont-care-about-any-poor-people-little-miss-flint-1793742165

Kirshner, B. (2015). *Youth activism in an era of education inequality.* New York, NY: New York University Press.

Klein, A. (2018, February 20). *10-year-old 'Little Miss Flint' helped hundreds of underprivileged kids see 'Black Panther' over the weekend.* Retrieved from https://www.washingtonpost.com/news/inspired-life/wp/2018/02/20/10-year-old-little-miss-flint-helped-hundreds-of-underprivileged-kids-see-black-panther-over-the-weekend/

Kwon, S. A. (2013). *Uncivil youth: Race, activism, and affirmative governmentality.* Durham, NC: Duke University Press.

Larson, R. (2006). Positive youth development, willful adolescents, and mentoring. *Journal of Community Psychology, 34*(6), 677–689.

Levengood, V. (2017, February 17). *Michigan civil rights commission report: Race and racism played roles in causing the Flint Water Crisis, and both Blacks and Whites are victims.* Retrieved from https://www.michigan.gov/mdcr/0,4613,7-138—405318—,00.html

Levin, S. (2016, September 27). 'We shouldn't have to feel like this': Girl, nine, gives tearful speech in Charlotte. *The Guardian.* Retrieved from www.theguardian.com/us-news/2016/sep/27/keith-scott-killing-charlotte-little-girl-speech-viral

Logan, G. (2017, October). *Black girls can fly.* Poster presentation at the Learning Sciences Graduate Student Conference, Bloomington, IN.

Logan, G. (2018a, May). *Towards an emergent theory of Black girl civics.* Short paper presented at the Next Generation Leadership, Pretoria, South Africa.

Logan, G. (2018b, June). Towards radical healing praxis for Black girls: Imagining learning environments that foster the sociopolitical learning of adolescent Black girls. In J. Kay & R. Luckin (Eds.), *Rethinking learning in the digital age: Making the learning sciences count,* 13th international conference of the learning sciences (Vol. 2). London, England: International Society of the Learning Sciences.

Logan, G., Lightfoot, B. A., & Contreras, A. (2017). Black and Brown millennial activism on a PWI campus in the era of Trump. *The Journal of Negro Education, 86*(3), 252–268.

Love, B. L. (2012). *Hip hop's li'l sistas speak: Negotiating hip hop identities and politics in the new South.* New York, NY: Peter Lang.

Mackey, J. Z. (2015). *Counter-stories of my social science academic and career development from a critical "praxticioner" and "conscious-preneur": Through the lens of critical race theory and the "sociological imagination."* Retrieved from ProQuest Dissertations & Theses Global. (1598301)

Mackey, J. (2017). Forsaking neutrality in political science: Making the case to intellectually assassinate. *Curriculum and Teaching Dialogue, 19*(1/2), 35–170.

Meyer, K. (2016, April 27). *Asked and answered: President Obama responds to an eight-year-old girl from Flint.* Retrieved from https://obamawhitehouse.archives .gov/blog/2016/04/27/asked-and-answered-president-obama-responds-eight -year-old-girl-flint

Mueller, C. (2004). Ella Baker and the origins of "participatory democracy." In J. Bobo, C. Hudley, & C. Michel (Eds.), *The Black studies reader* (pp. 79–90). New York, NY: Routledge.

Nam, C. (2016, June 23). What is participatory politics? Retrieved from https:// yppactionframe.fas.harvard.edu/blog/what-participatory-politics-0

Pittman, K. J., & Fleming, W. E. (1991). *A new vision: Promoting youth development: Testimony of Karen J. Pittman before the house select committee on children, youth, and families.* Washington, DC: Academy for Educational Development.

Ransby, B. (2003). *Ella Baker and the Black freedom movement: A radical democratic vision.* Chapel Hill: University of North Carolina Press.

Ryan, L. (2019, August 6). *How a 12-year-old is single-handedly taking on the water crisis in Flint, Michigan.* Retrieved from https://www.parents.com/news/little -miss-flint/

Saltmarsh, J. (1996). Education for critical citizenship: John Dewey's contribution to the pedagogy of community service learning. *Michigan Journal of Community Service Learning, 3*(1), 13–21.

Westheimer, J., & Kahne, J. (2004). What kind of citizen? The politics of educating for democracy. *American Educational Research Journal, 41*(2), 237–269. https:// doi.org/10.3102/00028312041002237

Wyn, J., & White, R. (1997). The concept of youth. In *Rethinking youth* (pp. 8–26). London, England: SAGE.

Youniss, J., & Hart, D. (2005). Intersection of social institutions with civic development. *New Directions for Child and Adolescent Development, 2005*(109), 73–81. https://doi.org/10.1002/cd.139

Zuckerman, E. (2014). New media, new civics? *Policy & Internet, 6*(2), 151–168. https://doi.org/10.1002/1944-2866.POI360

SECTION 1

KINSHIP REFLECTIONS

CHAPTER 1

GENERATION TO GENERATION

Learning to Othermother

Kel Hughes Jones
University of Michigan–Dearborn

After fellowshipping at my mom's church one Sunday, I stopped by a local grocery store to pick up a few items. While I currently reside on my own in a multicultural suburb, I enjoy visiting my parents' neighborhood (where I grew up), which is a thriving middle-class Black suburb. When my family first moved there, we were one of the few Black families in the city, as the population was primarily Jewish and Chaldean (Iraqi Christian). However, before I graduated high school, White flight took place and the town became majority Black. Thankfully, the school district adapted to meet the needs of the changing demographic. As more Black students came into the school system, we slowly saw more educators of color in our buildings. The curriculum evolved as well, becoming culturally relevant.

That Sunday, as I was pushing my cart through the store, I saw a familiar face talking with others by the meat section. As I drew closer, I saw the face looked a little older, and the hair slightly grayer, but the voice was still the same.

Black Girl Civics, pages 3–18

It was the first Black teacher I ever encountered (aside from family), Mrs. Jefferson, who taught in my elementary school and was also my childhood Girl Scout troop leader, along with my mother. I chased her down, gave her a big hug and began chatting. Years had passed by, yet she still remembered details about my life. She gave me words of encouragement, asked about my friends from grade school, and let me know she was proud of me. I watched her make her way through the grocery store and noticed she could only go so far without another former student, parent or community member speaking to her.

This encounter with Mrs. Jefferson constantly comes to mind as I think about educators who employ care in the classroom, specifically Black female teachers who *othermother*. Furthermore, it causes me to reflect on my own practice, as a Black female educator who has been teaching for 11 years in a multicultural school district, and to see myself transitioning into the space of an othermother. Care work is often gendered; it is assumed women are innate caregivers, particularly as mothers. Examining care and othermothering through a Black feminist lens, the purpose of this study is to understand how Black women learn to othermother by asking, "How is othermothering taught?" and "How do Black girls learn to othermother?"

REMEMBERING MY PAST: UNDERSTANDING MY ROOTS

Mrs. Jefferson may have been the first othermother whom I experienced at my school, but I can think of many other Black women in my life who have held the honor. For decades, my great-aunt has taken in students from the local university, giving them spiritual guidance, love, and a good meal. She has one biological son, but many affectionately call her "Ma." On my dad's side of the family, my aunt, a teacher-turned-principal in a major urban school district, cared for the physical and emotional well-being of her students, and created a familial school culture. Her caring drove her to adopt one of her students, as a means to best support him. My late maternal grandmother raised three of her grandchildren after raising three daughters, and served as an elementary school crossing guard and Vacation Bible School director at her local church. She was so well-known in the community that even after her death, a funeral home employee jokingly recollected on how my grandmother used to "whoop" him in the church basement as a young boy, as though he were her own son. In examining how these women cared, I pull from a Black feminist framework.

Black Feminist Thought and Care

The women in my family, along with Mrs. Jefferson, went above and beyond to provide social, emotional, and intellectual support to children as a form of care. The act of caring is a moral obligation (Gilligan, 1982), where individuals transcend individual feelings to respond to the needs of others (Noddings, 2003, 2010), regardless of gender. This transcendent care is also referred to as an active virtue (Noddings, 2003, 2010), an ethic shown through ideals, or memories that trigger actions (Bass, 2009; Noddings, 2003, 2010). In order to virtuously care, one must push past feelings into what Bass (2009, 2012) describes as corrective action.

However, when understanding how Black women care as othermothers, and how Black girls learn this skill, a multiple-identity framework must be applied. Black women and girls have multiple intersecting identities (Cooper, 2017; Crenshaw, 1989; hooks, 1994) impacting how care is displayed, taught, and learned. Therefore, Collins' (2000) Black feminist thought (BFT) will be explored in conjunction with the ethic of care, providing a foundation for Black feminist care (Bass, 2012), with a focus on othermothering.

Black Feminist Thought

BFT provides a space for Black female voices to be heard, which has historically occurred as Black women have taught, led, and uplifted the race through agency (Lindsay-Dennis, 2015). BFT deals specifically with the unique experiences of Black women in the United States (Collins, 2000; Lindsay-Dennis, 2015) and their ability to be activists. Black women involved in social justice from a BFT perspective recognize that our struggles are part of a larger movement for equity, empowerment, and justice for all humans (Collins, 2000).

The Black woman as an advocate for social justice reminds me of another example of an othermother in my family, my late great-grandmother, who was a school bus driver in her community, active in her church, and civically engaged. As a small girl, I remember sitting at her feet as she told a story about attending a city meeting to protest a policeman's wrongful, fatal shooting of an unarmed, special needs, young Latino male. During this public hearing, townspeople had two minutes to speak, signified by a bell. When it was her turn, my great-grandmother, who was short in stature, but made up for her height with her thunderous voice, approached the podium with confidence, proclaiming, "Don't ring that bell for me!" Her positionality granted respect from the council members, who retired the bell as she spoke. She would tell this story many times over the years, and it was my own personal example of community activism.

Black Feminist Care

These tenets of Black feminism—social activism, uniquely lived experiences, and multidimensionality, in conjunction with the ethic of care and personal accountability (Lindsay-Dennis, 2015), create Black feminist care

(BFC). Bass (2012) writes that BFC "frames an ethic of care within [BFT] as a foundation of Black women's epistemology that combines history, culture, and experiences with individual uniqueness, expressiveness, emotion and empathy" (p. 77). BFC places the unique experiences of Black women at the center of care ethics (Bass, 2012), creating a multidimensional framework. There are various aspects to BFC; however, for the purpose of this case study, the focus will be on othermothering.

Othermothering.   Through fictive kinship (Collins, 2000; Fordham, 1996; James, 1993), othermothers use their wisdom and stature to extend care to Black youth. Othermothers have the ability to reach young people in a way their biological mothers may not be able, providing wisdom, insight, safety, mentoring, and counsel (Lindsay-Dennis, Cummings, & McClendon, 2011). Additionally, othermothering liberates the Black woman and allows her to work as an activist, both in the community and abroad (Collins, 2000), much like in the example of my great-grandmother.

Typically, othermothering is a cultivated skill, passed through generations (Case, 1997). At younger ages, this nurturing ability is viewed more as a "sister friend" than an othermother; the woman does not yet have enough community stature, in regards to influence and tenure (Case, 1997; Collins, 2015; Lindsay-Dennis, et al., 2011). However, according to the literature, after the age of 40, the woman has matured and been in the community long enough to gain respect and begins to work on behalf of others (Case, 1997). I believe it is imperative to examine length of service and age together, because they create balance and multidimensionality for who an othermother may be. For instance, some othermothers may be in their late thirties but have served in the community for a significant amount of time, thus gaining stature. Additionally, some othermothers may be new to a community, but gain respect because of their age and commitment to service.

Historical perspective of othermothering.   While the ethic of care stresses a moral responsibility to care for others (Gilligan, 1982), African ethics focuses on the interdependence of God, community, family, and individuals (Paris, 1995). Morals and virtues are embodied by individual people, yet it is the responsibility of the entire family and community to cultivate these values in others (Paris, 1995). This interdependence cultivates communalism amongst African peoples, including the shared mothering of children. Historically, West African women who were part of polygynous households often shared nurturing responsibilities for children outside of their own individual biological offspring (Collins, 2015; James, 1993). In the Gold Coast, women were expected to marry, reproduce, and care for children while simultaneously being economically active by means of fishing or working the family farm (James, 1993). Taking care of other's children by women within the community-at-large was an honored tradition that promoted communalism and provided relief (Collins, 2015; James, 1993).

As West African people were enslaved, family patterns became disrupted. Africans were exposed to the gender ideologies of slaveholders, where women cared for the home as men worked (Collins, 2015). However, the demands of slavery made it impossible for women to solely nurture while men provided (Collins, 2015). As slaves, Black women continued this trend of caring for children while being responsible for household chores within the slave quarters (James, 1993). Enslaved families often experienced high amounts of instability, as male partners were often sold (Case, 1997; Guiffrida, 2005; James, 1993). Shared care of children was vital during slavery as families were split up and child-rearing extended beyond bloodlines; orphaned children would become the responsibility of other women within the slave quarters (Case, 1997; Collins 2015; Guiffrida, 2005; James, 1993). After slavery, most women became agricultural workers for low pay. Black women worked as farm sharecroppers, and children became cared for by other women in the community (Collins, 2015).

Othermothing in schools. As slavery ended and segregated schools emerged, the role of the othermother eventually included the classroom teacher (Foster, 1993; Guiffrida, 2005). Nowadays, classroom othermothers hold high expectations for students and create a warm atmosphere for learning (Case, 1997). They use their positions as teachers to work to shift hegemonic systems to prepare children for life (Thompson, 2004). As othermothers, educators show care to students by treating them as if they were their biological children. While I encountered this through Mrs. Jefferson in my youth, the greatest example of a classroom othermother could be found in my own home growing up, through my mother, who is now a retired adult and alternative education teacher.

My favorite time of day as a child was when my mom would come home from work and recap the day's events. My father was always reserved about discussing his work as a mechanical engineer, but I think my mother found it therapeutic to share daily teaching highlights. Her stories fascinated me—she would talk about ways staff members used music to motivate students and challenges students had with the legal system as they tried to further their education. The majority of her students were Black and needed a second chance to complete their high school education. Each year, she talked about students as though they were members of our family. I would listen as she would tell stories of helping students get lunch if they could not afford it, building rapport with their parents in the parking lot, and occasionally providing transportation for those who needed it, especially in the winter, as many students relied on a delayed city bus system. Most importantly, I watched former students come up to her in public and thank her for impacting their lives. She would quietly respond by stating how proud she was of them. My mother's life and career heavily influenced me, along with other Black women in my sphere who were displaying Black feminist care through othermothering.

LIVING IN THE PRESENT:
LEARNING FROM MY SURROUNDINGS

Through a series of twists and turns, I became a classroom teacher. Originally, I was a school librarian for 2 years, but due to a recession, budget cuts, and school closures, I found myself in the classroom as an ESL and science teacher, where I have been ever since. I knew I wanted to obtain my master's in library and information science degree even before graduating high school. My parents encouraged me to get a Bachelor of Science degree in elementary education and English as a second language so I could have something to fall back on, and I am glad I heeded their advice. The first and only district I have worked for is a multicultural suburb, where I also reside, with nearly 80 languages spoken by students. Although our student population is diverse, our teaching staff is not. I am one of a few Black teachers in the district and have now been employed for over a decade. Through the years, I have advocated for equity and inclusion in our district, and developed relationships with many Black families. Now in my mid-30s, when I reflect over my career, I often think of how I am moving out of the sister friend space and becoming an othermother, especially as I have established myself as an educator in my community and advocated for Black children and families, thus gaining influence and respect. In exploring how Black girls learn to othermother, I must examine my own lived experience as well. Therefore, phenomenology is the chosen methodology, and I position myself in writing through self-reflexivity.

Methodology and Methods

The phenomenological approach allows for reflection on the life and work of the othermother and creates a space for me as a researcher to intertwine my reflections, experiences, and beliefs (Groenewald, 2004; van Manen, 2016). Specifically, I will focus on utilizing hermeneutical phenomenology, which is focused on lived experiences and interpreting life (Creswell, 2013; van Manen, 2016). Furthermore, phenomenology will allow me to understand the essence of othermothering and the experience of learning to othermother. I have personally benefited from othermothering and see myself stepping into that role in my community. As I reflect introspectively upon the data and make connections to the phenomenon of othermothering, I will write with self-reflexivity, by being conscious of my biases and experiences as a Black female researcher, and discuss my positionality throughout this chapter (Creswell, 2013). This methodology will allow me to analyze the data, using my positionality as a strength.

Site Selection and Subject Identification

After compiling background research on othermothering, it was determined the Parker family (pseudonym) was ideal for the case study. A Black family of eight, the Parkers were selected from an urban homeschooling co-op. They were chosen because their oldest child was a female adolescent, the wide range of ages amongst their children, and the mother's age, stature and roots extending beyond the homeschool community. At the time of the study, the mother and father (referred to as Monique and Jerome) were 40 and 42 years old, respectively, and had been married for 14 years. The six children, all single births, are spaced roughly two years apart each, as shown in Table 1.1.

I have known Abigail since she was a baby, and I felt she would feel comfortable with being a participant in the study. I also felt my relationship with the family would create easy access and serve as a strength in the study. Because of my relationship, I knew Monique and Jerome had also trained their oldest daughter, Abigail, to take on more responsibilities because of her birth order position, which made me curious about how she was learning to care.

Over the years, Monique has taken extended family members, women from her church, and others from the community into her home to mentor. She has counseled many young women and believes those who are older should give back to those who are younger. Monique is looked up to as a sister and othermother by many in her community. The care and leadership she has extended to other Black women in her network throughout the years reaches beyond her bloodline.

Nearly a decade ago, Monique and Jerome became disgruntled with the public school system after enrolling their eldest daughter. They decided Monique would quit her corporate job, stay home, and educate their

TABLE 1.1 The Parker Children		
Name	Age (Years)	Gender
Abigail	12¾	Female
Benjamin	11	Male
Caleb	9	Male
Deborah	7	Female
Ezekiel	5	Male
Gideon	3	Male

Note: This figure assembles the names, ages, and genders of the Parker children.

children. She was one of the first in her "village" of friends and family to homeschool and paved the way for many other Black families. Women who are new to homeschooling often ask Monique for advice. Monique also started a homeschooling network (called a co-op), comprised of other families in the inner-city and collaborates with those in the group to create educational opportunities for their children.

Ethical Considerations

To remain ethical, subjects had their anonymity protected through the use of pseudonyms. They were also ensured of informed consent prior to interviews. My proximity to the family and identity as a Black female helped to strengthen the study because of my emic perspective. Groenewald (2004) explains, in phenomenology, "The researcher cannot be detached from his/her own presuppositions and that the researcher should not pretend otherwise" (p. 7). Therefore, my insider status was a strength to better understand and interpret the culture and phenomenon. I remained insightful and reflective through the process in order to convey the richness of the object at hand, othermothering (Creswell, 2013; van Manen, 2016). Before beginning research, the study received approval of the university review board. This required submitting an online proposal, which also checked for objectivity and subjectivity. Upon approval, the study commenced.

Data Collection

The study was conducted over the span of 13 weeks in four different locations. The first three interactions were observations, and the fourth was a joint interview with Monique and Abigail. Each session was approximately one hour long, described in more detail in Table 1.2.

During the first three sessions, I served solely as an observer. The family knew I was present and conducting a study. If necessary, I asked Monique or Jerome to fill me in about the setting or interactions between the homeschooling children. Notes were recorded during the sessions, via my smartphone and then transferred to my computer afterwards. Anecdotal information and reflections were recorded within 24 hours of the session. A

TABLE 1.2 Sessions and Interactions	
Session	Interaction
1	Observation at music recital for children in the homeschooling network.
2	Observation during field trip to local helmet factory with the homeschooling network.
3	Observation during homeschooling network mathematics instruction at the library.
4	Joint interview with Monique and Abigail in the Parker household.

Note: This table describes what happened during each session.

final in-home interview was conducted with 10 questions centered around care and mothering, which was audio-recorded, transcribed, and coded.

Data Analysis

While reflecting upon the research questions, I read through the data from the observations, notes, and interview. Using what Creswell (2013) describes as "phenomenological data analysis" (p. 82), I highlighted key phrases and statements that demonstrated subjects' essence of learning to othermother—how they experienced othermothering and how they learned to care. The statements were then clustered by commonalities and developed into four themes related to the subjects' experience with care. The four themes were that care is intentional, more than service, mimicked, and interdependent.

EMBRACING MY FUTURE: MAKING MEANING AND MOVING FORWARD

In considering the questions—"How is othermothering taught?" and "How do Black girls learn to othermother?"—I noticed the majority of the findings connected strongly to different aspects of care. Some findings answered the initial question—"How do Black girls learn to othermother?"—while others were linked to care as a moral attribute. Othermothering is a trait of Black feminist care and the data will be presented through that lens. There are four data categories, describing care as intentional, more than service, mimicked, and interdependent. In alignment with phenomenology, I will reflect on the personal influence of each category as a Black female educator, followed by a discussion and a concluding self-narrative.

Care is More Than Service

As stated earlier, care is an active virtue and a corrective action (Bass, 2012; Noddings, 2003, 2010). Caring is often shown through physical actions. When asked about the roles of mothers and othermothers, Abigail stated things people do for her. "My mom does a lot of house cleaning . . . She does the yard work sometimes. She cooks for us . . . [othermothers] have fun with us. [Othermothers] take us out to places we usually don't go." From a first glimpse, care can be and is shown through service.

However, I observed care transcends beyond task work. The actions Abigail associated with care are a very basic understanding of care and othermothering. In talking with Monique, I found care has deeper roots that may not be directly observed. She described mothering and care as "selfless," "loving," "[going] the extra mile," "integrity and character," and "constantly thinking of others before herself." The verb *love* was used several times when describing the work of mothers and othermothers.

SELF-REFLECTION

As an educator, the more I extend myself, the more I have begun to care about my students and their well-being. Going the extra mile, looks like volunteering to tutor students without extra pay, attending closely to classroom details and mentoring former students. As a Christian educator, it even includes praying for my students' personal needs in my private time. The care I show to each student goes beyond simple, everyday actions. My mind is constantly fixed on showing selfless care.

Care Is Intentional

Additionally, I learned that caring actions are often purposeful. A few weeks after the study was conducted, I went to lunch with Monique and Jerome. I inquired who was watching their children, and they proudly proclaimed that Abigail was. In past conversations with the Parkers, I learned the parents have been intentional in instilling leadership values in their children and give Abigail slightly more responsibility because she is the eldest. In one conversation Monique said, "[Abigail] thinks she is everybody's mama...but that's how we raised her." I took this statement to mean Monique and Jerome have purposely trained her to care for and look out for others.

Other intentional practices transpired throughout the case study, particularly in the relationship of the two sisters. On two separate occasions, Abigail was seen giving Deborah nonverbal signs of encouragement. Before giving a speech at the violin recital, Deborah nervously looked to Abigail. Abigail gave her a thumbs up and then Deborah nodded and began her speech with full confidence. In another instance, while the children were being homeschooled in small groups at the library, Abigail cheered on Deborah across the room as she was working on a math problem. In both instances, Abigail was intentional about showing care to her sister; it was care that drove her actions.

During our interview, the intentionality of care was discussed as well. Monique described caring for children as "walking a journey with them...nurturing them, teaching them...providing wisdom and discipline." These are all actions requiring a decision of care. Monique takes her responsibility to "[mold] all these little people" seriously and makes time to read books to best meet the needs of each child. She has figured out what each of their "love languages" are (Chapman, 1992) and adapts to reach each one. She said it is important to "treat [each child] as individuals," meaning she must be intentional in the ways she cares for each one.

SELF-REFLECTION

Within the classroom, I differentiate instruction to reach a variety of learners. We learn terminology through study, repetition, song, movement, and other art forms. I greet and talk to each child individually during passing time. When I see students and/or their families out in public, I actively engage in conversation, to intentionally show I am a part of the community. My mother's example of being relational is now something I embody. Being intentional and selfless go hand in hand.

Care Is Mimicked

One interview question asked the subjects how they learned to care. Abigail said she learned "because I have my mom and dad in the house and from reading the Bible." She then went on to say she watched her parents take care of her siblings, which is how she learned to do most things. Monique stated she "learned first from imitation." She referred to her younger years of playing with dolls and imitating "things our mothers, aunts and all the women in our family do and we mimic. We imitate what we see going on." Monique even described caring too much—a behavior she learned from her own mother. She discussed sometimes worrying too much about others' opinions, much like her mom, and having to unlearn that behavior.

In one observation, Abigail was seen mimicking Monique's behavior. While a student was playing a violin piece at the music recital, two of the older Parker brothers were whispering amongst themselves in the audience. Abigail quickly turned around, dragged her fingers across her lips and glared. The Parker brothers immediately complied and stopped talking. At first, I wondered how an adolescent could know the effectiveness of such a gesture. A few moments later, I saw Monique give the same nonverbal signal to the younger children, who also quickly altered their behavior. I realized Abigail was mimicking her own mother.

SELF-REFLECTION

The caring actions I employ as an educator often mirror things I remember my mom, Mrs. Jefferson, and other classroom othermothers doing. I make a point to stay in touch with former students, much like Mrs. Jefferson. I attend extracurricular events when students invite me, just as my mother would. I find myself writing reference letters for and celebrating major life milestones with former students, because I remember my teachers doing the same for me.

My cousin, a teacher-turned-principal, is another example of this. Her mother is my aunt, the retired principal previously mentioned. My cousin became a rising star in her urban school district, as her classes had extremely high test scores, and also for the rapport she developed with the community. She employed many of the caring tactics she watched her mom exhibit, from taking students under her wing to creating familial workspaces, which is now second-nature in her practice.

Care Is Interdependent

Caring is a moral obligation for all humans, regardless of gender (Gilligan, 1982). Furthermore, African ethics focuses on interdependence and the impact that the community has on the moral development of an individual (Paris, 1995). As I spent more time with the Parker family, I realized the truth of these assertions. It was not just Monique who influenced Abigail to show care; it was also Jerome. Additionally, as Monique and Jerome demonstrated care to their children, Abigail was not the only one to mimic it. The other children, particularly the older ones, did so as well.

The Parker children's paternal grandmother came to the music recital, as she is also the piano instructor for the homeschool co-op. When she came into the room, Benjamin made it his responsibility to assist her as needed (she was walking with a cane). Later on, Caleb helped her to get around as well. The two boys were constantly looking out for her. Through prior knowledge, I knew the boys' extension of care also came through a male youth development program. In the interview, Abigail described how even her father and uncles have shown her how to care. She said, "They tell us stuff because even my uncles sometimes . . . they're kind of like my 3rd or 4th dad. So yeah I think that [caring] could be my mom or dad." She was stating that demonstrating care is a communal responsibility.

Towards the end of the co-op field trip to the helmet factory, I struck up a conversation with Jerome, who was helping to chaperone. Through our time of discussion, I learned he too helps educate his children. He is responsible for teaching history and began sharing with me his pedagogy. I noticed how he cared for his children—through direct instruction, redirecting behavior, and positive reinforcement. As someone who is active in his children's lives, he is another factor influencing Abigail's othermothering skills.

SELF-REFLECTION

Furthermore, I realized it was not just female teachers who taught me how to display care. I still contact my Black, male, high school music teachers for classroom assistance. These teachers showed me care by remaining relevant, approachable, and simply being a good listener. They taught me how to actively engage students and garner attention. They modeled care through flexibility and switching plans to meet students' needs. Their influence had a strong impact on my development as an educator.

DISCUSSION

Reflecting on the data, I saw how each factor influenced Abigail's sense of othermothering, as illustrated in Figure 1.1. In becoming an othermother, an individual must have a transformed mind, ready to extend oneself. Monique described this as "going the extra mile." An othermother has also learned from others and knows the importance of intentionally demonstrating care. Abigail was seen mimicking Monique's actions, and my cousin and I learned educational care through the model of our mothers. The

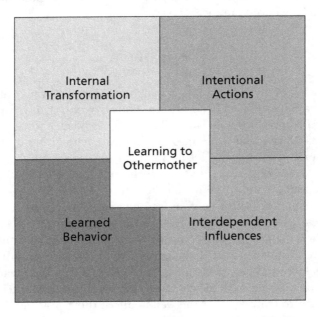

Figure 1.1 Influences on othermothering. The figure shows the factors impacting othermothering.

work of care is interdependent, and there are many individuals within the Black community who are responsible for modeling care to and for Black girls. Abigail experienced this through her father and other male kin, in addition to her mother; I encountered it through Black male teachers that I had, in addition to the other Black female teachers in my life.

Othermothering lays in the center of these factors because they equally impact it, non-sequentially. The process of learning to othermother is complex. Although four factors were identified in this study, further research may uncover additional influential aspects. Othermothering is a journey beginning at an early age, and deepens as Black girls and women mature. Othermothers are shaped by relationships and the community, including the journey of one's teaching career as well.

The ethic of care asserts that caring is a moral obligation (Gilligan, 1982). From a Black feminist care perspective (Bass, 2012), caring is something we should all strive for, and as Black women, we have an obligation to demonstrate care to Black girls. Doing so has an impact on their development, providing a model of community that shapes generations. Black girls can learn care from a variety of influences, but it is our responsibility as Black women to use care as a form of agency (Lindsay-Dennis, 2015), and show Black girls how to harness this power. When I think about my work as an educator, I needed the influence of the othermothers in my life, modeling care, to be where I am today.

CLOSING

During the fall of my eighth year of teaching, I stopped by my local grocery store after a weeknight church service. On my way out, I bumped into a father of a former student of mine. The family is Black and very intentional about instilling racial pride in their children. The father and I hugged and got caught up on life; I let him know I was working on my EdD and he wanted to know if I planned to still be in the district by the time his youngest daughter would be in middle school. I then inquired about my former student, and with a solemn face he said, "Things aren't going well Ms. Hughes . . . they aren't well. Please call my wife when you get a chance."

As I exited the grocery store, mostly worried about what could be going on with my former student, I recognized my growth as an educator. No longer was I a brand-new, bright-eyed, bushy-tailed, first year teacher, but I was someone who had become a pillar in the community, whom individuals could rely on to truly care for the well-being of their children. I had a history of going above and beyond, being approachable, and getting results. Pushing my cart through the dark parking lot, I felt myself walking in the shoes of my mother, Mrs. Jefferson, and all the othermothers who paved the way for me. I was on my way to joining their ranks.

REFERENCES

Bass, L. (2009). Fostering an ethic of care in leadership: A conversation with five African American women. *Advances in Developing Human Resources, 11*(5), 619–632.

Bass, L. (2012). When care trumps justice: The operationalization of Black feminist caring in educational leadership. *International Journal of Qualitative Studies in Education, 25*(1), 73–87.

Case, K. I. (1997). African American othermothering in the urban elementary school. *The Urban Review, 29*(1), 25–39.

Chapman, G. (1992). *The five love languages: How to express heartfelt commitment to your mate.* Chicago, IL: Northfield.

Collins, P. H. (2000). *Black feminist thought.* New York, NY: Routledge.

Collins, P. H. (2015). The meaning of motherhood in Black culture and Black mother-daughter relationships. In M. B. Zinn, P. Hondagneu-Sotelo, M. A. Messner, & A. M. Denissen (Eds.), *Gender through the prism of difference* (pp. 285–295). New York, NY: Oxford University Press.

Cooper, B. C. (2017). *Beyond respectability: The intellectual thought of race women.* Urbana: University of Illinois Press.

Crenshaw, K. (1989). Demarginalizing the intersection of race and sex: A Black feminist critique of antidiscrimination doctrine, feminist theory and antiracist politics. *The University of Chicago Legal Forum, 140,* 139–167.

Creswell, J. W. (2013). *Qualitative inquiry and research design: Choosing among five approaches.* Los Angeles, CA: SAGE.

Fordham, S. (1996). *Blacked out: Dilemmas of race, identity, and success at capital high.* Chicago, IL: University of Chicago Press.

Foster, M. (1993). Othermothers: Exploring the educational philosophy of Black American women teachers. In M. Arnot & K. Weiler (Eds.), *Feminism and social justice in education: International perspectives* (pp. 101–123). Washington, DC: The Falmer Press.

Gilligan, C. (1982). *In a different voice: Psychological theory and women's development.* Cambridge, MA: Harvard University Press.

Groenewald, T. (2004). A phenomenological research design illustrated. *International Journal of Qualitative Methods, 3*(1), 1–26.

Guiffrida, D. (2005). Othermothering as a framework for understanding African American students' definitions of student-centered faculty. *The Journal of Higher Education, 76*(6), 701–723.

hooks, b. (1994). *Teaching to transgress: Education as the practice of freedom.* New York, NY: Routledge.

James, S. M. (1993). Mothering: A possible Black feminist link to social transformation? In S. M. James & A. P. A. Busia (Eds.), *In theorizing Black feminisms: The visionary pragmatism of Black women* (pp. 44–54). New York, NY: Rutledge.

Lindsay-Dennis, L. (2015). Black feminist-womanist research paradigm: Toward a culturally relevant research model focused on African American girls. *Journal of Black Studies, 46*(5), 506–520.

Lindsay-Dennis, L., Cummings, L., & McClendon, S. C. (2011). Mentors' reflections on developing a culturally responsive mentoring initiative for urban African American girls. *Black Women, Gender + Families, 5*(2), 66–92.

Noddings, N. (2003). *Caring: A feminine approach to ethics and moral education.* Berkeley: University of California Press.

Noddings, N. (2010). *The maternal factor: Two paths to morality.* Berkeley: University of California Press.

Paris, P. J. (1995). *The spirituality of African peoples: The search for a common moral discourse.* Minneapolis, MN: Fortress Press.

Thompson, A. (2004). Caring and colortalk: Childhood innocence in White and Black. In V. Siddle Walker & J. R. Snarey (Eds.), *Race-ing moral formation: African American perspectives on care and justice* (pp. 23–37). New York, NY: Teachers College Press.

van Manen, M. (2016). *Researching lived experience.* New York, NY: Routledge.

CHAPTER 2

A TALE OF TWO BLACK GIRL CIVIC IDENTITIES

A Mother/Daughter Critical Autoethnography on Language, Literacy, and the Black Lives Matter Movement

Celicia L. Bell
Florida State University

Jasmine A. Clayton
Florida State University

This is an autoethnography about an African American mother (Celicia) and daughter (Jasmine) and our Black girl civic identities. For Celicia and Jasmine, Black girl civics is civic engagement by Black girls for the betterment of society at large, with a special emphasis on minoritized communities. Civic engagement, according to Thomas Ehrlich (2000),

> Means working to make a difference in the civic life of our communities and developing the combination of knowledge, skills, values and motivation to

Black Girl Civics, pages 19–34
Copyright © 2020 by Information Age Publishing
All rights of reproduction in any form reserved.

make that difference. It means promoting the quality of life in a community, through political and non-political processes. (Preface, p. vi)

Jasmine and Celicia have negotiated our civic identities through language, literacy, and the Black Lives Matter movement, while also straddling both sides of our cultural identities at different points in our lives. In this chapter, we use autoethnography to explore our emergent sociocritical civic literacy (Mirra, Coffey, & Englander, 2018) through a discussion of our respective experiences with nigrescence (Cross, 1991), double consciousness (Du Bois, 1994), and *The Hate U Give* novel (Thomas, 2017).

THEORETICAL FRAMEWORK

We use autoethnography to depict a form of sociocritical civic literacy that "insists upon considerations of identity, contexts, and practices when defining civic engagement, as well as analyses of structural barriers to an equitable civic life" (Mirra et al., 2018, p. 427). Our developing sociocritical civic literacy encompasses our raced and gendered cultural identities within the historical context of space and time, which includes our past and present experiences in and out of schools and universities. The cultivation of our nigrescence and Black girl civic identities requires embracing and advocating our cultural heritage through culturally relevant and sustaining traditional literacies, as well as new literacies (The New London Group, 1996), which disrupts the status quo by making visible the issues and concerns of minoritized communities.

Throughout history from the founding of the United States to the present new millennium, mainstream society has used print literacy to oppress minoritized groups by implying that there is only one way to be literate. New Literacy Studies (The New London Group, 1996), however, incorporates various forms of literacy and multiple ways of knowing that have involved activism as well. Examples of activist stances with new literacies includes (a) activating multimodal, multiliteracies, and popular cultures to communicate in a digital participatory culture that is more inclusive of various forms of literacies and meaning making and (b) using critical literacy to question White, hegemonic, systemic inequalities; racism; and colorblind ideologies.

New millennial literacy activism is one way to engage in civic literacy. New millennial literacy activism (re)mixes new literacies with the old forms of African American literacy activism that Lathan (2015) calls gospel literacy. Reminiscent of gospel literacy, Angie Thomas (2017), a Black female author, engages in Black girl civic practices with her young adult (YA) novel, *The Hate U Give*, to spark difficult conversations about racial issues and prompt people to action. "I look at books as being a form of activism because a lot of time they will show us a side of the world that we may not have known about," Thomas says in a YouTube video (Epic Reads, 2017). The novel, which dominated the bestseller lists, was birthed from the Black Lives Matter movement and tackles the hard-to-stomach realities of police brutality, racism, civic activism, identity, nigrescence, and double consciousness from the perspective of a teen protagonist, Starr. The novel speaks to the present generation, millennials and Generation Y, who are experiencing a present-day cultural trauma deeply rooted in past cultural traumas and a past generation scoffed at for being seemingly weak and ineffectual.

Haddad (2018) writes about Black Lives Matter protest novels like Thomas (2017) and the "potentiality of the novel[s] to expand and animate the politics of Black liberation" (p. 40). *The Hate U Give* (Thomas, 2017) has impacted public education through social justice oriented teachers who teach the book to spark racial, critical, and civic literacies within K–12 schools (Ebarvia, Parker, & Schmidt, 2018; Ellenbogen & Buckley-Marudas, 2019; German, 2019), as well as teacher education programs in colleges and universities (Dyches & Sams, 2018). Ebarvia et al. (2018) calls books like *The Hate U Give* (Thomas 2017) "literatures of resistance" and asserts that the book "is sparking a movement all its own: students, teachers, and readers—all mesmerized and uncomfortable—are reading this tale and grappling with the implications about our society" (p. 93).

Jasmine and Celicia's Black girl civic literacies position us "as civic agents of change who can [help] transform society through [our] literacy skills" (Mirra et al., 2018, p. 425). We can be change agents because our experiences with nigrescence and double consciousness grants us access to mainstream and minoritized communities; our second sight (Du Bois, 1994) is an opportunity to bridge two cultural worlds. Cross (1971) conceptualizes his version of nigrescence, which means becoming Black, from a Black perspective by detailing Blacks' identity formation in five stages: pre-encounter, encounter, immersion-emersion, internalization, and internalization-commitment. Neville and Cross (2017) develops an "emerging racial awakening model" (p. 105) that highlights how education, personal experience and/or observation, and activism could influence each other as well as racial awakening (p. 105), which we display in our autoethnographies.

As *African Americans,* we recognize the two conflicting sides of our heritage, our double consciousness (Du Bois, 1994). We are American with an African heritage that has been stolen and lost to us because of slavery. We are also *Black* as a member of the African diaspora, the community of people whose ancestors were Africans dispersed throughout the world by the transatlantic slave trade, especially the Americas and Caribbean. Du Bois (1994) describes double consciousness, or second sight, as "a peculiar sensation," a "two-ness," and "two warring ideals in one dark body" (p. 2). In our autoethnographic accounts, we discuss our double consciousness and nigrescence as a complicated process of picking up and putting down Black girl civic identities, in a quest to balance contradictory imperatives of embracing Blackness. Through our journeys to find our place and our voices, our civic identities are refracted through the literary, film, popular culture, and community landscapes that we navigate daily.

METHODS

Autoethnography is the study of one's self in society in relation to culture. We use critical autoethnography as the research method to expound on theories related to culture, nigrescence, and civic identity formation, like other researchers (Gooden, 2014; Hernandez & Murray-Johnson, 2015) who have used autoethnography to analyze their various identity positions. As Black girls, critical autoethnography allows us to insert our voices and personal narratives into scholarship at the intersection of race, gender, community, and academia while interpreting the relationship of ourselves to our sociocultural contexts (Boylorn & Orbe, 2016; Chang, Ngunjiri, & Hernandez, 2016). We wrote the narratives in an informal, first-person point of view to maintain the authenticity of our two individualized voices.

Despite a 21-year professional career as a knowledge worker in various capacities, Celicia is currently pursuing a doctoral degree for primarily civic reasons: to position herself to better serve the Black community through academic and research endeavors strengthened by school, university, and community partnerships. Jasmine took a gap year after earning her bachelor's degree to write her first YA novel with main characters of color, which she hopes adds to the reading selection possibilities for minoritized readers.

Connecting Our Experiences to a Young Adult Novel

In *The Hate U Give* (Thomas, 2017), the main character, Starr, a Black young lady, experiences double consciousness because she has two identities. Williamson Starr goes to a White school in a White neighborhood, while Garden Heights Starr lives in a poor, Black neighborhood where she does not feel like she belongs in the neighborhood because she is sheltered. Celicia and Jasmine have similar as well as different experiences from Starr. Like Starr in *The Hate U Give* (2017), we have navigated nigrescence in various ways and experienced racially epiphanous events that sparked a heightened consciousness of racial stereotypes and disparities. Starr struggles to find her voice during her civic identity formation. Starr's bravery with activism is her liberating response to her horrific experience with police brutality. For Jasmine and Celicia, our Black girl civic identities manifest alongside our nigrescence through sociocritical civic literacy. We have used our multimodal multiliteracies not only to assist in our nigrescence but also to activate and engage with our civic activism in print and social media.

JASMINE'S STORY

For as long as I can remember, reading has always been my favorite thing to do. It's an escape for me, an opportunity to immerse myself in another world, to experience life from another person's vantage point. As a young girl, the YA novels that I read were a major influence on my life. Even though I owned a small collection of books at home, I was a voracious reader and went to the library often to supplement my book addiction, which was expensive. I can't recall checking out a single book from the library with a protagonist that looked like me and shared my experiences as a Black girl growing up in American society.

Growing up, I never thought much about race, so it's difficult for me to look back on my memories through a racial lens. Like Starr in *The Hate U Give* (Thomas, 2017), I went to a predominantly White school. I spent kindergarten through 12th grade at a research school in a suburban White neighborhood. There were times when I was the only Black kid in class. I was aware of racial bias, of course, but it never affected me in a negative way (that I was aware of) so I didn't dwell on it. I'd overhear conversations among my family about racial issues and for the longest time I didn't understand their discontent and disillusionment with American society. I was a proponent of colorblindness, fully buying into the facade of a post-racial society taught in school. Slavery was ages ago! Jim Crow is no more! We elected a Black president! "Why can't we all just get along?" I wanted to ask. "Why does race even matter?"

In elementary school, although most of my friends were White, the friend that I was closest to was a mixed girl, Black and White. Even though I didn't realize it at the time, I think that the reason I connected with her so much was because of the cultural similarities. I'd always felt inadequate around my White friends, like I had to hide a part of myself, but I didn't know the reason. At that young age, I hadn't yet realized how comforting it could be to have friends who shared your cultural experiences. As I transitioned into middle school, I became more aware of my Blackness, and my friend groups started to reflect that change. As a shy and socially awkward girl who just wanted to fit in, my dark skin made me feel like even more of an outsider. I used chemical relaxers even though it was destroying my hair. I wore baggy clothes to hide the curves that I was developing. I avoided being in the sun for too long and my skin became pale and lackluster. Still, I couldn't change my genetics and that set me apart from my White peers.

I remember sitting in class and envying the White girl next to me for her naturally straight hair and slender nose. I thought to myself, "Why did I have to be born Black? It would be so much easier if I were White."

In high school, I started to accept my Blackness more, but there was still a disconnect. Much like Starr, I felt like I had two personas. There was the Jasmine that I pretended to be when I was with my White peers, and the Jasmine that I was ashamed to be when I was with my Black peers. I acted like the R&B that I grew up listening to wasn't my favorite genre of music and embraced pop music instead. I distanced myself from anything that might label me as *ghetto*. I laughed at jokes with negative racial undertones that my White peers made even though the jokes made me uncomfortable because I didn't want to seem like *that angry Black girl*. White people thought they were complimenting me by saying, "You're not like other Black girls," because I didn't fit their stereotyped image of what a Black girl was like. If a White girl was loud and obnoxious that was just her personality. If a Black girl was loud and obnoxious, it was because she was Black. If a White girl was quiet and demure, that was just her personality. If a Black girl was quiet and demure, like myself, she was *not like other Black girls*. That comparison separated me from my Black identity even more. When around my Black peers, I was teased constantly for *talking White*. I didn't use African American Vernacular English (AAVE) or listen to rap/hip-hop. The first time someone called me an *oreo*, I laughed because that was what was expected, but it hurt. Once again, I was accused of not being Black enough, and for what?

When I think back on my childhood, I associated negative racial experiences with my Black peers, but I have realized now that I was isolating myself from them, insecure in my Blackness, rather than it being the other way around. I felt out-of-place around my White peers as well, always feeling inadequate, but back then, I just attributed it to my shyness. It wasn't until I started college that I really began to develop a healthy relationship with my Black identity. I loved my melanin-rich skin and naturally kinky hair. I loved Black culture. As an adolescent, I was blind to the plight of my fellow Black Americans. The racially fueled backlash following the election of President Obama in 2008 and the #BlackLivesMatter movement opened my eyes.

It was in 2015, when I saw the film *Selma* (Colson, Winfrey, Gardner, Kleiner, Duvernay, 2014) for the first time, however, that was a turning point for me. Just like Starr felt compelled to act after witnessing the murder of her best friend by a White cop, viewing *Selma* (2014) moved something in me. It literally made me sick to the stomach. As a result, I began to educate myself, learning about American history from Black perspectives instead of whitewashed history textbooks. I observed the social upheaval all around me, and it was like a modern version of what I'd been reading about—we hadn't progressed nearly as much as I had been taught to believe. I turned to social media as a form of civic engagement that paralleled my evolving critical consciousness (see Figure 2.1). Now, I used Twitter and Facebook daily to enlighten myself and others on the social issues affecting this nation since these issues were rarely discussed in more traditional arenas like school or the mainstream news.

Jasmine Clayton
July 12, 2015 · 🌐 ▾

I hate to bring this up again because honestly, I am quite tired of this debate, but I feel as if this needs to be said. I have seen so many people defend the Confederate flag, for a multitude of reasons, throughout the past weeks. Some of you have even posted about how the taking down of the flag in SC on Friday was "such a shame."

I saw Selma for the first time last night (late, I know lol) and I literally became sick to my stomach as I watched it. It made me angry. Angry at this country and the people in it who still continue to do some of the same things that were portrayed in that film. As a result of the events that have come to light in the past few years, for the first time in my life it is in the back of my mind, that hey, there is an actual possibility that I might become the victim of a hate crime because of my race. That I might lose my brother or father because of the color of their skin, something that they have no control over. In 2015! Insanity.

My point is, however, that the Confederate flag was shown several times throughout the film. This was 50 years ago. Many who fought in the civil rights movement are still living today. These people were disparaged, bruised, and beaten, and watched their friends and family be murdered in cold blood under the name of that flag. I can't even imagine what they feel every time that they have to look at it. That flag is insensitive and an insult to those who suffered just to ensure that generations of people to come would be treated like human beings and citizens of this country and to be given the rights that they are privy to.

The Confederate flag is not Southern heritage. Apparently it wasn't even the official flag of the Confederacy. It was a battle flag that was adopted by hate-filled people to be a symbol of their hatred. It should be in a museum, as a reminder of the injustices committed against people of this country, not flying on state grounds. The fact that this is even a debate, that people are fighting so vehemently for this flag, people actually in my life... I can't comprehend it. It's just stupid tbh.

Figure 2.1   Viewing Selma, a racially epiphanous encounter, compelled Jasmine to action.

Throughout high school, I volunteered weekly at the public library in my hometown of Tallahassee, Florida and would check out several books before leaving. I must have gone through the YA section several times over. The Black characters that I came across (infrequently, mind you) when reading were always relegated to the *sassy best friend* archetype or throwaway side characters that were either overly stereotyped or White characters in blackface, usually with a cringy descriptor comparing their skin tone to some type of food. Of course, there were Black authors out there who wrote Black stories about Black characters, but I never encountered them in the library's YA section. As a library volunteer, I also noticed that most of the kids that I serviced were Black and Brown, like myself. Why, then, were we not represented on the bookshelves?

I was in my third year of college when I first heard about *The Hate U Give* (Thomas, 2017) and was immediately intrigued. The social commentary on police brutality and White privilege really spoke to me, but it was more than that. It was rare to find a Black female protagonist in mainstream YA fiction. The great thing about literary and popular fiction was that it was incredibly easy to put yourself in the shoes of the characters that you were reading about. Skin color was never something that I thought mattered. After so many years of reading novels from White perspectives, I didn't understand the value of reading from a cultural perspective similar to mine. Reading *The Hate U Give* (2017) was an enlightening experience and inspired me to write stories from the Black perspective.

My growing Black identity forced me to reexamine the direction that I wanted to take in life. I felt a need to help my people so I adjusted my two dreams, becoming a clinical psychologist and a published author, to accommodate that desire. Promoting mental health in the Black community and increasing access to and the quality of mental health services to underserved populations was now a priority for me. Moreover, I've started writing YA novels with Black female protagonists so that young Black girls can have stories that they can relate to, since I never did. I will do my part in helping fill the shelves of libraries and bookstores with authentic and diverse Black stories. Growing up Black in America can be very confusing for kids who don't have a strong sense of who they are. Everywhere we turn, Whiteness is portrayed as superior, the standard. That is why representation is important. I truly believe that if I had books like *The Hate U Give* (Thomas, 2017) and well-developed Black female characters like Starr to read about when I was growing up, I could have avoided a lot of the self-hatred that I was afflicted with. Now, as Issa Rae, the writer and star of the HBO series *Insecure* (Rae et al., 2019) says, "I'm rooting for everybody Black."

CELICIA'S STORY

I am *always* Black and I love it! Wouldn't have it any other way. My mom instilled positive cultural values in me at a young age. She used to recite to me Langston Hughes' poems "The Negro Speaks of Rivers" and "Song for a Banjo Dance." She loved to say, "I've known rivers" and "shake your brown feet honey." As a military brat, I lived in various places including Germany. I have always been a minority attending predominantly White schools; however, because we lived on or close to military bases I was exposed to other cultures. My best friend in elementary school was a White girl. I still remember her name. We twirled batons together in our front yards. Once I spent the night at her house for a sleepover (my parents didn't tend to let me spend the night at people's houses). I called my parents to come get me because I felt out of place (I pretended to get sick). You know, the whole wearing a headscarf to bed so you wouldn't mess your hair up thing. Alternatively, I also had similar experiences to Sekani's experiences in *The Hate U Give*, where Thomas (2017) wrote that

> in Garden Heights, kids play in the streets. Sekani presses his face against my window and watches them. He won't play with them though. Last time he played with some neighborhood kids, they called him "white boy" 'cause he goes to Williamson. (p. 87)

I remember in elementary school visiting cousins in rural Florida who used to circle around me and force me to talk so that they could ogle at the fact that I *talked White*. Unlike Starr and her siblings, I also lived in predominantly White neighborhoods.

My parents taught me about race and living in American society. I was always taught to strive to do my best and represent our race because we were blessed with access to educational opportunities. We were just as good or better despite racialized beliefs by some people that our skin color meant that we were valued *less than* White people.

I have coexisted in White mainstream society as well as the Black community; however, I have always felt like I stuck out in both, straddling both communities with double consciousness. In mainstream society, at times in my life, I have been cognizant of my skin color, like when we studied slavery in history or social studies class or during a junior high school bus ride where a White girl called me the "n" word. In the Black community, I could blend in until I danced or attempted to play the dozens (I was not good at either). And like Starr's family, I have experienced and given "the talk" "about what to do if a cop stopped me" (Thomas, 2017, p. 20). I have not really experienced overt racism that I could remember, until recently when I was called the "n" word for the second time in my life by a homeless or drug addicted White woman.

When my daughter was in K–12, I often touched base with her on what she was learning in school to ensure she was learning about Black history throughout the year and not just in February. That seemed to be the case; however, still she grew up in a faux post-racial society and went to a school with some diversity. Even though she had Black history facts, she was a novice when it came to Black pop culture despite it being all around her outside of school. I played Black music, watched Black movies, read Black books—but she wasn't interested; she preferred Disney channel, *High School Musical*, and *Glee*. I could tell that she didn't really have a concept of race, of being Black in America, in the way that I did growing up in the '70s, '80s, and early '90s. She didn't see color, and that was fine by me, so I embraced it because I embraced diversity and multiculturalism; terms that were now problematic because of the overused, disingenuous way the terms were incorporated into society, specifically institutions like school and the workplace. Clary-Lemon (2009) talked about how race is coded in these murky terms (p. W8). I was waiting in the wings for Jasmine when she embraced her Black identity, ready to happily and proudly feed her intellectual resources, as well as catch her up on all the Black classics so that she could understand Black pop cultural references related to things like *The Color Purple* for instance.

Like my daughter, my predominantly White K–12 public education was through the lens of White mainstream society. In high school, my critical and sociopolitical consciousnesses were awakened to the oppressed state of the Black community by my parents, popular media, and participation in a school-sponsored after school club that catered to Black students called Harambee Club. My high school senior year, I was president of Harambee (which is Swahili for togetherness). My experiences with Harambee Club included decorating the locked, glass case by the school's cafeteria with a Black History Month display donned in black, green, and red. I still remembered cutting out construction paper letters spelling the Marcus Garvey quote, "A people without the knowledge of their past history, origin, and culture is like a tree without roots." That one sentence has stuck with me throughout life. I used it every chance I could and I currently used it as the annual theme for our church's Black History Month exhibit and program. During college my nigrescence flourished because of personal exploration, college elective coursework, and a communal bond with the other Black students at my predominantly White university outside of class, through dorm life, and organizations like the Black Student Union.

For me, learning to value the multiple ways of knowing and being for a person of color in a White, hegemonic society has altered the way I viewed and civically engaged with the following Black youth: (a) my daughter and her participation in the Black Lives Matter movement; (b) my church's youth while coordinating our annual Black History program; and (c) a literacy research participant, a 19-year-old young Black man who recently graduated from alternative high school after participating in a gang diversion program. I began my doctoral studies from a deficit perspective, wondering why kids couldn't read; now, I was asking very different questions related to the necessity of transformative, culturally relevant and sustaining, and positive cultural identity forming educational experiences for youth and the societal implications of not doing so.

BLACK GIRL CIVICS AND NEW MILLENNIAL LITERACY ACTIVISM

New millennial literacy activism pervades the social importance of Thomas's (2017) novel, as well as Jasmine and Celicia's Black girl civics identities and literacies. The power of *The Hate U Give* (2017) stems from its new millennial literacy activism in various ways: (a) the call and response between the past and the present; (b) the use of social media to extend and perpetuate the conversation about police brutality, civic literacy, and activism through outlets such as the Black Lives Matter movement; and (c) the multimodality (available in various formats such as print books, audio books, social media, and movies). New millennial literacy activism recalls the civil rights movement of the past and mixes it with the present, creating new relevance for a movement that a trending toward post-racial society almost forgot or considered irrelevant to present, contemporary lives. New millennial literacy activism bridges the generational gap between the past and present collective identities of African Americans: the cultural trauma and double consciousness of being African and American. According to Lathan (2015), "In the gospel tradition, historical knowledge empowers activism" (p. 35).

Angie Thomas (2017) seems to deliberately incorporate historical figures and messages in her Black girl civics novel, as well as gospel literacy, which is rooted in the African American cultural tradition of community organizing and activism. In the novel, the characters display various forms of activism: Starr's father's involvement with the Black Panthers, Starr's uncle's assimilationist approach to progress, Ms. Ofrah's form of legal justice that is tied to the civil rights tradition, and Starr's way of negotiating civics as a Black girl who lives in a faux post-racial society. For instance, in *The Hate U Give*, Thomas (2017) sends out a *call* by reenacting a shared experience (i.e., police brutality, racism, nigrescence, and double consciousness). The *response* should resist dominant thought and lead to action while reading or after completing the book. Call-and-response is also a teaching tool. For Black girl civics authors, this involves teaching the reader how to respond to current events that are marginalizing, oppressive, and seemingly hopeless. Readers read and respond in various multimodal, multiliterate ways. Thomas, who experienced in college similar double consciousness and code-switching moments like Starr, Celicia, and Jasmine, expands her activism beyond authoring a protest novel. She tweets on Twitter and participates in YouTube interviews as well as in-person talks promoting the need for youth to engage in activism.

The participatory culture of new media allows individuals or communities an avenue for responding to our world(s). If we're not active in the response, we will not have a role in the composing or composition of our world(s). As a mother, Celicia is watching and mentoring her daughter through the first four of the five stages of racial identity formation (Cross, 1971), while her daughter simultaneously cultivates a civic identity by voting; sharing her opinions about America's sociopolitical upheaval on social media, such as Facebook and Twitter; and participating in local social justice rallies.

Participatory cultures like Black Twitter offer marginalized groups an opportunity to advocate for change through hashtag activism by disrupting mainstream messages that perpetuate negativity towards a group of people and give voice to the voiceless. Black Twitter, a segment of Twitter organized by hashtags related to the Black community, is a microcosm of the African American community. Topics vary from playing the dozens to community activism. These conversations have always existed; however, now the general public is privy to them because of the openness of the Internet. Black Twitter has shown the ability to influence the news and "force" headlines. With cell phone cameras, citizens can record or live stream video instantly. In *The Hate U Give* (Thomas, 2017), "'People from the neighborhood are already talking about it on Twitter,' Seven says, 'I saw it last night.'" (p. 33). In the novel, Black Twitter, not the mainstream White media, is the central communication hub for hearing about the word on the street as well as the Black Lives Matter movement.

The visceral, physical reaction that Celicia had while reading *The Hate U Give* (Thomas, 2017), as well as the repeated mention of "all that blood" (p. 25) in relation to Khalil's murder and "I can't breathe" (p. 25), mirrored experiences Celicia has had while enduring the repeated loop of videos showing violence against Black citizens. Celicia created "Blood Cry," a poetic graphic, because she was compelled and needed a creative outlet to express her frustrations and release pent up emotion while trying to embody a positive, activist message. Do *something* to advocate for or inspire change. She created and posted the poetic graphic to her various social media accounts such as Instagram, Facebook, and Twitter.

Celicia expressed her voice and Black girl citizenship through writing and has attempted to submit op-ed pieces (not published) to several national newspaper outlets because she felt compelled to *do* something. She later posted the pieces on social media like Facebook and Instagram, which granted her access and control to share her perspective despite the ever-present information gatekeeping of the mainstream media. In July 2016, she submitted "Blood Cry: On Modern Day Lynchings and White Silence" to the *New York Times*.

The following is an excerpt from one of the excluded op-ed pieces titled "I. CAN'T. BREATHE.—the Perpetual Brutalization of BEING WHILE BLACK" (Bell, 2018).

I am so sick and tired of being sick and tired. . . . I am personally offended and mentally and emotionally sick and tired of the constant, perpetual victimization and brutalization of African American CITIZENS in this country that I love. But now it is more than that. The grief and sometimes rage that I feel has turned to fear. Fear that I too will become a victim of hate. Hate given and received. I don't want to hate. We should all love and look out for each other regardless of our skin color and despite and in spite of our flawed characters . . . On many days I. CAN'T. BREATHE.

I can't breathe when I scroll through my social media timelines and have to endure reading and watching another African American CITIZEN being victimized and brutalized for merely BEING WHILE BLACK.

Being at Waffle House.

Being at Starbucks.

Being at Yale.

Being in Nordstrom.

Being at an AirB&B

Being in a car.

Being on a plane.

Being at a golf club.

Being at school.

Standing.

Sitting.

In distress.

Stranded on the side of a road in a broken car.

Walking across the parking lot.

Walking in the neighborhood.

Wearing a hoodie.

Living.

Breathing.

Just BEING . . .

CONCLUSION

For both Jasmine and Celicia, their sociocritical civic literacies were closely connected to their Black identities because they chose to activate their civic engagement in ways to advocate for and benefit the Black community, especially by using digital, participatory culture. For Jasmine, the low-salience attitude and miseducation of her pre-encounter stage was disrupted by her encounters with the movie *Selma* (Colson et al., 2014), the social and traditional media saturation of the Black Lives Matter movement and police brutality, and the YA novel *The Hate U Give* (Thomas, 2017). After experiencing an intense immersion-emersion stage, in the dawning moments of the internalization phase she was set to venture out and navigate her place in society, while balancing her various developing identities as a Black, middle class, young lady with double consciousness experiences. For Celicia, embracing the participatory culture of Black Twitter and other social media outlets was a way to activate her Black girl civic literacies. At very tense moments in the Black Lives Matter movement and the continued execution of Black people in the public square, she has felt compelled to use her artistry as a writer as a call for action in a multimodal way.

Educators and community leaders should incorporate more outreach practices and pedagogies targeted to marginalized youth that encourage embracing cultural heritage. The incorporation of new literacies with in-school and out-of-school literacies is important in an increasingly diverse, global society. The National Council of Teacher of English's (2019) position statement on critical literacy states that educators should "model civic literacy and conversation by creating a supportive environment where students can have an informed discussion and engage with current events and civic issues while staying mindful and critical of the difference between the intent and impact of their language." Future research should examine the impact of incorporating youths' racial and critical consciousnesses and new literacies with civic engagement.

ACKNOWLEDGMENTS

We thank Celicia's former doctoral advisor and committee chair, Dr. George L. Boggs, for his assistance with the initial conceptual development of the chapter, as well as his mentorship, enthusiasm, and willingness to always provide insightful feedback.

REFERENCES

Bell, C. L. (2018). *I. CAN'T. BREATHE.—The perpetual brutalization of BEING WHILE BLACK* [blog post]. Retrieved from https://www.cecibell.net/wordpress/2018/05/i-cant-breathe-the-perpetual-brutalization-of-being-while-black/

Boylorn, R. M., & Orbe, M. P. (Eds.). (2016). *Critical autoethnography: Intersecting cultural identities in everyday life (Writing lives: Ethnographic narratives)*. Abingdon, England: Taylor and Francis.

Chang, H., Ngunjiri, F., & Hernandez, K. A. C. (2016). *Collaborative autoethnography*. Abingdon, England: Routledge.

Clary-Lemon, J. (2009). The racialization of composition studies: Scholarly rhetoric of race since 1990. *College Composition and Communication, 61*(2), W1–W17.

Colson, C., Winfrey, O., Gardner, D., & Kleiner, J. (Producers), & Duvernay, A. (Director). (2014). *Selma* [Motion picture]. United States: Paramount Pictures.

Cross, W. E., Jr. (1971). The Negro-to-Black conversion experience. *Black World, 20*(9), 13–27.

Du Bois, W. E. B. (1994). *The souls of Black folk*. Mineola, NY: Dover.

Dyches, J., & Sams, B. L. (2018). Reconciling competing missions of English education: A story of pedagogical realism. *Changing English: Studies in Culture & Education, 25*(4), 370.

Ebarvia, T., Parker, K., & Schmidt, P. S. (2018). #BlackLivesMatter: When real life and YA fiction converge. *English Journal, 107*(5), 92.

Ehrlich, T. (2000). *Civic responsibility and higher education*. Phoenix, AZ: Oryx Press.

Ellenbogen, C., & Buckley-Marudas, M. F. (2019). Color bravery: On race from the page to the stage. *English Journal, 108*(4), 29–35.

Epic Reads. (2017, January 12). Tupac inspired Angie Thomas's new book | The hate u give [Video file]. Retrieved from https://youtu.be/H6ufAb82GJ0

Germán, L. (2019). To dismantle racism, we must discuss it. *English Journal, 108*(4), 15–16.

Gooden, M. A. (2014). Using nigrescence to recover from my mis-education as a 'successful' African American male. *Journal of African American Males in Education, 5*(2), 111–133.

Haddad, V. (2018). Nobody's protest novel: Novelistic strategies of the Black Lives Matter movement. *The Comparatist, 42*, 40–59.

Hernandez, K. K., & Murray-Johnson, K. K. (2015). Towards a different construction of Blackness: Black immigrant scholars on racial identity development in the United States. *International Journal of Multicultural Education, 17*(2), 53–72.

Lathan, R. E. (2015). *Freedom writing: African American civil rights literacy activism, 1955–1967*. Conference on College Composition and Communication/National Council of Teachers of English. Illinois.

Mirra, N., Coffey, J., & Englander, A. (2018). Warrior scholars & bridge builders: Civic dreaming in ELA classrooms. *Journal of Literacy Research, 50*(4), 423–445.

Neville, H. A., & Cross, W. E., Jr. (2017). Racial awakening: Epiphanies and encounters in Black racial identity. *Cultural Diversity and Ethnic Minority Psychology, 23*(1), 102–108.

Rae, I. (Writer), & Rae, I., Penny, P., Rotenberg, M., Matsoukas, M., Becky, D., & Berry, J. (Producer). (2019). *Insecure* [Television broadcast]. United States: HBO.

The National Council of Teachers of English. (2019, March 6). *Resolution on English education for critical literacy in politics and media.* Retrieved from http://www2.ncte.org/statement/resolution-english-education-critical -literacy-politics-media/

The New London Group. (1996). A pedagogy of multiliteracies: Designing social futures. *Harvard Educational Review, 66*(1), 60–93.

Thomas, A. (2017). *The hate u give.* New York, NY: Balzer + Bray.

CHAPTER 3

HOOD CIVICS

Intergenerational Healing and the Quest for Educational Justice For/With Black Girl Artivists

Jeanelle K. Hope
Texas Christian University

Vajra M. Watson
University of California, Davis

In 2017, Mercy Lagaaia—a Sacramento Area Youth Speaks (SAYS) student—competed in the International Brave New Voices youth slam poetry contest. She stepped to the mic and performed her award winning piece, "Bored of Education." Drawing from her own experiences navigating Sacramento schools, Mercy rhymes about witnessing her peers being misdiagnosed with attention deficit and hyperactivity disorder (ADHD); the school-to-prison pipeline; and her frustration with having her intelligence, civility, and humanity be decided by disengaged teachers and traditional systems of assessment that lack cultural responsivity. She spits, "I know I'm smart, but I was taught to never forget where I came from. So for u to see the good in

Black Girl Civics, pages 35–54
Copyright © 2020 by Information Age Publishing
All rights of reproduction in any form reserved.

me, best believe u gon see the hood in me." As personified in her poem, Mercy evokes important connections between good *and* hood to accentuate the richness, resistance, tenderness, and eminent love on the block in spite of harsh material conditions and oppressive social systems. In embracing her own truth and identity as a youth that has been greatly shaped by her neighborhood—a predominately Black, Southeast Asian, and Latinx community that stands in the shadow of the California State Capitol—Mercy complicates notions of what it means to be civically engaged.

Mercy's poetic testimony is part of a larger legacy. Black women have a formidable tradition of leading fights for freedom that impact society. Unfortunately, within discourses on resistance, there is a tendency to focus on public political activity (i.e., protests) that overlooks the varied ways Black women *and* girls embody less visible, yet no less significant, change-making efforts (Perlow, Wheeler, Bethea, & Scott, 2018). While some scholars see a "civic empowerment gap," that is, as "large and as disturbing as the nationally recognized reading and math achievement gaps" (Levinson, 2010, p. 316), others critique this entire notion. Our work directly challenges traditional modes of civic engagement by examining and celebrating how Black girls locate and reimagine civics.

Far too frequently, civics is defined as the belief of and participation in a democratic process, including voting, paying taxes, lobbying, and often respectable ways of servicing one's community. It is essential that we problematize this, given the realities faced by Black people, particularly Black women and girls. From Jim Crow laws and policies that restricted Black women from voting to recognizing the disproportionate ways in which capitalism and other power structures impact Black women, often limiting their ability to run for public office or even to be present for city council and local school board meetings, Black women and girls have been historically and systematically marginalized from democracy.

In our work, we reject hegemonic notions of civics and turn to the recent work of Bettina Love (2019), where she posits that within education, civics is,

> the practice of abolitionist teaching rooted in the internal desire we all have for freedom, joy, restorative justice (restoring humanity, not just rules), and to matter to ourselves, our community, our family, and our country with the profound understanding that we must "demand the impossible." (p. 7)

Building on Love's rewriting of civics and Watson's conception in *Learning to Liberate* (2012) that "it takes the hood to save the hood," we coined the term *hood civics*. This term destabilizes traditional notions of civic engagement that do not always capture how Black girls see themselves in relation to broader society and in service to their communities. The use of *hood* grounds the communities in which Black girls navigate and fight for. Hood civics is the localization of civic engagement; an explicit rejection of the belief in a nation-state, American essentialism, patriotism, and other characteristics of nationhood that are commonly associated with civics. Thus, hood civics informs abolition, allowing Black women and girls to reimagine the possibilities of their communities, while fighting for justice block by block via artivism, restorative justice, direct action, solidarity, and everyday acts of resistance.

"As long as Black girls contend with society's perpetuation of perfection and femininity as an embodiment of whiteness, schools will not be a place where they can practice epistemic or identity agency, and simply be while learning" (Carter, Brown, Castro, & Id-Deen, 2019, p. 2565). Building on this research, our study takes an intergenerational and intersectional approach to Black girl civics. In this chapter, we delve into the pedagogical possibilities and tensions of a high school elective course taught by Black women for Black girls. Specifically, we will use this case study to (a) consider notions of Black girlhood and what it means to be accepted and protected inside a class grounded in *sistahood*; (b) analyze the ways the students embody and enact a form of artivism rooted to their own lives, languages, and youth cultures—what we term *hood civics*; (c) argue for the necessity of this work to be intergenerational and carried out by Black women as the *pedagogy of our lives*; and (d) discuss radical love, intergenerational healing, and critical hope as a means to reclaim educational spaces for Black women's knowledges, identities, and realities to emerge, providing important subtext for *decolonizing spaces*—including inside school systems.

PEOPLE BEHIND THE PEN

Dr. Jeanelle K. Hope is a Black, queer woman educator whose work examines grassroots social movements and Afro-Asian solidarity building. As an advocate for ethnic studies implementation at the K–12 level, liberatory pedagogies, and social justice education, Jeanelle often works alongside school teachers, administrators, and state officials to transform curriculum and school spaces. She approaches all of her work from a Black radical feminist lens and aims to amplify the voices and experiences of Black women and girls.

Dr. Vajra M. Watson seeks innovative ways to align people and systems that advance social justice. As a White female scholar, she examines the culture of schools, the broad ecology of education, and the relationship between schooling and social change. Vajra is originally from Berkeley, California and was deeply impacted by the courses she took in the Black and Xicanx Studies Departments at Berkeley High School in the mid-1990s. In 10th grade her final exam question was: "What are you doing to stop and/ or curtail the spread of white supremacy in yourself, community, and this world?" This question still shapes her path and purpose.

RESEARCH CONTEXT

Founded in 2008, Sacramento Area Youth Speaks (SAYS) breaks the barriers of underachievement by elevating the voices of students as the authors of their own lives and agents of change.[1] With hip-hop and spoken word performance poetry at its core, SAYS community-based educators work inside middle and high schools to provide culturally relevant instruction to predominately Black, Latinx, and Southeast Asian students via workshops, courses, mentoring, and an annual youth empowerment summit that takes place at the University of California, Davis. Over the last decade, SAYS has developed an award-winning model that connects art, activism, and academics (Watson, 2013, 2016).

In 2016, SAYS piloted a yearlong elective course at a South Sacramento high school called *Project HEAL: Health, Education, Artivism, and Leadership.* This specialized course aimed to work exclusively and unapologetically to address the experiences of 25 Black girls who were disproportionately confronting oppressive social systems, including their school campus. At the onset, students were referred into the course by a teacher, administrator, or campus counselor based upon the following criteria:

- consistent absenteeism;
- receiving a D/F in more than one subject;
- multiple detentions, suspensions, and/or referrals;
- recently incarcerated and/or on probation/parole;
- from a high-poverty area of Sacramento;
- from a high-violence area of Sacramento;
- receive free/reduced-fee lunches;
- designated as emotionally disturbed by a school IEP;
- gang-involved or affiliated; or
- will be the first in their family to graduate high school and/or first in their family to attend college.

While many teachers and administrators considered these students to be menaces, as described in detail on their disciplinary records, this was not the case in the Project HEAL space. Led by two Black women poet-mentor-educators (PMEs) in their mid-30s, this course was designed to align with students' lived experiences and elevate their aspirations. Inside the Project HEAL classroom, Black women worked holistically to help Black girls tease through their trauma and discuss multiple forms of violence—gang, sexual, and emotional—as well as income inequality and health disparities.

Before delving into our findings, we will share the research questions that guided our inquiry, the process we used to collect and analyze data, and the literature base that informs the civics of Black girls.

METHODOLOGY

Throughout this study, we have been guided by four overarching research questions:

1. In what ways, if at all, does the Project HEAL elective course disrupt the oppressive nature of schooling for Black girls?
2. Does an identity-based Black girl empowerment course change the self-perceptions and academic trajectories of its students? If so, how and why?
3. How is this class transforming the students and teachers as artivists within the Black community?
4. How does intergenerational healing shape and inform our understanding of Black girl civics?

To answer these questions, we relied on various qualitative techniques. Casual conversations and in-depth interviews took place over the course of two school years (2016–2017 and 2017–2018) with the teaching artists and the students. We facilitated a focus group with students (we also use the term *sister circles*), accompanied the class on some of their field trips, and took field notes during our participant observation of the Project HEAL elective course. Additionally, we received copies of the students' writing from the in-class workshops, analyzed their school records (specifically examining data related to attendance, behavior, and academic progress) and received course lesson plans and syllabi. Altogether, these multiple data sources allowed us to triangulate responses for patterns, accuracy, and helped us develop our findings.

THE INTERSECTION: BLACK GIRLHOOD STUDIES, HIP-HOP FEMINIST PEDAGOGY, AND PLACE-BASED EDUCATION

Black girlhood studies markedly draws on Black feminist scholars whose pioneering work explored the intersection of race and gender (Crenshaw, 1991); challenged the mythologizing of Black women as super-human (Wallace, 1979); moved the voices and experiences of Black women "from margin to center" (hooks, 1984); and provided new theories on Black women's thought, history, epistemologies, identity formation, and cultural production (Collins, 2000; Davis, 1981; Shange, 1976). Black girlhood studies provides a similar space for Black girls to be examined with the same rigor and nuance.

In "Super-Girl: Strength and Sadness in Black Girlhood," Nia Michelle Nunn uses "super-girl" as a metaphorical tool to elucidate how Black girls aged 8–13 are seen as possessing an uncanny ability to confront issues of racism and sexism during their educational experiences, while little attention is paid to the sadness that they also endure as a product of their perceived and actualized strength. Nunn's (2018) work calls for the creation of spaces, tools, and strategies that can help Black girls work through this imbalance, specifically within education. Ruth Nicole Brown's work (2009, 2013) illustrates the radical potential of Black girlhood studies by providing concrete examples of Nunn's call in praxis. In *Hear Our Truths: The Creative Potential of Black Girlhood,* Brown examines how Saving Our Lives Hear Our Truths (SOLHOT), a youth intervention program, provides space for Black girls to express the strength and sadness that Nunn describes, as well as create room for Black girls to envision their freedom, be affirmed, and tell their truths. Utilizing a "performative and creative methodology of a visionary Black-girlhood practice," (p. 3) SOLHOT helps disrupt elitist configurations of youth interventionist programming by creating a space that centers Black girls. SOLHOT, like Project HEAL, is an educational space that critically grapples with Black girlhood and youth studies by engaging the lived experiences of Black girls through liberatory pedagogies and teaching philosophies.

As a space of creative expression, hip-hop serves as both a soundtrack and method for the students and teachers in Project HEAL. In *When Chickenheads Come Home to Roost: A Black Feminist Breaks it Down,* Joan Morgan (1999) provides Black women with a language to describe their relationship with hip-hop, a genre that has been used to discuss the Black experience, while simultaneously garnering an immense amount of criticism for its marginalization of Black women artists, and the perpetuation of sexism and gendered violence. Morgan posits that we can be radical Black feminists *and* critical hip-hop heads—hip-hop feminists. Morgan's framework of hip-hop feminism has inspired a new wave of scholarship within Black girlhood and education studies—hip-hop feminist pedagogy.

Beyond engaging hip-hop—which has arguably been a youth driven genre since its inception—and providing a space for girls, women, and feminists to challenge the genre while simultaneously finding pleasure and enjoyment, hip-hop feminist pedagogies prioritize the communities and spaces that surround students and shape their identities. This sentiment is also echoed by Love (2012) in her work, *Hip Hop's Li'l Sistas Speak: Negotiating Hip Hop Identities and Politics in the New South.* She examines how youth, in particular Black girls, make meaning of rap music and hip-hop culture as part of their identity development. This research also demonstrates that hip-hop can provide an essential text and common language for examining oppressive systems.

With Nunn and other scholars noting the significant role that familial and neighborhood commitments play in the shaping of Black girls' identities and how they are able to navigate school and educational experiences, finding ways to engage community in the classroom has been a successful pedagogical practice. Emerging in the mid-1990s, place-based education (PBE) is the integration of the local community's history, culture, and natural environment into learning (Watson, 2018). Black girlhood programs like Project HEAL and SOLHOT leverage components of PBE to help empower Black girls by drawing on the "funds of knowledge" (Moll et al., 1992) and "resistance capital" (Yosso, 2005) of a particular area. PBE provides a space for Black girls to discuss how they navigate their specific communities.

Altogether, these bodies of scholarship provide a necessary framework for illuminating how to create radical spaces for Black girls to unpack layers of personal and institutional trauma as a form of empowerment and collective resistance.

OUR KITCHEN TABLE TALK

Everyday, Denisha Bland (see Figure 3.1) and Patrice Hill (see Figure 3.2) teach a class at Jefferson High School[2] in South Sacramento for Black girls—Project HEAL. In a city with several programs focused on boys of color, Project HEAL filled a major void by addressing the needs of Black girls, who like their male counterparts, also had high suspensions, were involved in gang violence, and were in need of guidance and support as they grappled with a multitude of familial obligations and stressors. The course started in 2016 with 25 young women from various parts of South Sacramento. Hill, SAYS program coordinator and PME, states that much

Figure 3.1 Illustration of Denisha "Auntie Coco" Bland. Drawn by Tessa Russell-Harde, SAYS Poet-Mentor Educator.

Figure 3.2 Illustration of Patrice "Mama P" Hill. Drawn by Tessa Russell-Harde, SAYS poet-mentor educator.

of the first year of the course was spent building relationships; learning to be vulnerable with each other; exercising critical listening; and processing discussions around violence, trauma, the girls' often strained relationships with their mothers, navigating the foster care system, graduating from high school, and preparing for college.

Hill explains that when the class began, "We had all these big dreams" but reality quickly set in when the students were not getting along. To respond to these serious frictions, "We really had to scaffold back and meet them where they were at. Like not only in their consciousness and their identity, but how they felt about [being] a young person, a young woman living in Sacramento amongst gang violence, amongst drugs, amongst poverty, amongst abuse and neglect." To shift the classroom dynamics, Hill and Bland made a conscious decision to "put the curriculum to the side" and "share who we were... We had to open up our lives—like, *no, no, no baby, Coco Mama live right down the street... We shop at FoodMaxx too! We right here with you!*"

The notion of being "right here with you" is an important concept underscored repeatedly in interviews with the students and educators alike. The familiarity served as the foundation for a family-like atmosphere that would continue to develop throughout the course. Eventually, the students gave Bland and Hill new names; now, they are commonly referred to as "Auntie Coco" and "Mama P." This terminology demonstrates the closeness of extended kin and care created within the class (Hope, 2019).

Ashanti, one of the Project HEAL youth shares,

> In this class it helps to express and talk about things that I can't with my mom or certain family members. This class also is a good way to express how you feel in writing. Another thing is that you don't have to feel ashamed because the teachers won't judge you, they'll help you get through whatever you're going through. Lastly, Mama P and Coco are like moms.

For most of the girls, this class is the first time they have a Black woman teacher. With Hill and Bland often within the same age range of many of the girls' mothers and living in the same area as their students, they are able to foster a relational classroom environment that crosses the boundaries of the traditional role of student and teacher. For both Hill and Bland, these are not "other people's children" (Delpit, 1995), these students represent their younger selves and they often refer to them as "our babies." This ethic of care and kinship permeates their pedagogy.

Hill and Bland describe the first year of critical listening and building sistahood as "kitchen table talk," drawing on generations of informal gatherings Black women and girls have had at kitchen tables as they prepare dinner, socialize, gossip, vent, and fellowship with each other. Their reference to "kitchen table talk" also builds on the work of women of color feminist writers, like Audre Lorde, Barbara Smith, and Cherrie Moraga, who founded a women of color press in 1981, named *Kitchen Table: Women of Color Press*. Similar to the press, Project HEAL serves as a space for Black women and girls to express their experiences, knowledge, and feelings on their own terms; a space where they do not need to code switch or worry about surveillance from authority figures. And because of this level of safety, students consistently show up, open up, and grow.

Inside the Project HEAL course, students engage in a myriad of writing workshops and subsequently share their work during the sister circle. The sharing circles are highly personal and many times the participants have to hold space for one another to heal (Watson, 2017). Marcelle Haddix describes this act of critical listening as "listening face-to-face," an integral aspect of working with Black girls in educational spaces (2013). Haddix argues that when Black women listen to Black girls, they not only validate and legitimize the girls' experiences, but they also engage in a form of intergenerational wellness where they are able to center their own narratives as Black women as well as those within their families and communities across space and time. This theme was crystallized when Hill and Bland helped the girls advocate for a new school resource officer (SRO). Issues with an abusive SRO were emerging from the students' writing and classroom conversations. Instead of just hearing from the students, Hill and Bland organized to get the SRO replaced.

With the classroom acting as a symbolic kitchen table, Project HEAL has created a welcoming and affirming learning environment for Black girls, and often serves as a driving force for them to attend and succedd in school. Over the last 2 years, students in the SAYS classes had a significant drop in disciplinary infractions. The number of African-American female student referrals for fighting dropped by 31%. Moreover, we were able to track a 48% increase in attendance and a 17% decrease in suspensions, expulsions, and detentions. For these students, the smallest grade point increase was .5 and the largest increase was 2.8 points with an average increase of 1.6 points. In other words, after participating in the intervention class, a student with an average cumulative GPA of 1.8 improved to a 3.4. This stark leap in school engagement and academic success is the by-product of a classroom oasis that radically engages Black girls.

WRITE TO LIVE

Starting in the 1980s, South Sacramento developed a reputation for its gritty landscape—widespread poverty and drug addiction, thriving gang culture and street violence, and few community resources—which only worsened with "War on Drugs" policies. Black, Hmong, Vietnamese, Tongan, Latinx, and Samoan youth turned to the streets, redesigning South Sacramento's geography through gang lines, creating makeshift families of their own, and surviving from work within underground economies. Over the past 2 years, Sacramento County has also made the news on several occasions for officer involved shootings, with often unarmed Black civilians as victims. The March 2018 killing of Stephon Clark in his grandmother's backyard by the Sacramento Police Department (SPD) polarized the city. The shooting, similar to much of the city's gang violence, took place just a few miles from the school in the heart of South Sacramento. Being constantly surrounded by death has left many of the Black girls in a constant state of grief or at an impasse where they are desensitized to death.

During a writing workshop, Mikela explains this grief through a spoken word performance poetry piece:

Blood On the Streets

Fatal Attraction.
Trigger happy boys always claiming they're bout that action.
They cling to the streets like it's the latest fashion.
I'm just waiting for #RIP to go out of style.

Heard my brother just got shot 9 times and you expect me to smile.
Dead in a ditch with no friends beside him but a "friend" was the accused
and was standing on trial.
One color can end your life, one word can change their minds.
One word scars all our minds.
INJUSTICE!
114 between 2007 to 2018.
How many more dead teens before the truth can be seen?
There's rising violence in my city.
The Capital City.
Divided.
This definitely ain't one sided.
One against another.
Brother against brother.
Police against "other."
I'm waiting for the day when gun laws make a difference
and we can stop harming each other.

This poem succinctly captures the history of gang, street, and state-sanctioned violence in Sacramento, underscoring how perpetual violence impacts youth, in particular Black girls, as they continue to navigate through life without their loved ones.

While some school teachers expect students at Jefferson to block out and compartmentalize their trauma, this is antithetical to the Project HEAL pedagogy. Hill and Bland are adamant that it is unrealistic for students to "block out" their trauma. The only way to heal is to deal with the trauma head-on and heart open. "We got to be able to deal with that and confront that before we can get to learning," says Bland.

Part of democratizing the Project HEAL classroom is allowing the girls to curate the art, images, quotes, and overall décor of the space. With many of the girls having lost family members, intimate partners, and friends due to gang and state-sanctioned violence, they insisted on having a space within the classroom to memorialize folks—the RIP wall (see Figure 3.3). The wall is a space for the girls to post pictures of their loved ones, to serve as a reminder of the ills of violence, and to provoke discussions about how the girls can become agents of change. The RIP wall is part of the learning process, not an adjacent artifact.

As skilled facilitators, Hill and Bland use the RIP wall as space to build solidarity across South Sacramento. The wall is one of the few spaces where it is acceptable for people from rival gangs and neighborhoods to be seen in such close proximity of one another. The PMEs are able to delve into discussions around gang prevention by reflecting on the many lives plastered on the wall, using those images as cautionary tales, while leaving the girls

Figure 3.3 A photo of the "RIP Wall" in the Project HEAL class.

with hope and alternatives to what gangs often provide—security, family, and fast money. Many of those posted on the wall have been vilified and dehumanized in both life and death because of their connection to the streets; often seen as not worthy of being remembered. But even though their lives were riddled with violence, they were still someone's brother, sister, uncle, auntie, father, or partner. Bland posits, "We just wanted the youth to be able to keep those people with them because if that person means so much to you," explains Bland, "then how can you take that person [with you and] still navigate [through life so that] you don't die with them." Shawn Ginwright's article (2018), "The Future of Healing: Shifting From Trauma Informed Care to Healing Centered Engagement," challenges the ways trauma reinforces harm instead of creating space for healing. He asserts, "Without careful consideration of the terms we use, we can create blind spots in our efforts to support young people" (p. 3). To empower young people who are experiencing layers of grief, healing centered engagement is explicitly political, rather than clinical. The Project HEAL classroom reverberates with this philosophy. "We [accept] that death is something that everyone has to face and go through; it's a part of life," explains Bland. "It is part of the common humanity that binds us. So instead of breaking apart we find ways to bond." The RIP wall and the discussions that unfold are often therapeutic and one of the few forms of grief counseling available to the girls.

Similarly, Jeffrey Duncan-Andrade (2009) uses Tupac Shakur's metaphor of roses growing from concrete to describe educators' experiences in teaching youth in underserved communities. He argues that hope has been worn down in these communities, and youth have often been given a false sense of hope. Thus, it is the responsibility of educators to utilize a pedagogy that draws on critical and material hope—teaching that connects the violence, outrage, and trauma youth experience to actions that will help relieve their suffering. These acts—the RIP wall, writing and performing poetry and spoken word, conducting research on issues that stymie wellness in their communities, field trips, and even helping students find employment and/or extracurricular activities—literally and figuratively turn nouns, like hope, into verbs.

Thus, "hood civics" and "critical and material hope" are cornerstones of a grassroots pedagogy where Black girlhood survives and thrives, and Black women educators are empowered through their service to a younger generation—an act of reciprocity and hood civic engagement in itself.

THE PEDAGOGY OF OUR LIVES

The Black female students in this study were reluctant to open up to adults at school. This changed in the Project HEAL course where they trusted Hill and Bland with their secrets and stories. Bland remembers a hard day, "This year we had one young sister and she ended up catching an STD; she was hurt. She walked through the whole day of school carrying that she had this STD and when [she] got to seventh period, she just came in the classroom and she was *just crying*." Instead of probing to find out what was wrong, Bland explains that she "just hugged her. I hugged her for a long time." After whispering a prayer into this child's ear and letting her weep, she asked what was going on. This young girl shared that she had caught an STD." After taking the student to get the proper medical help, "We went out to eat so I could make sure that no side effects took place from the medicines." Bland, grinning and shaking her head states, "We just like spent damn near forty-eight hours talking about why protecting yourself is important."

Based upon this exchange, Bland designed a follow-up writing workshop for the entire class. She was taken aback that many of the girls did not know about safe sex. As one student told her, "Ms. Coco, I never had a talk about this. I never knew why condoms was important." Bland's response to this health scare demonstrates a pattern inside the Project HEAL classroom—student's lives *are* the curriculum.

Even though the class focuses on real-life strife and struggles, this is only part of the pedagogy. To avoid an entrapment of low expectations—where everyone wallows in the pain—writing exercises are designed to turn pain into power. Reality must meet rigor in order for the curriculum to become empowering (Watson, 2017).

An essential component of Project HEAL is using reality to unlock reality. In other words, how do lessons inside class impact larger issues of violence at school and in the neighborhood? How does the curriculum shift student agency, advocacy, and sense of personal and collective responsibility within/for the Black community?

The answer, according to Hill and Bland, are consistent, methodical healing rituals that occur through dialogue, carefully crafted writing workshops, and sister circles. Writing individually but then sharing publicly has a layered impact:

- Even though there is usually a writing prompt to get the words flowing, the free-write process is a practice in freedom; there are no restrictions to what a student puts on the page.
- Most students open up in their writing, and there is a personal intimacy and innocence that lies beneath the hardcore masks and tough fronts (Dance, 2002) they often wear to survive.
- As students listen to each other share in class, it becomes clear that they actually have a lot in common. Being young African American women from South Sacramento with a range of struggles is actually a foundation for unity, instead of peer-on-peer brutality.

Learning and healing are reciprocal. Bland shakes her head, "I'm healing everyday with these girls. They're teaching me something new about myself. They're teaching me how to have my standards. It's helping me find my *queendom* and also helping me want to be able to walk and live better as well." Bland is describing what her colleague Patrice Hill calls, "a pedagogy of our lives," in that the educators are building a curriculum and employing a pedagogy that also speaks to their lived experiences and provides space for them to think through their own healing, especially around childhood trauma and educational justice. Hill and Bland provide a classroom experience that they believe could have greatly benefited them when they were Black girls.

During our interviews, Hill reflected on her own upbringing, "My Blackness was never protected because it was never acknowledged." Patrice carries these intimate, personal experiences into the classroom and is adamant that as a PME she will use Project HEAL to shift students towards taking pride in their Blackness. To achieve this goal, she asks herself a profound question each week: "How do I manifest Blackness and beauty with each lesson that I teach?"

HOOD CIVICS

With Bland, Hill, and the larger reputation of SAYS in the spoken word community, the presence of creative expression is salient in the Project HEAL course. Bland and Hill instill in the youth that poetry is practice in freedom; a tool of liberation and activism—*artivism*. Chela Sandoval and Guisela Latorre (2008) define artivism as, "A hybrid neologism that signified work created by individuals who see the organic relationship between art and activism" (p. 82). They posit that for Chicanx youth, artivism is often deployed as a means to transform themselves and their communities (see Figure 3.4). Bland has a similar outlook on artivism and its utility for Black girls. She defines artivism as,

> Using your art to do better for your community. Or using your art to speak about something... I actually learned it over the years, but just political art. So, like, using my voice and my agency to do better for my community, in some type of way. And I always have that on my mind every time I sit down to write a poem that's like one of the first things I think about. Is this poem, is this poem for me first? Is it something I just need to write and put in my book? Or is this a poem finna be something that I need to give to the people... SAYS actually helped me learn that.

Similarly, Bland states: "I think when you are conscious of your art and how it affects people, then you become an artivist." Inside the classroom, Bland consciously demonstrates that "art can educate people." Art helps "create a third space," she explains.

Historically, marginalized populations have leveraged poetry as a genre and method to articulate their politics, and often to dissent, on their own cultural terms. Sandra Faulkner (2009) argues that poetry often pays attention to the "particulars" of embodied knowledge, providing insight on developing politics and new realities. Furthermore, women and youth have utilized poetry within social movements where they have been silenced. Cheryl Clark (2005) and Ruffin and Mack (2018) posit that Black women

Figure 3.4 A group photo from the restorative justice gathering at UC Davis Law School. Project HEAL youth were featured speakers.

and youth in the 1960s were major poets of the period as they often used poetry as a form of activism after experiencing sexism and misogyny within grassroots organizations. Thus, youth artivism in praxis is using art, in this case poetry, to elevate the voices on the margins, help develop and articulate youth politics, establish youth agency, and to employ spoken word performance poetry as a vessel for youth to become authors of their own lives and agents of change.

In the next piece, Destiny, a Project HEAL student, declares who she speaks for and why.

"My Story"

My story is for the depressed kids.
My story is for the neglected kids.
My story is for the stressed kids.

I come from a city of Black crime and dangerous times.
My eyes see a crazy city and a work in progress.
My ears hear yelling, gunshots.
My city is hate and people dying.
My home is full of stress and babies crying.
My school is full of ignorance, discrimination and stereotypes.
My voice screams love and peace.
My voice demands control and power.
My voice dreams of justice.

Written during a 2016 writing workshop, the poem is centered around Destiny finding her voice to share and critique her surroundings, later calling for justice and demanding control, power, and to be heard. Project HEAL youth, like Destiny, have shared their poems at city council meetings, performed on local and national slam poetry contests, and presented at local protests and demonstrations. The pieces that they perform in public often discuss Sacramento's current affordable housing crisis/resegregation/gentrification, police brutality, racism, public and mental health, domestic violence, and critiques of the foster care system. Project HEAL students, like Destiny, have used their artivism to amplify and unapologetically center

Figure 3.5 A group photo of some Project HEAL students.

the narratives of their communities, to organize the masses through school walkouts, to call out elected officials and hold them accountable, and to inspire their own communities to engage in hood civics.

CONCLUSION

Many studies focus on the leaves—that is, the facts and figures that are the byproducts of certain kinds of programs. Then, there is research that emphasizes the branches—those correlations of how, why, and where the leaves connect. And, there are plenty of examinations that simultaneously consider the historical context: the roots. Our intention, however, was to dig (literally and figuratively) through layers of discoveries, constantly triangulating among multiple sources, to uncover the seed that holds the soul of the story—the lifeline (Watson, 2014). Extending this metaphor of a tree, neither policymakers, scholars, nor practitioners can plant a tree with leaves, limbs, or even roots. To authentically sustain and replicate this work in Sacramento and beyond, the seeds of liberation need to be identified and planted abundantly; this is how a single tree sprouts into a world of Black girl magic.

Why is the seed so important? Because it holds the essence and presence of being and becoming. As a lesson, nature implores us to re-center the seeds of transformation and growth towards a Black feminist epistemology. What if to be civically engaged meant to be away from the White gaze? What if this is the praxis of freedom that grows, shapes, and reconfigures society at the social, material, racial, cultural, and intellectual levels? What does it mean to not only teach, but nurture the next generation towards greatness? As a small process of inquiry, we delved into a classroom that reverberates with the heartbeats of Black life, Black sistahood, and Black artivism.

This is precisely what Mercy is urging us to do at the beginning of the chapter. By seeing the hood in Black girls, and them claiming it, we not only rewrite a text for Black girl empowerment, but also see how this generation is redefining the politics of place and complicating how to be, *civically*.

ACKNOWLEDGMENTS

Funding for the Project HEAL courses as well as this study was provided by the City of Sacramento's Office of Violence Prevention, the UC Davis Feminist Research Institute, Sacramento City Unified School District, and most importantly, the young people and Project HEAL educators who opened up their classroom doors and hearts to this exploration of #HoodCivics and #BlackGirlMagic.

NOTE

1. http://www.says.ucdavis.edu
2. For the sake of anonymity, we use a pseudonym for the name of the high school where the Project HEAL course takes place. Additionally, we opted to only use the first names of the students.

REFERENCES

Brown, R. N. (2009). *Black girlhood celebration: Toward a hip-hop feminist pedagogy.* Bern, Switzerland: Peter Lang.

Brown, R. N. (2013). *Hear our truths: The creative potential of Black girlhood.* Champaign: University of Illinois Press.

Carter Andrews, D. J., Brown, T., Castro, E., & Id-Deen, E. (2019). The impossibility of being "perfect and White": Black girls' racialized and gendered schooling experiences. *American Educational Research Journal, 56*(6), 2531–2572.

Clarke, C. (2004). *After Mecca: Women poets and the Black arts movement.* New Brunswick, NJ: Rutgers University Press.

Crenshaw, K. (1991). Mapping the margins: Intersectionality, identity politics, and violence against women of color. *Stanford Law Review, 43*(6), 1241–1299.

Dance, L. J. (2002). *Tough fronts: The impact of street culture on schooling.* London, England: Routledge.

Davis, A. (1981). *Women, race, and class.* New York, NY: Vintage Books.

Delpit, L. (1995). *Other people's children: Cultural conflict in the classroom.* New York, NY: The New Press.

Duncan-Andrade, J. M. R. (2009). Note to educators: Hope required when growing roses in concrete. *Harvard Educational Review, 79*(2), 181–194.

Faulkner, S. (2009). *Poetry as method: Reporting research through verse.* Walnut Creek, CA: Left Coast Press.

Ginwright, S. (May, 2018). The future of healing: Shifting from trauma informed care to healing centered engagement. Retrieved from https://medium.com/@ginwright/the-future-of-healing-shifting-from-trauma-informed-care-to-healing-centered-engagement-634f557ce69c

Haddix, M. (2013). Chapter 7 visionary response: Listening "face-to-face" and "Eye-to-Eye": Seeing and believing Black girls and women in educational practice and research. *Counterpoints, 454,* 191–199.

Hill Collins, P. (2000). *Black feminist thought: Knowledge, consciousness, and the politics of empowerment.* Brandon, VT: Psychology Press.

hooks, b. (1984). *Feminist theory: From margin to center.* Boston, MA: South End Press.

Hope, J. K. (2019). "I'm an artist and I'm sensitive about my city": Black women artivists confronting resegregation in Sacramento. *American Studies, 58*(3), 59–85.

Levinson, M. (2010). The civic empowerment gap: Defining the problem and locating solutions. In L. Sherrod, J. Torney-Purta, & C. A. Flanagan (Eds.), *Handbook of research on civic engagement* (pp. 331–361). Hoboken, NJ: Wiley.

Love, B. (2012). *Hip hop's li'l sistas speak: Negotiating hip hop identities and politics in the new south.* New York, NY: Peter Lang.

Moll, L., Amanti, C., Neff, D., & Gonzalez, N. (1992). Funds of knowledge for teaching: Using a qualitative approach to connect homes and classrooms. *Theory Into Practice, 31*(2), 132–141.

Nunn, N. M. (2018). Super-girl: Strength and sadness in Black girlhood. *Gender and Education, 30*(2), 239–258.

Perlow, O., Wheeler, D. I., Bethea, S. L., Scott, B. M. (Eds.). (2018). *Black women's liberatory pedagogies: Resistance, transformation, and healing within and beyond the academy.* London, England: Palgrave Macmillan.

Ruffin, H. G., II, & Mack, D. A. (2018). Poetic justice: Bay area Afro-Asian women's activism through verse. In J. Hope (Ed.), *Freedom's racial frontier: African Americans in the twentieth-century west* (pp. 128–145). Norman: University of Oklahoma Press.

Sandoval, C., & Latorre, G. (2008). Chicana/o artivism: Judy Baca's digital work with youth of color. In A. Everett (Ed.), *Learning race and ethnicity: Youth and digital media* (pp. 81–108). Cambridge, MA: The MIT Press.

Shange, N. (1976). *For colored girls who have considered suicide/when the rainbow is enuf.* New York, NY: Scribner.

Wallace, M. (1979). *Black macho and the myth of the superwoman.* New York, NY: The Dial Press.

Watson, V. (2012). *Learning to liberate: Community-based solutions to the crisis in urban education.* New York, NY: Routledge.

Watson, V. (2013). Censoring freedom: Community-based professional development and the politics of profanity. *Equity & Excellence in Education, 46*(3), 387–410.

Watson, V. (2014). *The Black sonrise: Oakland Unified School District's commitment to address and eliminate institutionalized racism.* Final evaluation report submitted to Oakland Unified School District's Office of African American Male Achievement. https://www.ousd.org/cms/lib07/CA01001176/Centricity/Domain/78/TheBlackSonrise_WebV2_sec.pdf

Watson, V. (2016). Literacy is a civil write: The art, science and soul of transformative classrooms.] In R. Papa, D. M. Eadens, & D. M. Eadens, (Eds.), *Social justice instruction: Empowerment on the chalkboard* (pp. 307–323). New York, NY: Springer.

Watson, V. (2017, Winter). Life as primary text: English classrooms as sites for soulful learning. *The Journal of the Assembly for Expanded Perspectives on Learning, 22*, 6–18.

Watson, V. (2018). *Transformative schooling: Towards racial equity in education.* New York, NY: Routledge.

Yosso, T. (2005). Whose culture has capital? A critical race theory discussion of community cultural wealth. *Race Ethnicity and Education, 8*(1), 69–91.

CHAPTER 4

SISTERS, FRIENDS, AND KIN

Critical Pedagogies and Black Girl Civics

Sabrina J. Curtis
The George Washington University

We are the children of Africa. We practice Ma'at.
—*ARC* affirmation

The Africana Research Collective (ARC)[1] is an intergenerational, public health, and social action organization whose mission is to improve the health and well-being of Black[2] girls and their families and to advance social justice in their communities. The ARC was established by Black women who desired to create leadership, research, and social action opportunities for Black girls beyond the confines of traditional educational spaces. Each summer, the ARC hosts civic camp, a month-long leadership development and social action training program grounded in the histories and cultures of African and African diasporic peoples. During the camp, girls who are entering the first through ninth grades are fully immersed within the ARC community, which includes program leaders, caregivers, visiting scholars, and artists from their local area. Each day, the ARC's members recite an affirmation that ends in this way: "Like the Sankofa bird, we look to our past, so that we can be our best, today and every day. Àṣẹ"[3] (personal observation,

Black Girl Civics, pages 55–69
Copyright © 2020 by Information Age Publishing
All rights of reproduction in any form reserved.

2018). *Sankofaism* is an Akan word and custom that has largely been translated to "go back and fetch it" (Quan-Baffour, 2012, pp. 2–3). It is a form of "cultural borrowing" (Temple, 2010, p. 128) signifying a "return to source" (p. 128) where knowledge, wisdom, and lessons from the past are used to contextualize contemporary life experiences.

Temple (2010) describes the practice of Sankofa as "orientations towards African consciousness" (p. 128), which privilege African ways of knowing and resist Eurocentric worldviews as dominant and solely defining of contemporary life (Temple, 2010). Civic camp's program philosophy is intentionally centered on Ma'atian principles. The Kemetic principles of Ma'at[4] are a set of ethics derived from an ancient Egyptian standard of conduct. Ma'at is a "way of rightness" (Karenga, 2003, p. 10) where principles of truth, order, balance, reciprocity, and justice are central to seeking and sustaining harmony among people living in a community (Karenga, 2003). Collins (2000) asserts, "People become more empowered primarily in the context of community" (p. 279), which is possible through engagement in dialogical processes leading to a sense of connectedness and harmony among the collective (Collins, 2000). African dialogical traditions are significant in shaping African and African American discourse modes—they validate Black women's knowledge claims, and ways of knowing, and connect and sustain harmonious relationships within Africana communities (Asante, 1987; Collins, 2000; Evans-Winters, 2015). This dialogical tradition plays a central role in meeting the ARC's program objectives, which are to celebrate a sense of shared heritage among its members and to increase awareness of health and social inequities that continue to disproportionately affect Black families, particularly Black women and girls.

The ARC's social action focus is defined by advocating for transformative policies and practices that reduce racial and gender disparities and foster equity (personal communication [ARC internal program documents], July 9, 2018). Annette,[5] the ARC's co-founder and a sociologist by training whose own extensive research chronicles the social inequities and public health challenges that imperil Black families and communities, asserts that the organization's goal is to foster a sense of cultural pride and civic agency and to "chip away at some of the myths and misleading information pertaining to health and social justice in Black communities" (personal communication, 2018). Annette believes, "Individuals who are poor in health cannot wholly enact change" (personal communication, 2018). Through the ARC's programming, the girls develop skills to identify and critique social issues impacting their communities. They are encouraged to construct social action projects that address issues they have identified as important, all while being immersed in culturally relevant academic and arts-based activities. The girls, notably, take leading roles in conceptualizing the social action projects, which are typically suited to the needs of their peers, as well as their extended community.

The ARC's programming includes civic camp, which takes place each July, and Civic Girls Society, which runs throughout the year. Civic Girls Society is a youth-led initiative comprised of a youth leadership team model where the girls serve in elected offices and other leadership positions that allow them to hone their skills in strategic planning, budgeting, and project management. In Civic Girls Society, the girls participate in leadership development trainings and healthcare internships. They also perform regular community service work with local organizations in addition to implementing larger social action projects. In order to join Civic Girls Society, they must attend civic camp, a summer intensive orientation (or, in some cases, a reorientation as many of the girls remain long-time members of the organization) focused on increasing cultural consciousness, developing research skills, and fostering creative ability through various art forms, such as African dance, drumming, step, and poetry.

THEORETICAL AND CONCEPTUAL FRAMEWORKS

This discussion draws from a larger study designed to explore how the ARC's members make sense of their cultural, ethnic, and civic identities and practices. This area of inquiry has personal significance for me as a Black woman, as I remain active in leading mentorship programs for Black youth outside of the context of this research site. Knowing that my personal background influences how I come to this research, I do not see my positioning as a limitation; rather, I believe that it enhances my analysis and the ways I am able to observe and interpret the data. This research is situated at the intersections of culturally relevant pedagogy and civic identity development. I place it within a framework that positions the ARC as a radical, creative space (hooks, 1990), out of which the girls' civic practices are born and their subjectivities are reaffirmed.

Culturally Relevant Pedagogy

In "Toward a Theory of Culturally Relevant Pedagogy," Ladson-Billings (1995b) articulated a pedagogical model that promotes academic achievement, develops sociopolitical consciousness (including students' abilities to identify and critique social inequities), and fosters a sense of cultural competence within students. The model emphasizes maintaining students' cultural integrity while nurturing their intellectual growth (Ladson-Billings, 1995b; 2014). As a critical pedagogy and a "pedagogy of opposition" (Ladson-Billings, 1995a, p. 160), culturally relevant pedagogy (CRP) counters cultural hegemony, which only identifies dominant forms of cultural capital "as socially legitimate" (Giroux, 1997, p. 6). CRP resists a culture of individualism and competition and insists on values of collective empowerment and social justice (Aronson & Laughter, 2016). It embraces the cultural values, worldviews, and ways of knowing that students and teachers bring to the classroom. CRP facilitates reciprocal learning processes where students are intellectually challenged and engaged in peer-to-peer dialogue in which they use individual and shared wisdom to critique their sociopolitical realities.

Since Ladson-Billings' groundbreaking scholarship challenged deficit framing of African American students and uplifted strengths-based approaches to teaching, scholars have now broadened the initial framing of CRP by proposing new models such as culturally sustaining pedagogy (Paris, 2012; Paris & Alim, 2014). Culturally sustaining pedagogy seeks to "sustain linguistic, literate, and cultural pluralism as part of the democratic project of schooling and as a needed response to demographic and social change" (Paris & Alim, 2014, p. 88). It values the multiplicity of knowledge and cultures within communities and repositions them within a skills and asset-based framework. This framework addresses students' abilities to navigate an increasingly global society that relies less on having sole competence of dominant White middle class norms (Paris & Alim, 2014, p. 87). While Ladson-Billings (2014) embraces the reimagining of CRP, I wish, for the purposes of this discussion, to *go back* to CRP as Ladson-Billings (1995a, 1995b) imagined it by focusing, primarily, on the need to raise young people's sociopolitical consciousness while nurturing their cultural ways of being and knowing.

Civic Identity Development

Youth civic identity is influenced by sociocultural orientations and political ideologies embedded within family units and discourse communities (Flanagan, Loreto Martínez, Cumsille, & Ngomane, 2011; Kirshner, 2009). What becomes meaningful for a young person's civic identity is largely determined by what their community believes to be important (Phinney & Baldelomar, 2011). Flanagan and Faison (2001) posited, "The civic identities, political views and values of young people are rooted in their social relations and in the opportunities they have for civic practice" (p. 4). In intergenerational community spaces, where youth and adults are working to address the challenges facing their communities, meaningful opportunities for social justice-oriented civic practices arise. These communities of practice undoubtedly influence how youth come to see themselves as civic actors and how they make sense of their cultural, ethnic, and civic identities.

Although much of the literature on CRP is contextualized within formal schooling contexts, the tenets of CRP have significant implications for educational programming that occurs outside of the classroom in both after-school, summer, and community-based education settings. Community-based education allows for flexibility in the curriculum and for the possibility of youth-driven civic programming. Not having the constraints of multiple layers of bureaucracy and neoliberal notions of schooling, which are often located in formal education settings (Costigan, 2013; Malone & Donahue, 2018), community-based education can raise sociopolitical consciousness and lend to civic identity development by providing opportunities for youth to engage in critical social analysis and to collectively envision, organize, and enact social change (Noguera, 2014; Watts, Diemer, & Voight, 2011).

Radical Creative Spaces as Sites of Resistance

Community and civic organizations are sources of critical social capital. Ginwright (2007) describes this as a form of capital "facilitated by intergenerational advocacy that challenges negative concepts about Black youth; is developed by building a collective racial and cultural identity; and is sustained by cultivating an understanding of personal challenges as political issues" (p. 404). Black women's activism can manifest in what bell hooks (1990) calls radical, creative spaces or "central location[s] for the production of counter-hegemonic discourse that is not just found in words but in habits of being and the way one lives" (p. 149). These spaces are sites of resistance, creativity, inclusivity, and transformation open to interruption by artistic, political, and literary practices where Black women's subjectivities are affirmed (hooks, 1990). Consequently, Black women are uniquely positioned to hold space for Black girls and to provide reaffirming educational experiences that are critically informed, culturally relevant, and attuned to the local and broader sociopolitical contexts in which Black girls' lives are situated. Thus, these spaces, such as those created by the members of the ARC, offer unique opportunities to explore how Black girls make sense of their cultural, ethnic, and civic identities.

METHOD

To conduct this research, I utilized a basic interpretive design (Merriam & Tisdell, 2016) to explore how Black girls theorize about civic engagement and to understand how culturally relevant programming shapes their cultural, ethnic, and civic identities and practices. A basic interpretive study, which is concerned with how people interpret their experiences, construct their worlds, and attribute meaning to their experiences (Merriam & Tisdell, 2016), is useful for exploring how the girls make sense of their experiences as members of the ARC. The overall study was guided by the following research questions: (a) "How do Black women develop the cultural and civic identities of Black girls through culturally relevant civic programming?"; (b) "How do Black girls who participate in the organization's programs articulate their cultural and civic identities?"; (c) "How do the program participants characterize their civic experiences and assert their civic agency?"; and (d) "How do the caregivers describe the influence of the program on the development of the girls?"

To explore these questions, I collected data through focus group discussions, individual interviews, and participant observations for 115 hours over the course of the ARC's 4-week civic camp in 2018. The general population of the ARC's members who were on site at any given time for the duration of the camp included youth participants (all girls), program leaders, caregivers (some of whom periodically led health or arts workshops), and visiting scholars and artists. During daily camp meetings, I shared details about the study and worked with members to determine the best times to hold discussions to ensure that as many members as possible had opportunities to participate. As visiting scholars and artists came to the site, I engaged them after their workshops and invited them to participate in an interview.

Out of the population described above, I collected data from the following participants who self-selected into the study (see Table 4.1). The camp program documents, which include camp philosophies, weekly schedules with workshop details, instructor bios, and public facing curricular documents available on the organization's web site, were also reviewed.

I used inductive analysis (Thomas, 2006) and thematic analysis (Attride-Stirling, 2001) to reduce and analyze the data. This chapter will only address the following aspects of the study's overall findings: (a) The girls theorize about civic engagement differently; (b) their civic practices are largely inspired by their individual interests and other forms of external socialization in addition to the ARC's public health focus; and (c) the girls' abilities to

TABLE 4.1 2018 Study Participants		
Participant Category[a]	**Data Collection Method**	**Number in Category**
Girls (5th–9th grades)	Focus Groups (2)	11 girls
Girls (5th–9th grades)	Semi-Structured Interview	5 girls
Program Leaders	Semi-Structured Interview	5 women
Junior Program Leader	Semi-Structured Interview	1 woman
Caregivers	Focus Group	7 women
Caregivers	Semi-Structured Interview	3 (2 women and 1 man)
Visiting Scholars/Artists	Semi-Structured Interview	3 (2 women and 1 man)

[a] All participants identify as Black or as having African ancestry.

engage in critical social analysis are being cultivated by the opportunity to interrogate social inequities contextualized within historical and contemporary Black experiences.

FINDINGS: SANDRA, DANA, AND BIANCA

In this discussion, we hear from civic girls youth participants, Dana (14 years old), Sandra (13 years old), and Bianca (10 years old) whose perspectives help explicate these themes and a couple of the tensions in the data. Dana and Sandra have been a part of civic camp since its inception in 2010. They are both instrumental in ensuring that the daily programming at civic camp runs smoothly, guiding younger members of the ARC through academic and creative activities; and filling in the gaps when extra hands are needed to facilitate a project or complete a task. Bianca was just in her second year, yet, she was very outspoken and thoughtful in the way she reflected on her experiences. Because it is important for me to center the girls' voices, I retain their commentaries in the representation of their sensemaking as much as possible. Additionally, when appropriate or for added context, I include a few anecdotes from their program leaders and caregivers here as well.

For clarity, it is worth noting that in initial conversations with the girls, the term civic engagement did not resonate with all of them; instead many of the girls used "community service" as a way to discuss their regular community service work and their larger social action projects. Since the girls both perform regular community service and design strategic, research-based social action plans, for the purposes of this discussion, the broader term "civic engagement" is used to capture their ongoing volunteer work and the term "social action projects" is used to define the larger social action plans the girls conceptualize, research, design, and implement into their communities.

Girls' Theorizing and Practice of Civic Engagement

During a focus group discussion, the girls were asked to describe what civic engagement or social action meant to them and to explain how they felt about doing community work. The ways in which the girls conceived of civic engagement ranged from small actions, such as picking up litter and giving away money to people in need, to more complex actions or strategic forms of organizing, such as identifying public resources to improve green spaces in their neighborhoods. Dana, specifically, noted:

> I believe it's using your passions in some cases and also using what you know your community struggles with or your community needs help with in order

to give them your resources and help attend to their needs that you know are most urgent. (Focus Group Discussion, 2018)

Bianca identified an emotional and psychological aspect of civic engagement:

Keeping your community clean is a really good way for people to feel good. If you have a community that has trash all over it and just doesn't look nice, you really won't feel as good. It's really important for someone to be able to be happy where they live. (Focus Group Discussion, 2018)

Sandra added,

Dana and I have been a part of this since we were six and five. Before that, maybe we didn't really understand the concept of community service and civic engagement. But at the same time, we were doing these little things. Even when I would play outside in my neighborhood with my friends I would pick up trash and throw it out, or I'd make sure you go inside to throw out your stuff. Don't just leave it on the ground. But I didn't really understand the word to use for that. (Focus Group Discussion, 2018)

In the girls descriptions of how they initially thought about community-facing work, it became clear that the girls did not all characterize civic engagement in the same way despite having close, ongoing ties to the ARC. When asked to describe how social action projects were conceived and implemented through the ARC, the girls explained how they take turns creating their initiatives, which are fully supported by the organization and its members. For example, three of the girls were co-leading an effort to design a positive mental health initiative for youth in partnership with local schools. Their ultimate goal was to encourage schools to designate time for school members to engage in activities that center youth voices in dialogue about youth mental health issues. Sandra explained,

We are trying to destigmatize the negative air around mental health because it's something that's not really brought up in schools, and when it is brought up, it's mostly talking about adult women or just adults in general and we never really talk about it in kids. We all have things that we struggle with and a lot of us do have anxiety especially when it comes to the beginning of school. (Focus Group Discussion, 2018)

Sandra's concerns illuminate how the generation of the mental health awareness campaign reflects the ARC's stated programmatic focus and how she and her peers are asserting their civic agency in ways that confront social issues within and beyond the classroom.

The girls intimated that the ARC's programming was not the sole driver in how they thought about their community's needs. For example, Sandra designed and implemented a project called Full Court Dress, an ARC initiative inspired by her interest in sports:

> I decided to have a drive for warm clothing and socks. I had a basketball game and a bunch of people came and played in the game. So, I took something I loved, which is helping people and another thing I like, which is basketball. I got like 500 socks and a lot of jackets. I thought it was important because I feel like everybody thinks about the adults but we never seem to think about the children. (Individual Interview, 2018)

Sandra's idea to collect warm clothing as admission to an ARC-sponsored basketball tournament came to her during one of the many trips to the school where her mother works and where she often saw kids going to school in the winter without jackets. For Dana, her initiative was sparked by in-class experiences that were tainting her strong interests in mathematics. Her mother, Marie, noted that when Dana was in third grade, she began having some difficulty with her math work and it had begun to affect her self-esteem. When Dana expressed the sentiment that only the boys in her classroom were being called on to answer math questions, she realized other girls in the program were experiencing similar issues in their classes at their respective schools. An informal dialogue between Dana and her peers turned into an opportunity to engage other girls in her community who might be facing similar challenges in school. Out of a desire to address the girls' concerns, Dana launched Math Whiz Games, a community-wide math games competition to help Black girls realize their potential to do well in math.

Conversations with the girls shed light on how their lived experiences influence their understandings of civic engagement and how they make connections between personal interests and concerns about larger social issues (Ginwright, 2007), such as addressing mental health challenges in Black communities and combating negative stereotypes and narratives pertaining to Black girls' mathematic capabilities (Pinkard, Erete, Martin, & McKinney de Royston, 2017). By identifying these connections, the girls find ways to extend their experiential knowledge into viable social action projects, which in turn, reifies the value and significance their experiences bring to the larger society.

Girls' Civic Socialization and Critical Reflection

To further explore how the girls were theorizing about civic engagement, I also met with program leaders and caregivers to identify what other factors were influencing the girls' civic identity development. The data reflected that the differences in the ways the girls theorize about and practice civic engagement is also influenced, in some cases, by the girls' individual socialization

(Flanagan et al., 2011), their prior civic experiences, and the amount of time they had spent in connection with others in the program (Phinney & Balde-lomar, 2011). For example, after being an active member of the ARC for al-most eight years, Dana provided that she now approached civic engagement with a different mindset:

> I had no real desire to do it, I guess. It made it seem like it was a chore, rather than something that's fun and something that could really affect your life in a positive way. I do think it's important because not only is it helping your com-munity and improving your well-being, but it's also a reciprocal engagement. As you help your community you are in the end term helping yourself more because it's enriching your soul and you get more inspired to take more ac-tion and to really just improve the lives of others. (Personal Interview, 2018)

During a focus group discussion with the caregivers, Dana's mother, Marie, who is one of the ARC's primary program leaders, alluded to Dana's trans-formation and to her own as well:

> I didn't realize that I had contempt for poor people. I was born poor. And, I remember Annette (the ARC's co-founder) saying that to me, and I was like, "How could she say that about me! I was poor!" You know, but I think that along the way, coming from Jamaica to here, and then believing in this prem-ise of, pull yourself up by the bootstraps, that it actually had a by-product...I was actually passing that onto my kid. So, she too was also systematically feel-ing this way. So, I had to unlearn some of those things...so that then my kid could authentically approach giving. (Focus Group Discussion, 2018)

In response to Marie, Angela (Bianca's mother) commented:

> And it's interesting that you say that, because that's a cultural difference. It's because of where you come from, versus this, as I call it, Black experience. So culturally, I understand what you're saying. We also live in the inner city, so it's [poverty] something that we see all the time, and my daughter wants to give to a fault. But we have a dialogue about it because where we live, she sees it. Where we own our business on the east side, she sees it. And we try to find ways to support the community. So it's not just something that she's taught about; it's a value that we have. (Focus Group Discussion, 2018)

Dana's reference to Annette's indirect comments about poverty and self-ad-vancement hints at a tension between some members of African American and African immigrant populations, but highlights the diversity of perspec-tives that the organization's members have held over time. Angela's differ-entiation between how she and Marie were brought up in the United States and Jamaica illustrated how they, as adults and mothers, held competing perceptions about civic engagement. When I spoke with Bianca individually, she both confirmed and challenged her mother's sentiments:

> Well, my mommy does do community service. Basically, my whole family does, yes. Before I thought community service was more like a punishment and something that you really wouldn't want to do. And now, I feel like I want to do that more. I want to help my community. (Personal Interview, 2018)

The reflections Marie, Dana, Angela, and Bianca shared illustrate how some of the girls' conceptualizations of civic engagement are also influenced by their familial experiences in addition to the training and civic opportunities initiated through the organization. Many of the girls expressed how their beliefs in the importance of civic engagement changed after they began participating in the ARC's programming. In some cases, like Bianca's, the girls and their caregivers held different views regarding how their daughters perceived the importance of civic work at different stages in their lives.

In addition to the messaging the girls were receiving at home about what it means to give, to practice civic engagement, or to be socially active, the intersections of the ARC's public health and Black history and culture programmatic foci were also apparent when the girls were theorizing about critical issues affecting their communities. I asked the girls if they believed what they were learning about health, wellness, and social justice was specifically important for Black families. In their replies, they alluded to the many ways intersectionality (Crenshaw, 1991) and issues of place had implications for Black families. Bianca offered,

> Well, in public health [workshop], we actually learned a lot about how your health impacts your community and where you live really impacts how you go out into the world and how you feel mentally, socially, and physically. In our state, there are also places that people don't have access to proper food. Like not all parts of our state are the same. (Focus Group Discussion, 2018)

Bianca's comments reflect how she is using information she learned at civic camp to make connections between environmental circumstances and personal health and wellness. During an interview, Dana spoke to how she makes sense of the way race and gender intersect and impact the health and well-being of Black bodies:

> I was learning about African descent and how as a Black woman in America or even just a Black person in America you are more susceptible to different sorts of diseases. These typically go hand in hand, like, if you're suffering from stuff you are more likely to suffer from a serious mental illness. It's important to have a clear mind, clear body, and how that's even more necessary as a Black woman in America as there is so much oppression coming upon

your shoulders. I think that was something really important I learned and that I found out I have a real interest in. (Individual Interview, 2018)

The girls' assessments of the many ways social inequities and health disparities impact Black communities reflect how they are critically analyzing social issues. Their insights describe how they are dissecting historical and contemporary social issues through intersecting gendered and racial lenses. The space the ARC provides for the development of girls' civic identities and civic practices reflects what Evans-Winters (2015) calls "Black feminism as praxis," which is a "historical legacy of connecting educational reform to consciousness-raising about the conditions affecting the Black community and women" (p. 140). The ARC's work reinforces the notion that civic engagement, when it is aligned with the interests of those involved in the work, has positive developmental impacts for youth and adults in the communities in which the efforts are targeted (Christens and Kirshner, 2011).

CONCLUSION

Ladson-Billings' (1995b) theory of culturally relevant pedagogy provides a framework for understanding how Black history and culture are made explicit in the ARC's programming and illustrates how being intentional in nurturing the girls' cultural and ethnic identities is significant for the development of their civic leadership skills and raising their sociopolitical consciousness. For example, Sandra's participation in civic camp enabled her to deconstruct and reframe what she was feeling in school as she was attempting to navigate discussions on race and history in her classes:

[Black history] basically teaches me that not everybody was enslaved, and that we were *enslaved*, we weren't *slaves*. In school, it seemed that there would be a book about a Black child and then everybody would just look at you, or when they brought up slavery, I don't understand that because it wasn't me who did that to myself. The real people who you guys should be looking at is the people who actually did that to my ancestors, and I never understood that. But when I came to civic camp, I actually felt that I belonged. Even the girls who I might have met just last week, it feels almost as if we're sisters and when we all leave from civic camp, and over the weekend, it makes me sad now as I look forward to seeing them. (Individual Interview, 2018)

Sandra's assertions begin to speak to the possibilities that radical, creative spaces, such as those born by Annette and her colleagues, provide for Black girls to resist positions of marginality and to foster a sense of belonging (hooks, 1990). The "politics of location," hooks (1990) proclaims, "calls those of us who would participate in the formation of counter-hegemonic cultural practice to identify the spaces where we begin the process of revision" (p. 145). Contextualizing civic learning within a culturally relevant framework that moves beyond a young person's immediate context and encapsulates African Diasporic identities and cultures can help young people dissect their evolving sense of self, identity, and place within community and society.

Black girls' experiences, in general, remain under theorized (Evans-Winters, 2019) and scholarship on Black girls' intellectual and civic activities outside of formal school spaces remains limited. There is more to learn about the utility of framing education for social justice within the local, sociopolitical, and cultural contexts of youth. In conceptualizing future possibilities for this work, there is a need to consider how youth are exploring expanded and more "fluid" identities (Ladson-Billings, 2014, p. 77) and to examine the agencies of Black girls beyond the deficit framings in which much of the early literature on Black girls is located (Evans-Winters & Esposito, 2010). Further analysis on the evolving theories of culturally relevant and sustaining pedagogies (Ladson-Billings, 2014; Paris, 2012; Paris & Alim, 2014) and on the sociocultural and political contexts of society—and the ways in which historically marginalized populations conceptualize their place within it (Cohen, 2006)—can provide alternative frameworks for interrogating cultural, ethnic, and civic identity development in Black girls.

ACKNOWLEDGMENTS

Thank you to the ARC community for allowing me to share space with you and to my advisor and readers for their review and commentary.

NOTES

1. The name of the organization is a pseudonyms.
2. I use the term *Black* to identify participants who self-identify as Black or as having African ancestry.
3. Àṣẹ represents a divine essence in which physical materials, metaphysical concepts, and art blend to form the energy or life force that activates and directs socio-political, religious, and artistic processes and experiences. For more on the concept of Àṣẹ, see Abiodun, R. (1994). Understanding Yoruba art and aesthetics: The concept of Àṣẹ. *African Arts, 27*(3), 68–103.
4. For the ontological origins of Ma'at, see Karenga, M. (2003). *The moral ideal in ancient Egypt: A study in classical African ethics.* New York, NY: Routledge.
5. All participant names are pseudonyms.

REFERENCES

Abiodun, R. (1994). Understanding Yoruba art and aesthetics: The concept of Àṣẹ. *African Arts, 27*(3), 68–103.

Aronson, B., & Laughter, J. (2016). The theory and practice of culturally relevant education: A synthesis of research across content areas. *Review of Educational Research, 86*(1), 163–206.

Asante, M. (1987). *The Afrocentric idea.* Philadelphia, PA: Temple University.

Attride-Stirling, J. (2001). Thematic networks: An analytic tool for qualitative research. *Qualitative Research, 1*(3), 385-405.

Christens, B. D., & Kirshner, B. (2011). Taking stock of youth organizing: An interdisciplinary perspective. *Youth civic development: Work at the cutting edge. New directions for child and adolescent development, 2011*(134), 27–41.

Cohen, C. (2006). African American youth: Broadening our understanding of politics, civic engagement and activism. *Youth Activism.* Retrieved from http://ya.ssrc.org/african/Cohen

Collins, P. H. (2000). *Black feminist thought: Knowledge, consciousness, and the politics of empowerment.* New York, NY: Routledge.

Costigan, A. T. (2013). New urban teachers transcending neoliberal educational reforms: Embracing aesthetic education as a curriculum of political action. *Urban Education, 48*(1), 116–148.

Crenshaw, K. (1991). Mapping the margins: Identity politics, intersectionality, and violence against women. *Stanford Law Review, 43*(6), 1241–1299.

Evans-Winters, V. (2015). Black women in qualitative educational research. In V. Evans-Winters & B. Love (Eds.), *Black feminism in education: Black women speak back, up, and out.* New York, NY: Peter Lang.

Evans-Winters, V. (2019). *Black feminism in qualitative inquiry.* New York, NY: Routledge.

Evans-Winters, V., & Esposito, J. (2010). Other people's daughters: Critical race feminism and Black girls' education. *Educational Foundations, 24*(1–2), 11–24.

Flanagan, C., & Faison, N. (2001). Youth civic development: Implications of research for social policy and programs. *Social Policy Report, XV*(1), 1–14.

Flanagan, C. A., Loreto Martínez, M. L., Cumsille, P., & Ngomane, T. (2011). Youth civic development: Theorizing a domain with evidence from different cultural contexts. *New Directions for Child and Adolescent Development, 2011*(134), 95–109.

Ginwright, S. A. (2007). Black youth activism and the role of critical social capital in Black community organizations. *American Behavioral Scientist, 51*(3), 403–418.

Giroux, H. A. (1997). *Pedagogy and the politics of hope: Theory, culture, and schooling.* Boulder, CO: Westview Press.

hooks, b. (1990). *Yearning: Race, gender, and cultural politics.* Cambridge, MA: South End Press.

Karenga, M. (2003). *The moral ideal in ancient Egypt: A study in classical African ethics.* New York, NY: Routledge.

Kirshner, B. (2009). Power in numbers: Youth organizing as a context for exploring civic identity. *Journal of Research on Adolescence, 19*(3), 414–440.

Ladson-Billings, G. (1995a). But that's just good teaching! The case for culturally relevant pedagogy. *Theory into Practice, 43*(3), 159–165.

Ladson-Billings, G. (1995b). Toward a theory of culturally relevant pedagogy. *American Education Research Journal, 32*(3), 465–491.

Ladson-Billings, G. (2014). Culturally relevant pedagogy 2.0: Aka the remix. *Harvard Educational Review, 84*(1), 74–84.

Malone, H. J., & Donahue, T. (2018). The role of out-of-school time programs in bridging the diversity gap and improving educational opportunities for African American students. In M. Sanders, K. Lewis-Watkins, & K. Cochrane (Eds.), *The growing out of school time field: Past, present, and future* (pp. 71–86). Charlotte, NC: Information Age.

Merriam, S. B., & Tisdell, E. J. (2016). *Qualitative research: A guide to design and implementation.* San Francisco, CA: Jossey-Bass.

Noguera, P. (2014). Organizing resistance into social movements. In E. Tuck & K. W. Yang (Eds.), *Youth resistance and theories of change* (pp. 71–81). New York, NY: Taylor & Francis.

Paris, D. (2012). Culturally sustaining pedagogy: A needed change in stance, terminology, and practice. *Educational researcher, 41*(3), 93–97.

Paris, D., & Alim, H. S. (2014). What are we seeking to sustain through culturally sustaining pedagogy? A loving critique forward. *Harvard Educational Review, 84*(1), 85–100.

Phinney, J. S., & Baldelomar, O. A. (2011). Identity development in multiple cultural contexts. In L. A. Jensen (Ed.), *Bridging cultural and developmental approaches to psychology: New syntheses in theory, research, and policy* (pp. 161–186). Oxford, England: Oxford University Press.

Pinkard, N., Erete, S., Martin, C. K., & McKinney de Royston, M. (2017). Digital youth divas: Exploring narrative-driven curriculum to spark middle school girls' interest in computational activities. *Journal of the Learning Sciences, 26*(3), 477–516.

Quan-Baffour, K. P. (2012). Sankofa: 'Gazing back' to indigenous knowledge and skills for socio-economic development of Ghana. *Studies of Tribes and Tribals, 10*(1), 1–5.

Temple, C. N. (2010). The emergence of Sankofa practice in the United States: A modern history. *Journal of Black Studies, 41*(1), 127–150.

Thomas, D. R. (2006). A general inductive approach for analyzing qualitative evaluation data. *American Journal of Evaluation, 27*(2), 237–246.

Watts, R. J., Diemer, A., & Voight, A. M. (2011). Critical consciousness: Current status and future directions. *Youth Civic Development: Work at the cutting edge. New directions for child and adolescent development, 2011*(*134*), 43–57.

SECTION 2

TOWARD EDUCATIONAL JUSTICE

CHAPTER 5

STANDING UP AND SPEAKING OUT

Black Girls' Agency and Activism in Elite Independent Schools

Charlotte E. Jacobs
University of Pennsylvania Graduate School of Education

*I thought it would be cool to just be in a space where someone finally wanted
to hear what we had to say. At Olympia they always emphasize wanting our voices
to be heard but they want ALL OF OUR VOICES* [students from all racial
groups] *heard and no one can be singled out and the more voices from one group,
the more that voice is listened to and that smaller groups gets sucked up and ignored.*

—Tasha,[1] a 10th grader at Olympia School,[2]
explaining why she joined the Black girls discussion group

In this chapter,[3] I will identify and trace the different perspectives, strategies, and tools that high school-aged Black girls in two elite independent
schools[4] used to display their agency and activism in carving out spaces for
themselves in school cultures that are not always inclusive of their needs
and identities as Black girls in elite predominantly White spaces. In defining agency and its relationship to activism, I draw on Brown's (2016)
definition of agency, which is the "capacity to use what they [girls] know

from their own experiences to imagine creative solutions and to transform thoughts and strong emotions into meaningful action" (p. 96). Similar to Freire's (1970) notion of praxis, this definition of agency highlights how authentic reflection of one's experiences and the imagining of transformation logically leads to actions that attempt to create change. In defining activism, I also draw on Brown's (2016) description of "girl-fueled activism," which is "the opportunity to identify a problem, work in coalition, leverage allies and energize people, think critically, listen well, speak up, stand up, and take calculated risks" (p. 28). Brown's (2016) definitions illustrate how agency and activism are dependent on girls' critical awareness of their experiences and how those experiences often evoke strong emotions that influence the actions that girls choose to take.

Another central component of agency and activism for Black girls is resistance. As a result of their marginalized status in U.S. society, when Black girls engage in activism, that work necessarily draws on beliefs and actions that will push back against, disrupt, and ultimately move towards a dismantling of systems of oppression with the goal of creating a more equitable society. Throughout my work with the girls in my research study, I saw them resist in a myriad of ways—from talking amongst themselves and questioning why certain school policies seemed tone-deaf to their experiences, to making presentations to their classmates and faculty members about their experiences and advising where change needs to happen in school practices, to forming an organized student group that would serve the purpose of being an affinity space as well as a space for activism.

I come to this work as a middle-class Black woman who attended a diverse suburban public high school; attended elite, predominantly White institutions for post-secondary education; and taught at an elite, predominantly White independent school. These experiences inform my beliefs surrounding Black girls and education, particularly those who are attending predominantly White independent schools. My experience as a 7th grade teacher at a predominantly White, elite independent school also influences the way that I approach, understand, and interact with Black female adolescents. I look for the strengths, resilience, and authentic wisdom that Black girls emanate as they go throughout their daily lives rather than focusing on how their differences from the dominant norms of society are evidence of social and character detriments. As a researcher, my stance stems from my identity as a Black feminist who is dedicated to pursuing social, political, and economic equity for Black girls and women.

In this chapter, I will first present an overview of the existing research about Black girls' academic and social experiences in independent schools, then I will describe the theoretical lenses of this chapter, which stem from critical feminist and developmental frameworks. Next, I will present my findings, which explore the foundations of Black girl activism in schools and also illustrate what Black girl activism looks like in two different independent schools. I will close the chapter by discussing the implications of Black girl activism for Black girls themselves as well as for members of broader school communities. I will also offer recommendations for how educators and practitioners can cultivate and support Black girl activism in their schools.

REVIEWING THE LITERATURE: BLACK GIRLS' ACADEMIC AND SOCIAL EXPERIENCES IN INDEPENDENT SCHOOLS

When reviewing the literature on the academic and social experiences of Black girls who attend independent schools, one dominant theme that emerges is the struggle of fitting in and feeling uncertainty about their status in the academic and social worlds of their elite schools (Alexander-Snow, 1999; Horvat & Antonio, 1999). Another theme that the research highlights is what Horvat and Antonio (1999) term "symbolic violence" (p. 320, adopted from Bourdieu [1979]) to describe the status of Black girls in independent schools. In this context, symbolic violence manifests itself in that Black girls feel pressured to adopt a habitus (Bourdieu, 1979) that aligns with the ways of being and knowing of their elite, predominantly White independent schools.

In the academic realm, Horvat and Antonio (1999) found that Black girls also are confronted with assumptions from other students that the only reason that Black girls are accepted to their independent schools is because of their institution's commitment to fulfilling diversity and affirmative action-related quotas. This assumption, whether it is outwardly spoken or is a part of the ether of the daily school environment, has the potential to undermine the success of Black girls by calling their academic prowess into question from the day that they enter the classroom.

The devaluing of Black girls' academic skills within the independent school context continues with their marginalized status in the classroom. Through interviews with her participants, Alexander-Snow (1999) found that Black girls had learned that they had to fight for respect in the classroom concerning the curriculum by being strong and vocal about their opinions. Alexander-Snow (1999) and Chase (2008) both found that in order to gain more representation in the material that they were studying, Black girls had to continually question the curriculum and its lack of diversity.

Turning to the social/emotional experiences of Black girls in independent schools, a theme that arises repeatedly is how their *habitus* or ways of being are inconsistent with the habitus of the independent school environment (Horvat & Antonio, 1999). The adoption of the independent school habitus for Black girls often means a trade-off in terms of feeling like they have to leave aspects of their identity (particularly those connected with race) behind when they enter the doors of their school. This takes the form of Black girls consciously changing parts of who they are while in school, such as feeling pressured to talk a certain way, changing the types of music they listen to, and "surrendering their sense of racial pride and belonging as a part of their effort to navigate life at a school where their racial heritage did not appear to be acknowledged or valued" (Horvat & Antonio, 1999, p. 334). Similar to the research findings about the academic experiences of Black girls in independent schools, early on Black girls receive the message that they do not fit into the typical independent school student profile and are continually viewed as outsiders.

In spite of their feelings of not fitting or completely belonging to the academic and social worlds of their independent schools, Black girls show resilience and take pride in their outsider status as providing them with experiences that are "normal and part of life in the real world" (Horvat & Antonio, 1999, p. 337). Additionally, other researchers point out that another source of solidarity, resilience, and community for Black girls in independent schools is the presence of other Black girls and women (Chase, 2008; White, 2014). Through the existence of both formal (affinity groups, cultural clubs, etc.) and informal (lunch tables, before and after school, etc.) gathering spaces in school, Black girls in independent schools carve out places for themselves where they can feel validated in their experiences, valued for their presence, and feel like they belong at their schools.

THEORETICAL LENSES

Black Girlhood

As a pedagogical and methodological framework, Black girlhood emphasizes the agency, creativity, and resistance of Black girls (Brown, 2013). As most of the literature focusing on girls' activism either focuses on the work of White middle-class girls, or presents a whitewashed picture of girls' activism (Brown, 2016), Brown (2013) draws on Bambara's (1980, 1982) descriptions of the elements of Black girlhood to create an attuned framework for researchers and adult allies who work with Black girls. Using the findings from her qualitative study working with a girls' group for adolescent Black girls as a guide, Brown (2013) developed five principles that describe the Black girlhood framework:

- Articulate visionary Black girlhood as a meaningful practice.
- Showcase Black girl inventiveness of form and content.
- Expand our vision of Black girlhood beyond identity.

- Sense radical courage and interdependence.
- Honor praxis, the analytical insight that comes only by way of consistent action and reflection. (p. 3)

Another element of Brown's Black girlhood framework is that it can be used as an organizing framework in order to encourage and move Black girls towards the collective action of critiquing their status in U.S. society. While there is a significant amount of literature that chronicles Black female activism including their work in the abolitionist movement (Logan, 1999; Yee, 1992), the Civil Rights movement (Anderson-Bricker, 1999), and the rise of Black feminism (Collins, 1989; Hull, Scott, & Smith, 1982; Roth, 1999) and womanism (Collins, 1996; Phillips, 2006), it follows the common trend of looking at the activist work of college-aged and adult women, and not teenage girls. The Black girlhood framework suggests not only that we should focus on the activist work of Black girls, but also an approach to adopt when doing so:

> Black girlhood as an organizing framework allows for a repertoire of self-determined Black girl knowledge that may be used to improve practice inside of the very spaces that organize Black girls. Black girlhood as an organizing framework is a sound that moves us closer toward interrogating how the state works in and through us, challenging institutions that do not see us even when we are present, and practicing love. (Brown, 2013, p. 211)

The importance of Brown's (2013) description is that it emphasizes the presence and importance of the knowledge that Black girls possess, and also focuses on Black girls as agents rather than objects within the systems of power within our society. Brown's Black girlhood framework articulates the potential for Black girls to come together to create change when they take a critical stance towards the ways in which they are situated in society, degraded, and oftentimes ignored.

An Adapted Model of Positive Youth Development for Adolescent Girls of Color

This chapter also draws on a model of positive youth development adapted specifically for adolescent girls of color developed by Clonan-Roy et al. (2016). In adapting the PYD original model (Lerner et al., 2005), which presents six competencies that youth should master in order to successfully navigate adulthood, Clonan-Roy et al. (2016) infuse the PYD model with a critical race feminist framework (Carter, 2012; Wing, 2000) and hold that the developmental competencies of resistance (Ward, 1996, 2007), resilience (Smith & Carlson, 1997; Spencer, Dupree, & Hartmann, 1997), and critical consciousness (Freire, 1970; Kumagai & Lypson, 2009) are key to the optimal development of girls of color.

Similar to Brown (2013), the Clonan-Roy et al. (2016) model highlights the strengths that girls of color already possess as a result of having to navigate through a society grounded in racism, sexism, and adultism. The adapted PYD model for adolescent girls of color presents the potential of schools, educators, and girls group spaces to promote the development of critical consciousness, resistance, and resilience through intentional conversations with girls about their identity and status in society, adults situating themselves as allies to youth, and creating spaces that allow for girls of color to engage in resistance in order to develop action plans for change.

BLACK GIRL AGENCY AND ACTIVISM IN ELITE SCHOOLS

The findings presented in this chapter are based on data drawn from a phenomenological study that I conducted in two predominantly White, elite, independent schools located in the northeastern part of the United States, one co-ed (Grace School[5]), and the other an all-girls school (Olympia School). Creswell (2007) defines a phenomenological study as one that "describes the meaning for several individuals of their *lived experiences* of a concept or phenomenon" (p. 57). The phenomenological aspect of the larger study from which these data are drawn provides a contemporary perspective of the key issues that Black girls in elite, predominantly White independent schools encounter related to the structures of race, gender, and class.

The participants for this study were 25 adolescent self-identified Black girls in Grades 9–12 who attended weekly discussion meetings over a period of 5 months, which I facilitated. About half of the participants (13) also participated in one-on-one interviews with me as well. Below, I present two major findings that emerged from this study that describe the foundational elements of Black girls' agency and activism as well as how the participants engaged in activism in their schools. In order to protect the identity of participants, all of the names used are pseudonyms, including the names of the schools.

The Roots of Agency and Activism: The Development of Critical Consciousness

One main finding from the overall study is that the components of a developing critical consciousness and agency and activism have a reciprocal and integrated relationship with one another, so that each is enhanced by the presence of the other in Black girls' lives. A deeper analysis of this finding focuses on how a growing critical consciousness serves as a foundation for larger acts of activism. A point that stands out in the majority of the activism work that the girls displayed throughout this project was that the work was deeply connected to their own identities and experiences as Black girls. Some of these examples were how the girls focused on their status as Black girls in independent schools through presentations to the school faculty, how one participant explored the status of Black girls and women in the United States in her assembly speech to her school community, and how one participant took stock of both her own and the general experiences of Black students in independent schools through conducting interviews with other students. What all of these cases have in common is that at the roots of their activism was an acute awareness that the experiences that they were having were somehow tied to their identities as Black girls who exist in the predominantly White elite environment of their school as well as within a U.S. society that is dominated by patriarchal and racist ideologies.

The example below is an excerpt from an assembly speech given by Andrea, a 12th grader at Olympia. The excerpt illustrates how a developing critical consciousness tied to her own experiences led to Andrea engaging in the activism of creating a public speech:

> It's human nature to put people into categories; however, in an all-White school, when there are so few Black students, the tendency for the majority is to expect that those few of us represent all of our kind. A common example is history class: many of the [Black] students I interviewed for this assembly felt awkward when discussing anything about Black history because the students and even sometimes the teachers would look at them for the "Black perspective"; but the reality is that there is not just one Black perspective. Another example inappropriately grouping Black students together is when other people confuse the names of Black students. I mean c'mon guys, do I really look like [name of a Black girl at Olympia]? Or [name of a Black girl at Olympia]? How about [name of a Black girl at Olympia]? But in all seriousness, sometimes it perplexes me that a teacher always seems to get me and the other Black girl in the class confused when there are 5 blond White girls in the classroom whose names the teacher never questions. This just reiterates the fact that people who are a part of the majority seem to inappropriately group Black students as just a group thereby failing to recognize their individuality.

Andrea displays her developing critical consciousness in the way that she contextualizes her observations of and experiences with how Black people are treated differently than White people in the United States, and uses her own experience as a Black girl in an elite, predominantly White all-girls school to localize the experience. When Andrea describes the microaggressions that she, her peers, and other Black students in independent schools have experienced, she traces those encounters to the larger societal beliefs and stereotypes that exist about Black people. Andrea's ability to link micro-aggressions and discriminatory policies to a legacy of racism and classism exemplifies critical consciousness.

In their ongoing work with Black girls committed to social justice, both Evans-Winters and Girls for Gender Equity (2017) and Brown (2009, 2013) highlight the importance of Black girls having control over their activism work. Historically, activism work focusing on girls has largely left Black girls out of the picture, where the stories and experiences of Black girls have been absent or minimized and folded into a larger whitewashed version of "girl power" (Brown, 2016). In a world where Black girls' actions are under constant surveillance in schools and in their communities (African American Policy Forum & Center for Intersectionality and Social Policy Studies, 2015; Evans-Winters & GGE, 2017; Morris 2016), and where their bodies are viewed as "dangerous" and therefore need to be controlled by others (Brown, 2009; Evans-Winters & GGE, 2017), it is important that Black girls are able to fully participate in their own liberation work. This means starting the work from a place where Black girls are encouraged to engage in a form of praxis (Friere, 1970) by examining their own experiences and then critically reflecting on them with the goal of moving to action, and hopefully transformation.

Demonstrating Agency and Activism Through Student Voice

Another finding from the study focuses on how the participants in the study engaged in activism through communicating their needs to the school community. The girls frequently demonstrated agency coupled with strategic thinking by using the platforms of public speeches and presentations as a way to share their experiences as Black girl students at their schools and about the status of Black women and girls in the United States. The activism element of their work was demonstrated through the ways in which the participants incorporated a call to action in their presentations. Similar to the beliefs of hooks (2000) and other critical scholars (Brown, 2013; Wing, 1996, 1997), it is not enough to awaken people's conscience and consciousness, but a goal of awakening a new awareness is to move people towards action that will create systemic change. In the case of the girls in this study, the changes they advocated for centered on how the members of their school community—administrators, teachers, and students—could act both individually and as part of a larger movement to make their schools more inclusive and equitable spaces, particularly for Black girls.

To illustrate this finding, I draw on two specific public presentations (one which I attended, and one that the girls described to me in their interviews, and later provided their presentation slides as an artifact) where different girls skillfully used school-sanctioned events to advocate for the changes they wanted to see in their school and in the world by establishing themselves as experts of their experience and by using their public presentations to begin to recruit allies for their larger work.

One of the public presentations was the community assembly speech of Andrea (introduced earlier in the chapter). Community assembly speeches are a requirement for 12th graders at Olympia. The students are expected to give a 10-minute speech on any topic of their choosing, and they work with two faculty advisors over a period of months to develop a speech that they will give in front of the entire upper school community. Andrea chose to focus her speech on the experiences of Black students at independent schools. For the second public presentation example, I look to the presentation that four of the Olympia participants gave about what they learned from attending the Student Diversity Leadership Conference (SDLC), a national diversity, equity, and inclusion conference for high school students who attend independent schools.

In both Andrea's speech and the SDLC presentation, the girls incorporated personal experiences as a way to legitimize the importance of their presentations and to communicate a sense of urgency about the changes that they wanted to see happen in their school. Andrea opened her speech, "A Guest in a Strange House," by purposely drawing attention to the fact that the speech will cover not only her experiences at Olympia, but also the experiences of other Black students who attend independent schools:

> This year commemorates the 60th anniversary of *Brown vs. The Board of Education*: the monumental supreme-court case that decided Blacks deserve equal rights in the field of education. As we reflect on our past, it is important to question what is it like for Black students in this space, in this time. By this space, I am referring to the type of elite educational environment where White is the majority and tuition is required to attend the school. Does this sound familiar? Good morning, my name is Andrea, and I truly believe that the unique journey of a Black student at a prestigious mostly White school deserves to be highlighted. Since 7th grade, I have attended Olympia, which is why I chose this topic: I want you all to understand how my personal experience has made me who I am today. Therefore, aside from exploring statistics, my research for this assembly has been internal: reflecting on my experience and comparing it with other Black students' in nearby schools like ours. I interviewed students from [names two other local independent schools] and Olympia. Although our experiences are diverse, there is one phrase that I believe captures the essence of all of our journeys; thus, my senior assembly is entitled "A Guest in a Strange House."

In this excerpt, Andrea established herself as an expert by not only calling on her own experiences as a valid source of information about the experiences of Black students in independent schools, but also indicated that she conducted her own small research study in which she interviewed Black students at two other independent schools and found that her and their experiences had similar themes. The effect of Andrea bringing in the stories of others works to counter the argument of "well, that's just your experience" that people from marginalized groups often encounter when they attempt to share their stories as a way to show larger trends and patterns of inequity (Delgado & Stefancic, 2012).

Throughout her speech, Andrea drew on her experience and the stories of other Black students to detail how Black students defined being Black versus the narrow definitions ascribed to them by their peers; microaggressions that she and her peers had experienced such as assuming that all Black students at independent schools are poor, and are relied upon to present the "Black perspective" in history and English classes; and the pressure to code switch in order to fit into "a strange house"—the independent school world being an environment where Black students do not always feel welcomed or included.

Similarly, Melanie, Adrienne, Nicole, and Lauren's (all students at Olympia) SDLC presentation also drew attention to their daily experiences around race, gender, and sexuality as Black girls at Olympia. In the slide titled "A Day in the Life" (see Figure 5.1), the girls listed negative and insensitive comments that they had received about their hair, about race and racism in the United States, and about their general appearance. By choosing to put this slide early on in their presentation (it was the third slide out of 14 slides), the girls attempted to make a personal connection with their

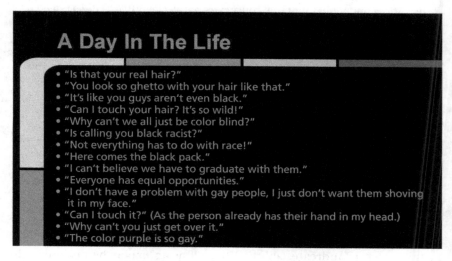

Figure 5.1 Olympia SDLC presentation, "A Day in the Life."

audience (their teachers) by presenting themselves as evidence. The effect of this action is that it humanized the points that the girls made in their presentation. Drawing on personal experiences moved the argument away from a hypothetical incident or encounter to issues that existed within the walls of Olympia.

Following the traditions of Black women activists who came before them, Andrea, Melanie, Adrienne, Nicole, and Lauren used their personal experiences of themselves and their Black peers as data. In doing so, they were articulating what Collins (1989) terms the "Black female standpoint" (p. 746), in which they articulated how "a subordinate group not only experiences a different reality than the group that rules, but a subordinate group may interpret that reality differently than a dominant group" (p. 748). They held up their lived experiences as evidence of their realities both inside and outside of school and formed a counternarrative to the dominant ideas that Black girls and Black students in independent schools are "doing ok" (Brown, 2012; Cary, 1991; Gaztambide-Fernández & DiAquoi, 2010).

Sources of Critical Consciousness Development Leading to Activism

As scholar and girls' activist Brown (2016) points out in her book *Powered By Girl: A Field Guide to Working With Youth Activists,* youth activism does not happen in isolation. In order for young people to be moved to engage in action that leads to constructive and productive change, they must first become aware of what the issue is, and then learn about effective ways in which to engage in action (Brown, 2016). A third finding of this study describes the importance of Black girls being able to find spaces where they are able to do the consciousness-raising work that develops their agency and activism.

The discussion group spaces at both Grace and Olympia served as a place where the girls were encouraged to ask questions, trust their observations, and offer suggestions related to their schooling experiences. Following the principles of critical pedagogy, the girls engaged in "problem-posing education" (Freire, 1970, p. 79, 80), where they took on the role of knowledge-producers by actively engaging in dialogues with themselves and with their adult allies about relationships of power, dominance, and privilege in their school lives. For the girls, their sources of critical consciousness development not only took the form of the structure and approach of the discussion sessions, but also videos the girls watched where they saw other Black girls engaged in activism, the online campaigns of #ITooAmHarvard and The Faces of Private Schools Tumblr that they looked through, as well as the advice and guidance they received from adult allies.

Outside conferences and forums also provided a foundation from which the girls could begin to contextualize their experiences within the broader landscape of systems, institutions, and ideologies. Melanie, Adrienne, Nicole, and Lauren's (students at Olympia) attendance to the Student Diversity Leadership Conference (SDLC) served as a site of critical consciousness development in that for 3 days they had the opportunity to be in community with 1,500 high school students and a faculty of 50 college students, teachers, and practitioners, who were all interested in having dialogues about issues of diversity, equity, and inclusion in independent schools and in U.S. society. When they participated in the discussions and exercises at SDLC, the girls learned new terminology and activist strategies. As an example, when describing their experiences at SDLC in their presentation to faculty members at their school, the girls included an image of the SDLC attendees using the well-known "Hands Up, Don't Shoot" position that was used as a form of protest following the shooting of Michael Brown in Ferguson, Missouri in 2014. This image illustrates the opportunities the girls were given to learn about and engage in forms of unified protest during the conference (Figure 5.2).

Similarly, much of the focus and content of Kendra's (a 12th grader at Olympia) assembly speech on #BlackGirlsMatter was inspired by her experience at the Breaking Silence Summer Camp, an activism, arts, and healing camp sponsored by the African American Policy Forum (AAPF; http://www.aapf.org/). Co-founded by legal scholar and intersectionality activist Professor Kimberlé Crenshaw, the AAPF is "an innovative think tank that connects academics, activists and policy-makers to promote efforts to

Figure 5.2 Olympia SDLC presentation, "Hands Up, Don't Shoot."

dismantle structural inequality" (AAPF website, 2016). The current work of AAPF focuses on using a lens of "intersectional social justice" to interrogate the status of girls and women of color in the United States. In particular, AAPF is leading three different social justice campaigns, #SayHerName, #BlackGirlsMatter, and #WhyWeCantWait, movements that focus on how women and girls of color have been victims of police brutality, how education systems have failed girls of color, and why it is imperative that we focus on the experiences of girls and women of color in the United States through the lenses of different institutional systems.

The awareness of the status of Black girls and women that Kendra displayed throughout her speech can be traced to the influence of scholars, activists, and media mentioned throughout her speech. Kendra drew on the work of scholars such as Professor Kimberlé Crenshaw and activists such as the founders of the #BlackLivesMatter movement and Assata Shakur to defend and support the points she made. Her access to reports written by the AAPF and her decision to follow the hashtags of the different campaigns provided Kendra with a particular perspective and a knowledge of statistics regarding the status of Black women and girls in the United States.

DISCUSSION AND IMPLICATIONS

The findings of this chapter have implications for interrogating the status that Black girls often occupy at their schools. In particular, a phenomenon that seems to emerge is how Black girls are put in the position of being "*the curriculum of diversity*" (Gazatambide-Fernández, 2009, p. 166) versus *contributing to* a curriculum of diversity. Another implication from this chapter focuses on the role of educators in cultivating and supporting Black girl activism in their schools.

Black Girls as Educators

One tension that this chapter highlights is that absent of any other support or dialogue, Black girls often are either put into or take on the role of educating others about their experiences and about larger race relations within the United States. In independent schools, the "educator" role often takes the form of students of color serving as experts about the experiences of their racial/ethnic group. In their qualitative study focusing on the experiences of students of color at an elite boarding school, Gaztambide-Fernández and DiAquoi (2010) captured how Black girls are often put in the educator position. The girls in their study describe often being looked to by peers to explain different aspects of the Black experience or answer any questions that their White peers might have about race. While the girls in Gaztambide-Fernández and DiAquoi's study often found themselves *placed in* the position of educators, in this study Kendra and Andrea seem to willingly *take on* the educator role. Similar to Kendra and Andrea, in her ethnography of an elite prep boarding school, Chase (2008) describes an instance in which Black girls used their speeches during an MLK Day assembly as a platform to call out the "ignorance" and inequalities that they had experienced while on campus.

Much like the examples described above, in this study the motivation behind much of the activism that the girls engaged in within the context of their school seemed to have the goal of awakening the awareness of their peers and teachers about the experiences of inequity that existed within their school, particularly along lines of race, gender, and class. The girls used their own experiences as the vehicle to heighten awareness and inspire emotions that they hoped would cause their peers and teachers to care.

The tension that arises in Black girls adopting the role of educators is that they are continually expected to do the work of educating the dominant group, rather than the dominant group taking it upon themselves to develop a competence and awareness of power relations in the school and how they are complicit in Black girls feeling excluded from the school community. Additionally, while public forums such as presentations and community assemblies serve as spaces where Black girls can share and offer a perspective about their experiences, in terms of structural support, the schools in this study did not demonstrate that there were mechanisms for follow-up conversations, action planning, or strategic development. Therefore, the reach of Black girls' activism and awareness-raising could only go so far in terms of creating change in their school communities.

Cultivating Black Girl Activism: Implications for Educators

Another factor to consider when working to cultivate Black girl activism is the opportunity for Black girls to create and claim their own space for the work. In creating "homespaces" (Ward, 1996) and "homeplaces" (hooks, 1990; Pastor et al., 2007) for themselves, Black girls are able to set the tone and focus of their work. Having a space in school where they are free to develop meaningful relationships while potentially overcoming any barriers that keep them apart is significant. In schools, where the focus on academics and, in the case of Black girls, control of their behavior, often takes precedence over socioemotional learning (Fine & Zane, 1989; Morris, 2007; Morris, 2016), making space for Black girls to explore their identities is central to their positive development. Additionally, Black girls being able to create their own space and decide who to welcome to that space works to support Black girls in feeling inspired to move to action and not be defeated by sharing their experiences, which are often painful, embarrassing, or enraging.

CONCLUSION

This chapter presented how agency and activism are enacted by Black girls within the context of independent schools. The core of Black girls' agency lies in the various ways through which they resist the dominant narratives that prescribe who they are and what they can and cannot do. This chapter illustrated how Black girls demonstrated resistance by engaging in "resistance for liberation" strategies (Robinson & Ward, 1991) that produced a counternarrative or counter-story of their experiences. By creating presentations and speeches that illuminated their daily experiences with microaggressions at school, the participants in this study intentionally placed the experiences of Black girls at the center and articulated how their school communities could be allies in supporting their needs and their sense of belonging at their school.

This chapter also highlights what scholar, researcher, and activist Evans-Winters (alongside members of the organization Girls for Gender Equity; 2017) describes as "Black girl power" which is "located in girls collectively questioning, exploring, engaging, and naming one's own reality throughout the research process" (p. 8). The girls' discussion group served as a place where the girls engaged in the research process of reflecting on what it meant to be Black girls in their schools, and where their schools served as places of support and where they as Black girls remained in the margins. The examples in the chapter of girls doing research by interviewing Black students at local independent schools, facilitating meetings with teachers about school life and protocols, and engaging in reflective and iterative decision-making demonstrates that an important part of agency and activism is Black girls being able to see themselves in the work that they do.

Lastly, this chapter highlights how agency and activism are not the sole work of the girls themselves. Thoughtful, genuine, and reflective adult allies are central to promoting Black girls' development in how to effectively and productively engage in changework where they will see the results that they want. In the context of schools, adults typically possess amounts of power and access to knowledge about school policies and procedures of which young people may not be familiar or aware. The role of adult allies is to provide "scaffolding" (Brown, 2016, p. 161) to young people's activism so that the required conditions exist for girls to do the activism work they want in order to create school-level and broader change.

NOTES

1. In order to protect the identity of participants in this study, I use pseudonyms for all participants.
2. This school name and all other school names referenced in this chapter are pseudonyms, and are not reflective of any schools that potentially have this name.
3. Excerpts from this chapter have been published in Jacobs, 2017.
4. Independent schools, according to the National Association of Independent Schools, the accrediting body for over 1,400 independent schools in the United States, are "non-profit private schools that are independent in philosophy: each is driven by a unique mission. They are also independent in the way they are managed and financed: each is governed by independent board of trustees and each is primarily supported through tuition payments and charitable contributions. They are accountable to their communities and are accredited by state-approving accrediting bodies" (NAIS website, 2015).
5. In order to maintain confidentiality, all participants and school sites have been given pseudonyms.

REFERENCES

African American Policy Forum & Center for Intersectionality and Social Policy Studies. (2015). *Black girls matter: Pushed out, overpoliced and underprotected.* New York, NY: Author. Retrieved from http://static1.squarespace .com/static/53f20d90e4b0b80451158d8c/t/54dcc1ece4b001c03e323448/ 1423753708557/AAPF_BlackGirlsMatterReport.pdf

African American Policy Forum & Center for Intersectionality. (2016). Retrieved from https://aapf.org/

Alexander-Snow, M. (1999). Two African American women graduates of historically white boarding schools and their social integration at a traditionally white university. *Journal of Negro Education, 68*(1) 106–119.

Anderson-Bricker, K. (1999). 'Triple jeopardy': Black women and the growth of feminist consciousness in SNCC, 1964–1975. In K. Springer (Ed.), *Still lifting, still climbing: African american women's contemporary activism* (pp. 49–69). New York, NY: New York University Press.

Bambara, T. C. (1980). *The salt eaters.* New York, NY: Random House.

Bambara, T. C. (1982). *The sea birds are still alive.* New York, NY: First Vintage Books.

Bourdieu, P. (1979). Symbolic power. *Critique of anthropology, 4*(13–14), 77–85.

Brown, E. (2012). "It's about race . . . no, it isn't!" Negotiating race and social class: Youth identities at Anderson School in 2005. In D. T. Slaughter-Defoe, H. C. Stevenson, E. G. Arrington, & D. J. Johnson (Eds.), *Black educational choice: Assessing the private and public alternatives to traditional K–12 public schools* (pp. 28–48). Santa Barbara, CA: Praeger.

Brown, L. M. (2016). *Powered by girl: A field guide for working with youth activists.* Boston, MA: Beacon Press.

Brown, R. N. (2009). *Black girlhood celebration: Toward a hip-hop feminist pedagogy.* New York, NY: Peter Lang.

Brown, R. N. (2013). *Hear our truths: The creative potential of black girlhood.* Urbana: University of Illinois Press.

Carter, N. A. (2012). Critical race feminism: An educational perspective. *PowerPlay: A Journal of Educational Justice, 4*(1), 249–261. https://corescholar.libraries .wright.edu/womensctr/5

Cary, L. (1991). *Black ice.* New York, NY: Vintage.

Chase, S. (2008). *Perfectly prep: Gender extremes at a New England prep school.* New York, NY: Oxford University Press.

Clonan-Roy, K., Jacobs, C. E., & Nakkula, M. J. (2016). Towards a model of positive youth development specific to girls of color: Perspectives on development, resilience, and empowerment. *Gender Issues, 33*(2), 96–121.

Collins, P. H. (1989). The social construction of black feminist thought. *Signs: Journal of Women in Culture and Society, 14*(4), 745–773.

Collins, P. H. (1996). What's in a name? Womanism, Black feminism, and beyond. *The Black Scholar, 26*(1), 9–17.

Creswell, J. W. (2007). *Qualitative inquiry and research design: Choosing among five approaches* (2nd ed.). Thousand Oaks, CA: SAGE.

Delgado, R., & Stefancic, J. (2012). *Critical race theory: An introduction.* New York, NY: New York University Press.

Evans-Winters, V. E., & Girls for Gender Equity. (2017). Flipping the script: The dangerous bodies of girls of color. *Cultural Studies ↔ Critical Methodologies, 17*(5), 415–423.

Fine, M., & Zane, N. (1989). Bein' wrapped too tight: When low-income women drop out of high school. In L. Weis, E. Farrar, & H. G. Petrie (Eds.), *Dropouts from school: Issues, dilemmas, and solutions* (pp. 25–53). Albany: State University of New York Press.

Freire, P. (1970). *Pedagogy of the oppressed.* New York, NY: Herder & Herder.

Gaztambide-Fernández, R. (2009). What is an elite boarding school? *Review of Educational Research, 79*(3), 1090–1128.

Gaztambide-Fernandez, R. A., & DiAquoi, R. (2010). A part and apart: Students of color negotiating boundaries at an elite boarding school. In A. Howard & R. A. Gaztambide-Fernandez (Eds.), *Educating elites: Class privilege and educational advantage* (pp. 55–78). Lanham, MD: Rowman & Littlefield.

hooks, b. (1990). *Yearning: Race, gender, and cultural politics.* Boston, MA: South End Press.

hooks, b. (2000). *Feminism is for everybody: Passionate politics.* Cambridge, MA: South End Press.

Horvat, E. M., & Antonio, A. L. (1999). "Hey, those shoes are out of uniform": African American girls in an elite high school and the importance of habitus. *Anthropology & Education Quarterly, 30*(3), 317–342.

Hull, G. T., Scott, P. B., & Smith, B. (1982). *All the women are White, all the Blacks are men, but some of us are brave: Black women's studies.* New York, NY: Feminist Press.

Jacobs, C. E. (2017). The development of black girl critical literacies of race, gender, and class in independent schools: Awareness, agency, and emotion (Doctoral dissertation). *Publicly Accessible Penn Dissertations*. 2356. Retrieved from https://repository.upenn.edu/edissertations/2356

Kumagai, A. K., & Lypson, M. L. (2009). Beyond cultural competence: Critical consciousness, social justice, and multicultural education. *Academic Medicine, 84*(6), 782–787.

Lerner, R. M., Lerner, J. V., Almerigi, J. B., Theokas, C., Phelps, E., Gestsdottir, S., ... Smith, L. M. (2005). Positive youth development, participation in community youth development programs, and community contributions of fifth-grade adolescents: Findings from the first wave of the 4-H study of positive youth development. *The Journal of Early Adolescence, 25*(1), 17–71.

Logan, S. W. (1999). *We are coming: The persuasive discourse of nineteenth-century black women*. Carbondale, IL: SIU Press.

Morris, E. W. (2007). "Ladies" or "loudies"? Perceptions and experiences of black girls in classrooms. *Youth & Society, 38*(4), 490–515.

Morris, M. (2016). *Pushout: The criminalization of Black girls in schools*. New York, NY: The New Press.

National Association of Independent Schools. (n.d.). Retrieved from https://www.nais.org/about/

Pastor, J., McCormick, J., Fine, M., Andolsen, R., Friedman, N., Richardson, N., ... Tavarez, M. (2007). Makin' homes: An urban girl thing. In B. J. R. Leadbeater & N. Way (Eds.), *Urban girls revisited: Building strengths* (pp. 75–96). New York: New York University Press.

Phillips, L. (2006). *The womanist reader*. Philadelphia, PA: Taylor & Francis.

Robinson, T., & Ward, J. V. (1991). "A belief in self far greater than anyone's disbelief": Cultivating resistance among african american female adolescents. *Women & Therapy, 11*(3–4), 87–103.

Roth, B. (1999). The making of the vanguard center: Black feminist emergence in the 1960s and 1970s. In K. Springer (Ed.), *Still lifting, still climbing: African American women's contemporary activism* (pp. 70–90). New York: New York University Press.

Smith, C., & Carlson, B. E. (1997). Stress, coping, and resilience in children and youth. *Social Service Review, 71*(2), 231–256.

Spencer, M. B., Dupree, D., & Hartmann, T. (1997). A phenomenological variant of ecological systems theory (PVEST): A self-organization perspective in context. *Development and Psychopathology, 9*, 817–833.

Ward, J. V. (1996). Raising resisters: The role of truth telling in the psychological development of African American girls. In B. J. Ross Leadbeater & N. Way (Eds.), *Urban girls: Resisting stereotypes, creating identities* (pp. 85–99). New York: New York University Press.

Ward, J. V. (2007). Uncovering truths, recovering lives: Lessons of resistance in the socialization of Black girls. In B. J. Ross Leadbeater & N. Way (Eds.), *Urban Girls Revisited: Building Strengths* (pp. 243–260). New York: New York University Press.

White, E. S. (2014). *When and where I enter: A study of the experiences of African-American girls in all-girls' independent schools.* Shaker Heights, OH: Center for Research on Girls at Laurel School.

Wing, A. K. (1996). A critical race feminist conceptualization of violence: South African and Palestinian women. *Albany Law Review, 60,* 943–976.

Wing, A. K. (1997). Brief reflections toward a multiplicative theory and praxis of being. In A. K.Wing (Ed.), *Critical race feminism: A reader* (pp. 27–34). New York: New York University Press.

Wing, A. K. (2000). *Global critical race feminism: An international reader.* New York: New York University Press.

Yee, S. J. (1992). *Black women abolitionists: A study in activism, 1828–1860.* Nashville, TN: University of Tennessee Press.

CHAPTER 6

#BLACKGIRLMAGIC IN THE EVERYDAY

Black Women and Civic Identity in Post Secondary Education

Alaina Neal-Jackson
University of Michigan, Ann Arbor

In the last decade, Black millennials have increasingly utilized social media platforms—Twitter, Instagram, Facebook, YouTube—to raise awareness around the injustices perpetrated against the Black community and to prompt national discussions on civic and political issues (Nielson, 2017). Social media outlets allow users to share personal messages about social issues, circulate articles and blog posts that discuss racial inequity, and inform others of breaking news in almost real time. These sites also allow users to create smaller shared communities within the larger base of users through hashtags that label and categorize content. Black girls and women have used hashtags to highlight the specific inequities they face given their intersecting marginalized racial and gender identities. One such tag is #Blackgirlmagic (#BGM). Started by CaShawn Thompson in 2013,

Black Girl Civics, pages 93–107
Copyright © 2020 by Information Age Publishing
All rights of reproduction in any form reserved.

#BGM created an online dialogue centered on celebrating the often ig-
nored achievements of Black women. In an interview in 2016, Thompson
stated that she hoped for #BGM to be a space for Black women to "name
and identify the ways [they] make space for themselves" in a society where
they are constantly denigrated (Thomas, 2016). Since its inception, #BGM
has served as an opportunity for Black women to share and celebrate the
ways that they persevere despite adversity in their lives. Though there has
been debate around the utility of the term *magic* given concerns about the
potential to call forth the stereotypic image of Black women as superhuman
and further perpetuate the erasure of Black women's vulnerabilities and
very real humanly needs (see Chavers, 2016), Ford (2016) explains that the
use of the word *magic* "is not about tapping into something supernatural,
it's about claiming or reclaiming what others have refused to see" (p. 7).
Thus, #BGM is fundamentally about making Black women visible in ways
that reveal the fullness of their identities including both the triumphs and
struggles they face in their daily lives.

Black girls' and young women's participation in #BGM is increasingly
becoming viewed as a form of participatory politics in online spaces (Hope,
Keeles, & Durkee, 2016; Keller, 2012). However, less is known about how
#BGM extends beyond the internet and into the physical world. Though
Nielson (2017) reports that Black millennials spend at least an hour a day
on social media and that many view their online presence as an extension
of their identities, the majority of their days are still likely filled with interpersonal interactions with others. As such, this raises questions: "How does
#BGM get embodied by Black women in their everyday lives?"; "Does it
function as a form of civic participation in the daily lived space/reality?";
and "How is it, if at all, used to transform the institutions they frequent,
particularly those that are challenging to their identities as Black women?"
The #BGM online movement is dynamic because of the way it captures
the resistance efforts of Black girls and women against multiple oppressive
forces in their lives. The translation of this online movement into on-the-
ground efforts could, and should, be examined.

PREDOMINANTLY WHITE COLLEGE
AND UNIVERSITY CAMPUSES

A particularly fruitful context in which to examine the real-world iterations
of #BGM is predominantly White university (PWI) and college campuses.
In the United States of America, there are 4,627 degree-granting postsecondary institutions with over 19.9 million enrolled students, accounting
for roughly 5% of the U.S. population (U.S. Department of Education

National Center for Education Statistics, 2017). Of these millions of enrolled students, only 13% are Black. Scholars have long documented that in these predominantly White spaces, existing societal patterns of racism and sexism are recreated such that Black students are often subjected to discrimination and marginalization both in and outside of the classroom. Black women in particular talk about being an "outsider within" in their college or university spaces, meaning that although they were invited to be a part of the campus community, they are invisible to others and treated as though they don't belong (Johnson, 2017). As undergraduate students, Black women often experience periods of isolation as the only one of their race in their classes (Patton & McClure, 2009), and in some STEM fields, the only one of their gender as well (Beasley & Fisher, 2012). They routinely experience microaggressions, most often in the form of stereotypes, that disparage their Black womanhood, question their admission to institutions of higher education, and position them as academically inferior (Solorzano, Ceja, & Yosso, 2000; Winkle-Wagner, 2015).

Patton and Croom (2017a) argue that postsecondary institutions have overwhelmingly been irresponsible in addressing the racism, sexism, classism, and other forms of oppression that affect Black women on their campuses. Even so, Black women still continue to enroll and matriculate from these institutions at an increasing rate. This suggests that in the midst of institutions failing to protect them, they are advocating and making space for themselves in ways that promote their academic success and overall well-being. Unfortunately, this is work that Black women have always had to do within an America that has never willingly given Black women opportunities to thrive. Given that #BGM highlights how Black women persevere despite adversity, PWIs are an ideal context in which to examine how the movement is embodied in the offline, everyday space.

Drawing upon 30 in-depth interviews, this chapter explores how undergraduate Black women enrolled in one PWI, Brennan University (BU[1]) and worked to transform the institution to be more accountable to their realities and needs as Black women. Analysis revealed that in the university context, the undergraduate Black women's civic participation was rooted in daily enactments of the primary tenants of #BGM: (a) asserting visibility as means of resilience and (b) displaying power. By engaging these tenants the Black women worked to combat the injustices they faced and reclaim the opportunities they were denied. In their real-world interactions, they did not literally use the hashtag but nevertheless embodied the spirit of the movement. Because the predominant narrative at BU was that undergraduate Black women were anything but "magical," embodying the mission of #BGM was the most powerful way to take a stand against efforts to marginalize and exclude them from the campus community.

METHODS

Theoretical Framework

This work was guided by Black feminist theory (BFT). BFT serves to "produce facts and theories about the Black female experience that will clarify a Black woman's standpoint for Black women" (Collins, 1986, p. 16). BFT allows researchers to privilege intersectionality and foreground the ways that race, gender, and class, amongst other meaningful social identities, come together to influence the way Black women move about and experience the world (Crenshaw, 1997; Johnson, 2017). It acknowledges that these identities are not lived separately and thus should not be analyzed as such. In this investigation, I privileged Black women's voices in order to recognize their right to tell their own truths and display the power with which they do so. Importantly, as a critical Black feminist, my research is always intended to be *with* and *for* the Black women with whom I interact and not just *about* them. By engaging in research in this manner, I also exemplify the core values embedded in #BGM.

Research Setting and Participants

Data was drawn from a larger study focused on undergraduate Black women's transition between their secondary institution and BU, a predominantly White institution. In order to recruit participants, I utilized a snowball sample methodology (Merriam, 2009). Upon the completion of an interview, I asked participants to (a) provide me with names of other undergraduate Black women who might be interested in the study or (b) to share my information with other undergraduate Black women so they could reach out if interested. In this manner, I drew upon the social networks of participants to create the sample. Ultimately, the sample included 30 self-identified Black women. For the purposes of this study "Black" was utilized in a diasporic sense. All participants were enrolled as undergraduate students at BU during the Winter 2014 and Winter 2015 semesters. Please see Table 6.1 for a snapshot of the participants. Following the 30th interview, I stopped recruitment because at that point I felt I had reached saturation as similar themes were surfacing in the participants' interviews. There is no agreed upon standard for sample sizes within qualitative research and the point of saturation will vary across studies (Rogers & Way, 2016).

TABLE 6.1		Participant Demographics	
Pseudonym	Status in BU	Major	First Generation
Alana	Jr	Gender and Women's Studies/Psychology	Yes
Amy	Jr	Business Administration	Yes
Adriana	Sr	Industrial and Operations Engineering	Yes
Anita	Jr	Gender and Women's Studies	No
Autumn	Sr	Education/Psychology	Yes
Alisha	Sr	Biopsychology, Cognition, Neuro-science	Yes
Bianca	Sr	African American Studies/Sociology	No
Brandy	Sr	African American Studies/Psychology	Yes
Christina	So	Music, Theatre, and Dance	No
Casey	Sr	Clinical Psychology/Biopsychology, Cognition, Neuroscience	No
Chastity	Jr	Business Administration & Accounting/Social Work	Yes
Cecilia	Jr	Education	No
Danielle	Jr	Education	No
Emerald	Jr	Gender and Women's Studies/Pre-Med	No
Eunice	Jr	Accounting	Yes
Fatima	Jr	Sociology/African American Studies	Yes
Farrah	Sr	Biopsychology, Cognition, and Neuroscience	No
Janelle	Jr	Gender and Women's Studies/Psychology	Yes
Jamie	So	Psychology	No
Lerraye	Jr	Psychology	No
Leslie	Sr	Nursing/Midwifery	Yes
Mary	Sr	Movement Science	Yes
Rochelle	Jr	Spanish/Pre-Med	Yes
Randy	Sr	Biopsychology, Cognition, and Neuroscience	Yes
Shanelle	Sr	Philosophy/Pre-Med	No
Shayna	Sr	Psychology/African American Studies	No
Trina	Jr	Psychology	Yes
Terrie	Jr	Education	Yes
Tanya	Sr	Sociology/Urban Studies	No
Tracy	Jr	Kinesiology	Yes

Procedures and Analysis

Every participant participated in one semi-structured interview. A semi-structured interview format was utilized given its flexible format that allows for the exploration of new ideas that could not be anticipated. The interview covered the participants' personal and educational background, decision-making relevant to attending BU, first moments on campus, and the major constraints and opportunities they encountered in BU's social and academic realms. Findings related to #BGM emerged as the women talked about navigating challenges on BU's campus. When applicable, the undergraduate Black women were prompted to speak to the differences they imagined between their experiences and that of Black men and White women in order to capture their intersectional identities as both Black *and* woman. After the completion of every interview, field notes were completed to catalogue initial reactions and questions for analysis (Emerson, Fretz, & Shaw, 2011). All participants signed consent forms that provided permission to audio record the interview, which was then transcribed for analysis.

Data analysis was conducted utilizing Corbin and Straus' (2014) analytical methods of asking questions about the data, making comparisons between data, and ultimately deriving concepts to stand for those data. I conversed with the data through a process of structured and open coding (Merriam, 2009). I created structured codes by translating the questions from the interview protocol into larger categories. For example, the question, "Have you encountered any barriers as a Black woman during your time at BU?" became "Black Women Barriers" or "BW-BARR." As I applied structured codes, I simultaneously engaged in open coding by creating new codes whenever data could not be captured by any preexisting structured code. The coding proceeded using Dedoose, an online coding software, until all interviews had been coded and I reached a level of saturation where no new codes could be developed within or across categories. In the final stage of analysis, I conducted axial coding where I examined the relationships amongst the codes and grouped them into larger, thematic categories (Corbin & Strauss, 2014). In order to create robust assertions about the relationships I observed, I used Dedoose to search through the entirety of the dataset for affirmative instances *and* disconfirming cases. When warranted, interpretations were nuanced to better capture the breadth of the data.

FINDINGS

The beginning of the 2015–2016 academic year at BU was like the many that had preceded it. The president welcomed the community of students, faculty, and staff into the new year with a proclamation that BU was deeply committed to equity, diversity, and inclusion for all of its members. However, many of the undergraduate Black women I spoke with raised questions about the authenticity of his professed commitment. Alana, a junior, used air quotes when speaking about the value BU placed on "diversity" and stated, "They're unwilling to listen to the students . . . even though they say they're about inclusion, I don't really think they are." Alisha, a senior, stated, "The university—It's like you want to promote diversity but really, is it diverse? Do you really care about diversity?"

These critiques of the president's professed commitment to diversity were based in the undergraduate Black women's daily gendered, racialized experiences in both academic and social spaces. They detailed daily interactions with White peers and faculty where they were denied the rights and resources they were owed as members of the campus community—interactions that obviously stood in stark contrast to the mantra of equity and inclusion for all. In the midst of these daily assaults, the undergraduate Black women took action in ways that were powerful displays of #BGM. As the remainder of the discussion will illustrate, though they did not use the specific terminology, they were engaged in the core mission of #BGM because they were intentionally and purposively asserting their visibility on campus to combat their experiences of marginalization. Their actions functioned as a form of civic engagement because the purpose of establishing visibility was to promote greater inclusion and equity for Black students on BU's campus as a part of their mission to secure justice for Black Americans more broadly. The visibility celebrated in #BGM was evident in the undergraduate Black women's (a) activism and community organizing on campus and (b) interactions with White peers where they confronted, and corrected, gendered racial stereotypes. While many themes emerged, the following discussion highlights the most robust themes present amongst the Black women with whom I spoke. I will discuss each in turn.

#BGM at BU: Activism and Community Organizing

One of the key assertions of the #BGM campaign is that Black girls and women have always been powerful playmakers within U.S. society despite White America's failure to acknowledge them as such. In fact, Ford (2016) points out that this lack of recognition is the "inside joke" embedded in the use of the term magic. In Ford's estimation, magic is about knowing something that others don't know or refuse to see. It is about putting at the forefront, the unrecognized power and skills with which Black girls and women have always drawn upon to resist the oppressive forces in their lives.

The undergraduate Black women at BU engaged directly with the mission to assert Black women's visibility, particularly as powerful playmakers, through their activism and organizing of the campus community. As Fatima stated, "[Black women on BU's campus are] leaders...and causing this uproar...Like challenging or pushing back on that dominant narrative [about Black students]." As campus leaders, they facilitated many events to bring awareness to the issues pertaining to the larger Black community, on and off campus. Concerning some of the initiatives regarding off campus issues that came out of their leadership, she shared that they "did this protest for Ferguson when that happened. We did the die-in." In her statement she mentions Ferguson, which referred to the murder of Mike Brown, an unarmed Black teenager, at the hands of law enforcement. In staging the die-in, the undergraduate Black women were demanding that BU acknowledge—and respond—to their whole identities beyond their student status. They were forcing BU to recognize the complexities in their experiences as Black students in that what was happening in Black communities across the country was meaningful to their everyday lives on campus. Their protest made the statement that BU was responsible for acknowledging these deaths and creating space for the community to reckon with them. Fatima also spoke about how Black female students helped to organize around on-campus issues facing Black students including an online social media movement "BEBU [Black Experience at BU]," and "talk[ing] with the regents...about our budget for BSU [Black Student Union] and how they made us these promises in the past." As Fatima highlighted, Black female students played important roles in multiple coordinated efforts at BU to address issues they faced on campus.

Brandy also talked about the BEBU social media campaign that Fatima briefly mentioned as a critical space where Black women were leading the efforts. In short, BEBU was a movement started by Black students at BU in order to bring awareness to the challenges they faced on campus. Students made statements using a shared hashtag that detailed the difficulties of being a Black student in classes, walking the halls, and interacting with non-Black peers at BU. The hashtag supporting the campaign trended on multiple social media sites and caught the attention of major news outlets in addition to the university administration. Brandy shared that as college students, she felt they were in the "perfect place" to command the nation's attention in this manner and cited examples of other collegiate activists such as the Black Panthers and Assata Shakur. She felt extremely proud that as a Black woman she was able to leverage her status as a college student to bring awareness to critically important issues. She shared, "If they want to kick me out of school because I decided to uplift my community, go ahead...At the end of the day that's what it's about for me. I care about being a part of history." It was apparent that Brandy felt there was immense power in protest as a means of teaching peers and others about the plight of Black students on BU's campus. It was also clear that she was willing to leverage that power and do the work of teaching others. Her comments revealed a deep commitment to being an activist and pushing for BU to be responsive to the needs of Black students.

Another student, Shanelle, also shared an instance of how she planned to meet with a university administrator, much like the regents Fatima talked about, as a means of exposing the unfair situations that Black students found themselves in. The impetus for the meeting was an interaction she had with a White male peer who verbally berated her because he felt that Black students were unfairly privileged on university campuses given their access to race specific resources that other (read: White) students didn't have. As she tried to get context to understand his perspective, he continued to push back in a way that made it a "terrible experience" for her, during which her professor failed to intervene. She shared that she would be speaking with the dean of students in the coming weeks because "that was just not—not okay. You don't say that . . . I'm taking action with this because if this happens with another student I'm going to feel bad that I didn't take action when I know that I'm equipped to do that." Shanelle clearly expressed feeling a strong responsibility for using the power she had to pave the way for students who came behind her to have a better experience. By rallying to secure a conversation with the dean, she was ensuring that her experience of being berated by a White male student with a racial chip on his shoulder (to put it nicely) would not continue to be ignored, like her professor had done, but would be acknowledged. Importantly, her ability to take this challenging experience and use it as a means to advance a less hostile space for future Black women enrolled in BU, was a poignant example of the resilience celebrated in the #BGM movement.

Lastly, Leslie, a senior, shared a story about a friend whose advocacy took the form of sending a message to the entire campus community, not just the university administration, about the racial discrimination Black students faced in their classes at BU. In this instance, the discrimination was related to a White professor's failure to address White students' routine mispronunciation of the names of African countries, extreme stereotyping of their economic status, and continued expression of pejorative misinformation about those residing in Africa. Frustrated by this, Leslie's friend "wrote a letter for the Brennan Newspaper about how terrible [the] teacher was" and provided a list of alternative ways to engage in conversation about Africa. By utilizing the Brennan newspaper as an outlet, Leslie's friend was commanding the attention of the campus community toward an unjust, and frankly unacceptable, classroom situation. Her letter called out her professor for being complicit in the discriminatory behaviors. Though the chair of the department in which the class was housed refused to address the professor's ineptitude directly, Leslie's friend had nevertheless been successful in making the issue one of public concern. Even if there were no immediate changes in the current iteration of the class, her activism laid the foundation for the department to be more responsive to how the course was taught. As these examples have demonstrated, the undergraduate Black women were displaying #BGM through their position as powerful playmakers whose activism and organizing was forging a path to a more inclusive context at BU.

#BGM at BU: Defining Black Womanhood in Interpersonal Interactions With White Peers

In addition to making themselves visible through their activism and community organizing, the undergraduate Black women also asserted their visibility through a deliberate set of actions within their interpersonal interactions with White peers. Remember, one of the core purposes of visibility in the #BGM movement is for Black women to make space for themselves in places that do not readily welcome them. As Michelle Hite quoted in Thomas (2016) denotes, #BGM is a way for Black women to speak to each other and say, "I see you excelling in a context that is hostile to your presence, which makes it all the more glorious" (para. 12).

Often in academic and social contexts, the undergraduate Black women encountered unwelcoming White peers who invoked pejorative stereotypes about Black women in ways that had the potential to circumscribe their access to critical educational resources. Rather than allowing these negative images to define who they were, the undergraduate Black women pushed back against their peers' deficit understandings. In interactions with their peers, they redefined a Black feminine identity in ways that celebrated the intelligence, resilience, and beauty of Black women. By deliberately engaging with their White peers in ways that directly challenged stereotypic perceptions, these women believed that they were enacting change on the ground level. Though they recognized the importance of holding BU accountable to Black women's needs at the institutional level, they knew that the everyday interactions between students was a significant place in which their rights were infringed upon. As such, challenging their peers was an important way to assert their visibility to hold BU accountable at every level towards meeting the needs of Black students in general and Black women in particular.

Alisha shared,

> For people to sit there and say, oh, I didn't know you could do this...You didn't think I was capable of greatness? Well, let me show you...that's just my incentive to prove to you more than what I'm capable of, and not just for myself, but for other people too.

Alisha detailed experiences working with peers who "didn't know [she] had it in her" to be great, though she had no doubts about her greatness and ability to be academically successful. For Alisha, the best response to these microaggressions (that came in the form of "snide remarks") was to engage in behavior that demonstrated their incorrect nature and to, in fact, "blow" the low expectations "completely up" so that her peers would have no choice but to recalibrate their expectations of her currently and in the future. Though she did not say anything directly to them, she believed her actions, and excellency, would speak loudly enough to challenge their perceptions. This was in line with #BGM's call for Black women to demonstrate their achievements despite other's refusal to recognize them as such. Importantly, Alisha did not see her actions as simply serving a selfish purpose. She saw it as a chance to alter the situation for the many other Black women who her peers would interact with in the future. Possibly, as a result of her own actions, these women would not be subjected to the same low expectations that she was.

Casey, a senior, also allowed her actions to speak against pejorative images she encountered from White peers about Black women. She shared her experiences of feeling marginalized in her classes because of peers who tried to act as though there were "prerequisites" for being a woman of color. For Black women specifically, these prerequisites were "crazy, loud, very opinionated, sassy—you know all those stereotypes." Casey continued to talk specifically about how this transpired in her classrooms when peers assumed that she was unintelligent and incapable of expressing clearly articulated opinions. She shared that "sometimes in class that if I say something that's smart sometimes people are just kind of... taken off guard." When asked how she responded in these kinds of situations, she stated that she took hold of her potential. She shared that she realized that "all the potential that I've always thought I had and that I thought I could do I can actually do... I do have something to give." In Casey's response, it was evident that her actions furthered a core tenant of #BGM which was to persevere despite being in a space where her identity as a Black woman was denigrated. She refused to back down when she encountered stereotypes in her interactions with her White peers and instead actively attempted to counter their expectations by demonstrating her intellectual prowess. Contrary to the messages she was hearing, she did in fact have worthy intellectual contributions to make. In making this realization and not allowing her peers' perceptions to limit her engagement in classes, she was not only making space for herself to reach her academic potential, she was also creating an opportunity for her White peers to witness an image of greatness that they had not believed possible from Black women.

Autumn asserted her visibility as a Black woman in interactions with White peers by verbally challenging them around their problematic reliance on pejorative stereotypes. She recounted a time she dealt with the presence of stereotypes about Black women's communication during a group project meeting. During this incident, a White female peer corrected her verbalization of "expresso" to "espresso." Autumn expressed that it led her to question, "Why did she just try to control my speech and control how I'm feeling?" As Autumn recounted her story, it was evident that she was baffled that her peer would feel it necessary, and acceptable, to correct her speech without even considering why she may have expressed it in that manner. Nearly instantly however, she arrived at the conclusion that it was because White students felt it necessary to "control" how she, as a Black woman, verbally expresses herself due to perceptions that Black women are not in control of their own communication and feelings. Implicit in her statement was that White students do not feel the need to control other students in this manner—just Black women. When asked how she addressed the situation, Autumn shared that she communicated to her peer, "I would just appreciate if you just did not try to correct my speech... there are differences in experiences, there are differences in culture... [and] I don't think you really understand what that really means." Though Autumn "hesitated" before confronting her peer about the situation because she did not want to appear overly aggressive and make her cry (which would conjure up another dangerous stereotype about Black women as angry and aggressive), she ultimately decided it was necessary that her peer know why the interaction was problematic. Her actions served as a display of #BGM in the way that she masterfully shifted the dynamics of the working relationship so that she would not continue to have to exist in a group space where she felt disrespected and unfairly surveilled. Importantly, in creating a more inclusive space for herself, she simultaneously created an opportunity for her peer to be educated around cultural differences in communication, which may have had an impact beyond the duration of the group project.

As evidenced through these narratives, the undergraduate Black women at BU engaged in #BGM in their interpersonal interactions with White peers by ensuring that negative stereotypical notions about Black women did not go unchecked. Whether verbally or indirectly through their behavior, they were intentionally shifting the narrative of who Black women were and making a space available for their peers to see them in a radically new way. These undergraduate Black women believed that, in part, systemic change for Black female students on BU's campus could be accomplished by pushing back against the deficit perspectives their White peers had and making visible the truth about the identities and capacities of Black women.

DISCUSSION AND CONCLUSION

Though BU expressed a commitment to diversity and equity, the under-graduate Black women I interviewed shared narratives that called into question the strength of this commitment. Nearly every Black woman with whom I spoke could detail more than one incident where she felt denied the rights she was owed as a member of the campus community—respect, value as a learner, and access to academic resources and support. In the midst of this exclusion, the undergraduate Black women resolved to trans-form their school conditions in order to make BU a space where they would not be denied their rights but would be treated fairly and equally as in line with their White peers.

Through asserting the visibility celebrated in the #BGM movement, these Black female students diligently made strides towards creating more equitable opportunities for themselves and Black students writ large. The undergraduate Black women were deeply engaged in participatory politics through #BGM—both in their activism and organizing on the campus— and in the use of their interpersonal interactions as agents of change. They saw the campus as a reflection of society, which was why the larger patterns of racism, sexism, and anti-Black discrimination were prevalent in their daily interactions with White peers and faculty. For them, there was a di-rect connection between the work they did on their university campus and the eradication of the larger societal racism and discrimination. As Brandy stated, some of the most powerful and prolific Black activists began their work as university students and on university campuses. It was evident that the women felt that serving the Black community at BU was a part of the effort to serve the Black community that existed outside of BU.

Importantly, the undergraduate Black women's narratives around per-sonal interactions with White peers illustrates the critical connection be-tween personal experiences and larger social and political structures. They operated with the understanding that change could, and should, happen both at the institutional level and on the ground. They recognized that the White peers who they shared classrooms with would not always be students at BU, but would leave the campus and be the very people they would en-counter in their jobs, communities, and other spaces. They saw an opportu-nity to use their interactions to disrupt the existing patterns of discrimina-tion in which these students participated in. Though these students came from different worlds before coming to BU and would likely return to those very worlds when done, they did not have to return as the same people they were when they had initially arrived.

Though the undergraduate Black women were doing the work to make BU a space that was more responsive to their needs as students, this is not their cross to bear. The additional work that these Black women take on can have deleterious effects on their mental health and academic achievement. When they were invited onto campus, it was to join the social and academic community as full citizens. Their activism should not be necessary for BU to be a welcoming space as they should be entering a campus that is already prepared to meet their academic and social needs. When campuses are not prepared, in reality, Black women are only being offered conditional acceptance; they are accepted to the university on the condition that they advocate for themselves to be respected. Postsecondary institutions must be willing to do more than simply espouse a commitment to diversity, equity, and inclusion for all. While professing commitment is a first step, it is nothing without meaningful enactment. I urge BU, and other selective PWIs like it, to reflect on their commitment to equity and inclusion by asking: "How does one meaningfully act upon a commitment to equity and inclusion?"; "What opportunities exist at the institutional level for the community to learn about Black women?"; and "How are community members held accountable when they fail to live up to the ideals embedded in this commitment?" As prestigious PWIs increasingly proclaim to anyone who will listen about their commitment to diversity and inclusion, they must recognize that it is their responsibility to create, and sustain, an equitable context to which all students are rightfully owed.

NOTE

1. All names in the manuscript have been changed to pseudonyms to protect the privacy of participants.

REFERENCES

Beasley, M. A., & Fischer, M. J. (2012). Why they leave: The impact of stereotype threat on the attrition of women and minorities from science, math and engineering majors. *Social Psychology of Education, 15*(4), 427–448.

Chavers, L. (2016). Here's my problem with #BlackGirlMagic: Black girls aren't magical. We're human. *Elle.* Retrieved from https://www.elle.com/life-love/a33180/why-i-dont-love-blackgirlmagic/

Collins, P. H. (1986). Learning from the outsider within: The sociological significance of Black feminist thought. *Social problems, 33*(6), 14–32.

Corbin, J., & Strauss, A. L. (2014). *Basics of qualitative research.* Thousand Oaks, CA: SAGE.

Crenshaw, K. (1997). Intersectionality and identity politics: Learning from violence against women of color. In M. L. Shanley & U. Narayan (Eds.), *Reconstructing political theory: Feminist perspectives* (pp. 178–193). University Park, PA: Pennsylvania State University Press.

Emerson, R. M., Fretz, R. I., & Shaw, L. L. (2011). *Writing ethnographic fieldnotes.* Chicago, IL: University of Chicago Press.

Ford, A. (2016). There is nothing wrong with Black girl magic. *Elle.* Retrieved from https://www.elle.com/life-love/a33251/there-is-nothing-wrong-with-black-girl-magic/

Hope, E. C., Keels, M., & Durkee, M. I. (2016). Participation in Black Lives Matter and deferred action for childhood arrivals: Modern activism among Black and Latino college students. *Journal of Diversity in Higher Education, 9*(3), 203–215.

Johnson, J. M. (2017). Choosing elites: Experiences of working-class Black undergraduate women at an Ivy League University. In *Critical perspectives on Black women and college success* (pp. 172–184). New York, NY: Routledge.

Keller, J. M. (2012). Virtual feminisms: Girls' blogging communities, feminist activism, and participatory politics. *Information, Communication & Society, 15*(3), 429–447.

Merriam, S. B. (2009). *Qualitative research: A guide to design and interpretation.* San Francisco, CA: Jossey-Bass.

Nielsen. (2017). *Young, connected and Black: African-American millennials are driving social change and leading digital advancement.* Retrieved from Nielsen website https://www.nielsen.com/us/en/insights/report/2016/young-connected-and-black/#

Patton, L. D., & McClure, M. L. (2009). Strength in the spirit: A qualitative examination of African American college women and the role of spirituality during college. *The Journal of Negro Education, 78*(1), 42–54.

Patton, L. D., & Croom, N. N. (2017a). *Critical perspectives on Black women and college success.* New York, NY: Routledge.

Patton, L. D., & Croom, N. N.(2017b). Critical perspectives on undergraduate Black women. In L. D. Patton & N. N. Croom (Eds.), *Critical perspectives on Black women and college success* (pp. 15–28). New York, NY: Routledge.

Rogers, L. O., & Way, N. (2016). "I have goals to prove all those people wrong and not fit into any one of those boxes": Paths of resistance to stereotypes among Black adolescent males. *Journal of Adolescent Research, 31*(3), 263–298.

Solorzano, D., Ceja, M., & Yosso, T. (2000). Critical race theory, racial microaggressions, and campus racial climate: The experiences of African American college students. *Journal of Negro Education, 69*(1), 60–73.

Thomas, J. (2016). "Black girl magic" is more than a hashtag; it's a movement. *CNN.* Retrieved from http://baltimoretimes-online.com/news/2016/feb/25/black-girl-magic-more-hashtag-its-movement/

U.S. Department of Education. Institute of Education Sciences, National Center for Education Statistics.

Winkle-Wagner, R. (2015). Having their lives narrowed down? The state of Black women's college success. *Review of Educational Research, 85*(2), 171–204.

CHAPTER 7

BLACK WOMEN'S ACTIVISM IN GRADUATE SCHOOL

Tracie A. Lowe
The University of Texas at Austin

Since the mid-1970s the overall enrollment numbers of Black women in graduate and professional programs has increased across the nation from 3.2% to approximately 9% in 2015 (National Center for Education Statistics, 2016, Table 306.10). Despite this growth, a historical tradition of exclusion from institutions of learning, de jure and de facto segregation, as well as institutional racism has significantly contributed to the glaring disparities related to access among Black women in graduate education. As a result, Black women graduate students remain highly underrepresented in higher education and are often one of a few, if not the only representative like themselves irrespective of their graduate disciplines (Joseph, 2012; Robinson, 2013; Schwartz, Bower, Rice, & Washington, 2003). Regarding degree conferment, Black women earned only 8% of master's degrees in 2015 in comparison to White women who received 34.9% (National Center for Education Statistics, 2016, Table 323.20). The total number of doctoral degrees Black and White women attained in 2015 was 5% and 31.8%,

Black Girl Civics, pages 109–124

respectively (National Center for Education Statistics, 2016, Table 324.20). Despite the statistic, Black women continue to pursue graduate levels of education to increase their access to better postgraduate opportunities (Gasman, Hirschfield, & Vultaggio, 2008).

Black women enrolled in graduate programs face a complex set of challenges related to their race and gender. Scholars have highlighted the prevalence of gendered racial microaggressions against Black women that adversely affect their experiences as students in predominately White spaces (Lewis et al., 2013). These microaggressions are characterized as "subtle, everyday verbal, behavioral, and environmental expressions of oppression based on the intersection of one's race and gender" (Lewis et al., 2013, p. 54). Though limited in number, research studies on Black women graduate students have indicated how differential treatment by faculty, staff, and students along with racial stereotyping elicits feelings of isolation, exclusion, and invisibility (Alexander & Hermann, 2015; Borum & Walker, 2012; Johnson-Bailey, 2004; Shavers & Moore, 2014). Black women contend with race-related issues in graduate school using an array of strategies, including various forms of coping and self-protective measures (Lewis et al., 2013). They also seek support from multiple sources such as mentors, family, and friends (Alexander & Bodenhorn, 2015; Patton, 2009; Patton & Harper, 2003). Resisting is an additional method that Black women graduate students use to deal with institutional racism, stereotypes, and prejudices toward them in their educational settings.

Though historical and recent accounts of Black women's activism have acknowledged the impact of their advocacy on transforming inequitable systems within institutions of higher learning, the experiences Black women have in graduate school in general, and specifically related to their activism remain vital topics for exploration. Therefore, there is a critical need to identify how Black women pursuing advanced degrees conceptualize and describe their activist participation. Hence, the purpose of this chapter is to discuss the findings from an empirical study which examined the activism experiences of 12 Black women graduate and professional students at a public research institution in the Southwestern United States. This investigation specifically addressed how the participants defined activism, factors that influenced their resistance work, and how their involvement in activism influenced their educational experiences. The chapter begins with a review of relevant literature on Black women in graduate education. A brief overview of the theoretical framework that informed the study is provided, followed by the methodology used for data collection and analysis. The section following highlights significant findings from the study and the chapter ends with a discussion of the implications this work has concerning Black girl civics.

REVIEW OF RELEVANT LITERATURE

Universities are often microcosms of society, meaning race-related issues that are prevalent in America for Black women also manifest in college settings (Johnson-Bailey, 2004; Lewis et al., 2013; Schwartz et al., 2003). Scholars have pointed to the multiple ways in which Black students experience similar instances of discrimination, feelings of isolation and invisibility at historically or predominately White institutions (Borum & Walker, 2012; Lewis et al., 2004). The university support systems that are meant to assist students in their transition to and completion of graduate programs are not privy to their needs, nor do these entities appropriately advocate for them (Lewis et al., 2004). For example, the socialization process for graduate students is a critical period that significantly shapes their expectations, satisfaction, and commitment to their graduate and professional programs (Ellis, 2001). A positive socialization experience may yield several benefits for students. Research suggests, however, that Black women encounter unique challenges, which negatively affect their acclimation into these environments (Ellis, 2001; Gasman et al., 2008; Lewis, Ginsberg, & Davies, 2004). The culmination of these experiences results in the lowest levels of satisfaction among Black women graduate students in comparison to their peers (Ellis, 2001).

Faculty advisors play a critical role in cultivating a sense of belonging among graduate students. Developing connections with them is necessary for graduate students because they serve as mentors who provide resources to help students accomplish their academic goals. Ellis (2001) noted, however, that Black and White students alike have difficulty forming meaningful relationships with their academic advisors. Of more significance is the fact that Black women's relationships with faculty advisors were reportedly more contentious than their Black male and White counterparts alike (Ellis, 2001). The absence of faculty mentorship leaves many Black women graduate students without the proper guidance to figure out the unwritten norms or "hidden curriculum" of graduate school (Gasman et al., 2008; Lewis et al., 2004). The hidden curriculum refers to the implicit rules or requirements of graduate students that are not explicitly expressed (Margolis & Romero, 1998). The exclusionary practices of the hidden curriculum result in the stigmatization of women of color as students who are less prepared to perform at the graduate level (Margolis & Romero, 1998).

Whereas a lack of support has negative implications for Black women in graduate school, the presence of mentorship from faculty has been critical to their success (Johnson-Bailey, Valentine, Cervero, & Bowles, 2008). For example, Black women faculty contribute to the retention of Black women graduate students when they provide affirmative spaces and establish opportunities for research and teaching that are scarce for students of color

(Johnson-Bailey, 2004). Supportive interactions with professors also affect the professional development of Black women graduate students, making them more competitive in the job market (Gasman et al., 2008; Johnson-Bailey, 2004). In summary, the networks that Black women in graduate school establish positively affect their self-efficacy and their persistence (Dortch, 2016).

To deal with the daily stresses of racial microaggressions at their institutions, Black women graduate students also utilize resistance, collective, and self-protective coping methods (Lewis et al., 2013). Collective coping, for example, involves using social networks as a safe-haven for Black women to express their frustrations or dissatisfaction with their experiences (Lewis et al., 2013). According to Patton and Harper (2003), family members such as mothers, grandmothers, aunts, sisters, and friends have been instrumental in giving the compassion and affirmation Black women graduate students need to remain resilient. These individuals supply a community of cultural wealth (Yosso, 2005) as well as life lessons on humility, independence, the value of education, and how to cultivate notions of personal self-worth (Patton, 2009).

Self-protective measures have served as a safeguard against the negative attitudes and behaviors that Black women graduate students experience in the classroom and during their interactions with others (Lewis et al., 2013). A case in point, some women choose not to engage in classroom discussions in which their peers fail to acknowledge the implicit biases they attribute to Black people. There are other instances in which Black women employ resistance coping and speak out against those who have treated them wrong (Lewis et al., 2013; Robinson, 2013). By voicing their opinions, however, Black women risk further marginalization when they are misjudged, silenced, or ignored altogether (Robinson, 2013). Research studies have given useful insights into the experiences of Black women graduate students and the ways they persist despite their circumstances. The next section introduces two dimensions of activism Black women use to combat the issues of race and gender in personal and professional settings (Collins, 2009)—struggles for group survival and struggles for institutional transformation.

THEORETICAL FRAMEWORK

As previously noted, Black women in higher education have experiences that are markedly different from those of their Black male counterparts and also of their White peers. Therefore, it is critical to select theoretical frameworks that move outside of the traditional lens of the dominant society and appropriately centralize the unique ideas and perspectives of Black women (Howard-Hamilton, 2003). Accordingly, Black feminist thought

(Collins, 2009) was used as the conceptual framework for the study because it focuses on the collective standpoint of Black women and their everyday shared experiences of oppression in the United States. Throughout history, Black women's resistance has been an integral part of their daily lives and has served as a means of combating multiple forms of institutional racism. Because of their historical exclusion from formal organizations, leadership, or authoritative roles, Black women have used their positions as outsiders-within to challenge the status quo and redefine their social standpoint (Collins, 2009). The approaches they utilize to accomplish their goals for social equity are, unfortunately, seldom acknowledged, often devalued, and at times misinterpreted.

Two dimensions of Black women's activism addressed by Collins (2009)—struggles for group survival and struggles for institutional transformation—were used in this study to explore how Black women have transformed their worlds in unconventional and innovative ways. Struggles for group survival consist of the indirect actions (i.e., providing positive messages for self-affirmation or cultivating mechanisms that uplift the Black community) taken to confront negative stereotypes or ideologies perpetuated by mainstream society. Education, for instance, is one sphere in which Black women have prepared future generations of activists through their liberatory teaching and leadership practices. More direct challenges to discriminatory laws and policies within schools, such as Black women's work within the civil rights movement, are representations of struggles for institutional transformation. Each of these dimensions provides a culturally relevant lens for examining the compelling stories of the participants.

METHODS

This study employed a qualitative phenomenological approach to "describe the meaning or essence of participants' lived experiences, or knowledge as it appears to consciousness" (Hays & Singh, 2014, p. 50). A phenomenological approach was best suited for this research as the goal was to understand the essence of Black women graduate students' experiences related to the phenomenon of activism as well as the meanings they attributed to the concept (Creswell, 2013; Hays & Singh, 2014). The study was conducted at a large, historically White, Research I University in the Southwestern United States, where Black students accounted for approximately 5% of the total student population. Purposeful and snowball sampling was used to recruit participants who were selected based on their self-identification as a Black woman or nonbinary individual currently enrolled in a graduate or professional program. A total of 12 participants, aged 22–33, were selected—11 of the participants in the study identified as Black women and one participant identified as Black and nonbinary. Of the 12 participants, two were professional students, six were doctoral students, and four were master's students pursuing professional or social science degrees at the university.

The participants completed a demographic survey that included questions where they reported their age, program of study, graduate level (master's, doctoral, or professional school), race/ethnicity, gender, and hometown. All the participants were interviewed twice using semi-structured interviews, which allowed for flexibility in questioning during the data gathering process (Creswell, 2013; Hays & Singh, 2014). The interview questions focused on their definitions of activism, how they described their activist involvement, factors that influenced their activism, as well as how their activism influenced their graduate student experiences. Participants also participated in a visualization technique activity in which they were asked to identify an item that represented their activism. As part of the second interview, the participants were asked to discuss how their chosen item related to their activism, an approach which elicited additional information used to triangulate the data from their prior responses.

An analysis of the data consisted of inductive coding in which codes emerged organically from the data and deductive coding in which codes were derived using the selected theoretical framework (Miles, Huberman, & Saldana, 2014). Three rounds of coding were utilized: first cycle pattern coding to identify emerging themes in the data, second cycle coding to group the ideas into more concise summaries, and the third round of coding using the theoretical framework for analysis (Miles et al., 2014). Member checking and triangulation of the data occurred through the use of clarifying questions and an analysis of data from two rounds of interviews (Hays & Singh, 2014). Each of the participants also received the findings to provide feedback before the completion of the final report. They were then invited to a formal presentation of the research, where several noted the positive impact of the study in terms of the encouragement they gained from being part of the project. Seeing their views and opinions represented and validated was meaningful to them, particularly in an educational space that seldom acknowledged their experiences.

FINDINGS

Findings from the study illustrated the contemporary ways in which Black women in graduate school spaces defined activism and how their relationship with the concept influenced how, when, and why they engaged in resistance efforts. The results discussed in this chapter focus specifically on four themes related to the development of their conceptualizations of activism over time. The first theme describes the race and gender-related experiences of the participants during their childhood to high school that would later influence their interpretations and performance of activism. The second theme explores the alternative ways in which the participants defined the concept of activism as well as the expectations assigned to those who identified as such. Next, a discussion of the different ways in which the participants integrated resistance measures into their educational work is provided. The section concludes with an examination of the relationship between the participants' activism and the theoretical dimensions—struggles for group survival and struggles for institutional transformation—which guided the analysis of the study.

Experiences During the Younger Years

During their childhood years, the participants began to grapple with issues of discrimination and racism that made them question why people were not treated the same because of their mere skin tone. These early encounters inevitably led them to deeply reflect on the inequities between their communities and those of others who lived in different areas or who looked different from them. Though the participants as children could not fully grasp or understand the magnitude of the problems they encountered, they knew they wanted to change their circumstances as well as those of others. Their cultivation of the desire to transform their environments from a young age was the primary impetus behind the participants' thoughtful reflections on the concept of activism.

Grace, a master's student, recalled a story where, as a child attending a predominately White elementary school, she felt the teachers were "culturally insensitive." She explained to her mom, "They were just treating minority children wrong...mainly Black kids...what they're doing isn't right." Her mother listened to these concerns and took actions to address them with Grace by her side. As a result of her mother's support, Grace gained the confidence to continue advocating for herself and the needs of others throughout her educational career. Similar to Grace, other participants encountered issues of race while growing up. However, as they aged, they developed a higher level of critical consciousness regarding how each of their identities influenced their interactions with others and how others treated them.

After noticing as a teenager, how the men and women in her family did not share the same domestic responsibilities, Melissa, a doctoral student in the study, decided to inquire into the reason why:

It just didn't seem fair...even in my household, as a middle child, my older brother got away with a lot that I didn't get away with. And then, whenever I asked my parents about it, or even just chores, their answer was, "You're the girl. You have to do this."

Melissa considered these moments to be "the early stages of [her] formulating and questioning certain things," and they ultimately served as a precursor to her later resistance work. The problematic issues of race for Grace and gender that Melissa uncovered would intersect to create unique challenges for the other participants as well.

Jasmine, a doctoral student, encountered gendered-racial microaggressions in one of her high school history courses. A project she decided to complete on the bombing of the 16th Street Baptist Church in Birmingham, Alabama, was not received well by her White male instructor. Jasmine explained that she was given a score that ultimately kept her from maintaining an A in the class, making her ineligible for the honor of being class valedictorian at her high school. Jasmine's teacher revealed the intent of his actions when he stated, "No way there would be a Black female valedictorian at [this] high school." She continued to say, "If I took the final exam, he would fail me. And so, I walked away." Despite Jasmine's dealings with the discriminatory behaviors of her history teacher, she would later become a history major who centered her scholarship on Black women. Grace, Melissa, and Jasmine learned at an early age how to reckon with circumstances they felt were unfair. Each of the situations they were involved in represented critical periods in their lives where intentional discussions on topics such as racial- and gendered-microaggressions might have provided a means for helping them understand their experiences. These incidents which influenced their identity development as a youth would later affect their perspectives on activism and how they integrated resistance work into their everyday practices.

Defining Activism

Surprisingly, the concept of activism was not a topic many of the participants had taken the time to reflect on in the past intentionally. Activism was admittedly a complicated thing to explain or describe for them. In defining the term for herself, Melissa expressed, "I just think it's something that . . . it's really fluid. It's hard to define and say, you know, who is or who isn't an activist." Although there were variations in how they made meaning of the term, generating change for the betterment of their surroundings, whether that be in their communities or their educational spaces, was a common theme threaded throughout the responses of the participants. Terms such as *advocacy* and *pushing back against systems* were also a component of how they defined the concept. As the participants reflected on their activism and what it meant to be an activist in the era of the Black Lives Matter movement, they noted how some of their longstanding preconceptions on the subject changed with time. The boundaries of what could be considered activism became more ambiguous in contrast to the more rigid notions of what it represented.

Sherri, a master's student, acknowledged that "I guess a part of me is hesitant to leave [activism's] old definition...And, that's like the protesting that I've been kind of taught. [It] was like, the real hard-hitting, make-a-change protesting." However, for other participants, activism could not be merely narrowed to more overt acts such as political marches or rallies. Harper concisely summed up the participants' responses when she stated activism could be "one of the most basic things. And it could be [the] extreme of things." Overall, the participants' responses in the study provided evidence of Collins' (2009) assertion regarding how Black women's interpretations of activism move beyond the traditional ideas and definitions typically associated with the concept.

Each of the participants also spoke of varying levels of activist engagement in their discussions and pointed to the fact that not everyone approached doing resistance work in the same manner. Jasmine, a doctoral student, indicated that although there were different degrees of commitment among activists, each of them was important:

> I think there are people who are activists for a moment. And we need those people. And then I think there are people who are activists for a movement. We need those people. And I think there are people who are activists for life, who just sincerely are interested in the betterment of their world and future worlds.

Every level of involvement was needed in the movement for social equity, according to Jasmine. Although the work was expressly important, everyone was not willing to formally accept the title of being an activist as it was not always viewed positively.

The participants asserted that the expectations and responsibilities associated with the activist title were unnecessary burdens; they did not want to assume them. As a result, most of them preferred not to label themselves as such. Breanna affirmed the sentiments of most when she stated, "I mean if someone's like, 'are you an activist?' I'd be like sure. But, I don't put myself forth like that." One reason for their hesitancy to accept the title stemmed from the fear that they would be criticized for any missteps in their work. Harper explained, "If you don't do XYZ, then like, how are you an activist? Or, if you say anything wrong, you will get dragged. And then it's like you're canceled. It's like, maybe. But is that really helpful? No, it's not." Although the assumed consequences of being a leader in the movement dissuaded the participants from formally associating with the activist role, they were still very much involved in social change projects within their various communities, including educational spaces.

Forms of Educational Activism

All of the participants engaged in educational forms of activism to improve the culture of their universities and the learning environments of other Black students they served in their schools. During her undergraduate years, Melissa explained how she and her peers helped to establish a new ethnic studies program at her institution:

> We didn't have like an African American Studies major or minor, which was interesting to us. The Black population was very small, but still, we were like, you know, these are things that people are interested in. We got a minor. Now they have like a whole program which is cool.

Melissa created an academic space that not only progressed her agenda for the inclusion of Black students in higher education but one that also provided an extraordinary legacy that others would benefit from in the future.

Jasmine's activist efforts focused on altering historical narratives in the K–12 setting that excluded conversations on the racial injustices against Black people in America. As a summer fellow in an organization dedicated to creating inclusive schools, she had the opportunity to develop a curriculum based on social justice tenets for the sake of creating an anti-biased education. She expressed that completing the program challenged her to think critically "about how do we get students in primary school to understand issues of race?" Jasmine wanted to develop a curriculum in which the teachers fulfilled their educational requirements for the test. However, she also wanted to assist in "creating informed, well-rounded citizens who can take up the [resistance] fight as they grow older." The task proved to be thought-provoking for her as it was challenging to figure out how to translate history to a younger population and tackle issues that were difficult to discuss. Her efforts, she realized, were a "great example of how activism gets applied to both a really academic space and a higher ed space." Cultivating the development of skills and knowledge was a method not exclusive to Jasmine's work. Others also utilized similar measures to empower the students of color they served.

Working in an institution of higher education gave Kai, a master's student, the opportunity to support students in ways that would increase their academic success. She was very thoughtful about the activities she facilitated for the undergraduates in her program. Kai had her students use a campus map to identify departments, offices, or personnel that were responsible for providing services that could aid in their success. She expressed that before her interactions with them, her students had never seriously considered how essential they were to the life of an institution. Kai found it gratifying to give tools of resilience to others so that they could achieve their goals in institutions that were not adept at responding to their needs. She explained,

> We look at higher education as this system that students come into, and [they] kinda have to use their autonomy to make [it] work for them to try and meet the standards that the school set. But I was like, no—everyone here works for you.

Similar to Kai's work, several other participants also alluded to advocating on behalf of their students to obtain the resources they were lacking. In other instances, the participants shifted their focus to the classroom as a space for change where they could present views and ideologies that were not represented in academic curriculums.

Nicole, a doctoral student, used innovative measures to stimulate differing viewpoints within the graduate conversations she facilitated. She, however, worked from an instructional standpoint to transform student thinking: "My AI [assistant instructor] class, it's already pretty much set out for me. The readings are all set for me. So, I have to like, bring in my own examples if I wanted [*sic*] it to be truly intersectional." Though she had a limited range of authority over the curriculum, Nicole found ways to incorporate new and diverse voices: "I can't pick the readings. But I can pick the examples that I have from the readings, and . . . will continue to center women of color."

In summary, activism in education was a priority for all of the participants, which was most likely because they had completed most of their education at institutions that historically excluded them and their experiences. When describing their experiences, the participants illustrated how multidimensional the work of activism was for them. Their responses suggested that the nature of resistance work was not "one size fits all," and there were a variety of measures that could be used to improve their educational experience.

Struggles for Group Survival and Institutional Transformation

Collins' (2009) two dimensions of activism—struggles for group survival and struggles for institutional transformation—were used as a lens to examine how the participants defined the concept and how they described and interpreted their experiences related to resistance work. There were many instances in which they partook in activist measures that were representative of each dimension. For example, the educational setting, as illustrated in previous findings, was regularly used as a space to empower others and encourage racial uplift through the passing along of skills, knowledge, and tools for self-affirmation. Actions such as these have been a prominent element of Black women's struggles for group survival for generations. Though at times unrecognized, the participants' roles as organizers and informal leaders for their students' causes were transformative within their spheres of influence.

Harper, for instance, discussed how she worked with her associate principal in high school to organize a panel for her peers to share their learning experiences in classrooms with all White teachers:

> I just felt like they needed to know what it was like to be a Black student here. And so, we organized [the panels] in the library, and it was a volunteer thing for teachers to come and listen. And we had students come and answer questions about what it was like [be]cause most of their Black students came from [the inner city].

The panels were necessary for creating a space in which Harper's peers of color could express their concerns. This example of struggles for group survival demonstrated how the participants used their outsider-within positions to identify problems and advocate on behalf of those who did not have the same levels of access to individuals with administrative authority. Though Harper did not directly challenge institutional policies, she used the informal power she possessed to bring attention to the experiences of Black students. She intended to increase their sense of belonging, which indirectly impacted their educational outcomes.

Representations of struggles for institutional transformation also emerged as the participants worked to change school policies and practices that were problematic. Jasmine's direct experience with participating in the Black Lives Matter movement is an example of the work done to eliminate institutional racism that affected the lives of Black individuals in the city where her university resided. Fighting against the police brutality within her college community placed her on the frontlines, a position where she learned several lessons on remaining hopeful despite the slow process of change:

> So, it would be one thing if you felt like you were fighting the good fight and things were improving. But I don't remember any of us saying, like, things are improving (laughs). I don't remember that ever being the mentality like, oh great. You finally got some change. We finally got what we wanted. I don't think that's how anybody felt. I think it was just like everybody's angry. Everybody's really frustrated. And everybody wants to evoke some sort of change. And, you know we'll be damned if we don't try. We're just gonna try. That's all we can do.

Jasmine realized how sustaining activism required an intentional shift in her mindset. There seemed to be periods where change was minimal or did not happen at all. However, her will to try and make things better never ceased. As illustrated in Jasmine's story, the development of an activist consciousness was a transformative process which helped her and the other participants understand that, despite the setbacks or trials that occurred, their work was still significant and ongoing.

DISCUSSION AND IMPLICATIONS FOR BLACK GIRL CIVICS

This study illuminated the innovative and comprehensive ways in which Black women graduate students conceptualized activism and how it manifested in their lives. Defining activism was not a simple process, and what represented activism could not be confined within certain traditional boundaries. Although the work of activists is known to bring about positive change, the participants in this study preferred not to label themselves as such. Their reasoning stemmed from a desire to avoid the underlying expectations and higher standards for living that were associated with the role. Despite their decision not to embrace the title, the participants did not shy away from the actual work involved in maintaining resistance struggles.

Gaining an awareness of the activism experiences of Black women in graduate school can help us understand how various circumstances cultivate or stifle their ability and willingness to resist throughout their lifetime. Cohen (2006) asserted the need for researchers to examine the politics of Black youth as doing so would broaden our knowledge of the new ways in which they engage within the political context. Rethinking the activism of Black women through a lens of struggles for group survival, institutional transformation (Collins, 2009), and other innovative measures of resistance is a starting point for expanding our definitions and conceptions of activism. Interventions that encourage the development of a liberation mindset are necessary for Black women of all ages and in all contexts who will significantly transform and redefine our society.

Ginwright's (2007) research on Black youth activism and critical social capital among Black community organizations highlighted how the development of civic engagement could be facilitated in several ways. He argued, "Critical social capital consists of intergenerational ties that cultivate expectations about the capacity for Black youth to transform the conditions that shape their lives" (Ginwright, 2007, p. 416). Black women's presence within organizations in the Black community can be beneficial for Black girls as the affirmation given between generations, coupled with shared collective experiences can create a safe-haven of learning (Collins, 2009). Connections to seasoned activists or individuals who have lived through and participated in movements can also provide a network of support to Black girls who are wrestling with the harmful dominant tropes and images of themselves and others like them (Collins, 2009). Reframing their identities in society from being viewed as problematic or deviant to being regarded as "civic problem solvers" might create a reality in which their wisdom is validated and utilized (Ginwright, 2007, p. 416). Having conversations with those who have experienced similar trials can foster a new lens in which Black girl's failures are no longer attributed to personal deficiencies or shortcomings (Ginwright, 2007). They can instead be conceived as the result of culturally insensitive institutional policies which can be addressed through politics (Ginwright, 2007).

Mentors and advisors also equipped the participants in this study with strategies and tools to use in their work against injustice. Black women who are biological mothers, extended kin, or as Collins states, "other mothers," are a unique group in the community that possesses the ability to cultivate positive relationships and positive images of self among a young generation of Black children (Collins, 2009). According to Collins (2009), "Black women's motherwork reflects how political consciousness can emerge within everyday lived experience" (p. 224). For example, some participants in the study noted how their moms, aunties, grandmothers, and other women they knew inspired them. Watching those close to them engage in social activism compelled the participants to grapple with how to address the issues they faced in their lives. Black women's knowledge and presence in the community is, therefore, essential to the growth and development of Black girls, women, and other individuals.

The participants also willingly acknowledged the value of their elders' expertise throughout their interviews. They tapped into the collective consciousness of their generation and those before them to produce new conceptualizations and approaches to activism molded to their specific needs, even at a young age. This finding affirms Cohen's (2006) research concerning the politics and civic engagement of Black youth. In her work, she emphasized the significance of acknowledging and examining their approaches to political participation:

> Whether we measure it or not, young people are using old and new ways to not only survive politically but re-create and improve upon their lived existence. Sometimes these forms are easily recognized, such as when they register to vote and show up at the polls. Other times their politics may be less visible, but no less profound—raising consciousness and disseminating oppositional ideologies through cultural vehicles. (para. 20)

Although much of the work the participants engaged in was not intentionally on display for others to observe, their labor undeniably served as a critical component of change. Ultimately, this study revealed that there are several lessons to be learned from the activism of Black women in graduate school. Their approach to dismantling systems of oppression are far reaching and provide a new framework for tackling some of society's greatest ills.

If we fail to examine the insight of these individuals, we risk limiting the opportunities we have to better our tomorrow.

REFERENCES

Alexander, Q., & Bodenhorn, N. (2015). My rock: Black women attending graduate school at a southern predominantly White university. *Journal of College Counseling, 18*(3), 259–274. https://doi.org/10.1002/jocc.12019

Alexander, Q. R., & Hermann, M. A. (2015). African-American women's experiences in graduate science, technology, engineering, and mathematics education at a predominantly White university: A qualitative investigation. *Journal of Diversity in Higher Education.* Advance online publication. http://doi.org/10.1037/a0039705

Borum, V., & Walker, E. (2012). What makes the difference? Black women's undergraduate and graduate experiences in mathematics. *Journal of Negro Education, 81*(4), 366–378.

Cohen, C. (2006). African American youth: Broadening our understanding of politics, civic engagement and activism. *Youth Activism.* Retrieved from http://ya.ssrc.org/african/Cohen

Collins, P. H. (2009). *Black feminist thought: Knowledge, consciousness, and the politics of empowerment* (1st ed.). New York, NY: Routledge.

Creswell, J. W. (2013). *Qualitative inquiry and research design: Choosing among five approaches* (3rd ed.). Thousand Oaks, CA: SAGE.

Dortch, D. (2016). The strength from within: A phenomenological study examining the academic self-efficacy of African American women in doctoral studies. *Journal of Negro Education, 85*(3), 350–364.

Ellis, E. M. (2001). The impact of race and gender on graduate school socialization, satisfaction with doctoral study, and commitment to degree completion. *Western Journal of Black Studies, 25*(1), 30–45.

Gasman, M., Hirschfeld, A., & Vultaggio, J. (2008). "Difficult yet rewarding": The experiences of African American graduate students in education at an Ivy League institution. *Journal of Diversity in Higher Education, 1*(2), 126–138. https://doi.org/10.1037/1938-8926.1.2.126

Ginwright, S. A. (2007). Black youth activism and the role of critical social capital in Black community organizations. *The American Behavioral Scientist, 51*(3), 403–418.

Hays, D. G., & Singh, A. A. (2014). *Qualitative inquiry in clinical and educational settings.* New York, NY: The Guildford Press.

Howard-Hamilton, M. F. (2003). Theoretical frameworks for African American women. *New Directions for Student Services, 2003*(104), 19–27. https://doi.org/10.1002/ss.104

Johnson-Bailey, J. (2004). Hitting and climbing the proverbial wall: Participation and retention issues for Black graduate women. *Race Ethnicity and Education, 7*(4), 331–349. http://doi.org/10.1080/1361332042000303360

Johnson-Bailey, J., Valentine, T. S., Cervero, R. M., & Bowles, T. A. (2008). Lean on me: The support experiences of Black graduate students. *The Journal of Negro Education, 77*(4), 365–381.

Joseph, J. (2012). From one culture to another: Years one and two of graduate school for African American women in the STEM fields. *International Journal of Doctoral Studies, 7*, 125–142.

Lewis, C. W., Ginsberg, R., & Davies, T. (2004). The experiences of African American PhD students at a predominately white Carnegie I–research institution. *College Student Journal, 38*(2), 231–245.

Lewis, J., Mendenhall, R., Harwood, S., & Browne Huntt, M. (2013). Coping with gendered racial microaggressions among Black women college students. *Journal of African American Studies, 17*(1), 51–73. http://doi.org/10.1007/s12111-012-9219-0

Margolis, E., & Romero, M. (1998). The department is very male, very white, very old, and very conservative: The functioning of the hidden curriculum in graduate sociology departments. *Harvard Educational Review, 68*(1), 1–32.

Miles, M. B., Huberman, A. M., & Saldana, J. (2014). *Qualitative data analysis: A methods sourcebook* (3rd ed.). Thousand Oaks, CA: SAGE.

National Center for Education Statistics. (2016). Table 306.10: Total fall enrollment in degree-granting postsecondary institutions, by level of enrollment, sex, attendance status, and race/ethnicity of student: Selected years, 1976 through 2015. In U.S. Department of Education, National Center for Education Statistics (Ed.), *Digest of education statistics* (2016 ed.). Retrieved from https://nces.ed.gov/programs/digest/d16/tables/dt16_306.10.asp?current=yes

National Center for Education Statistics. (2016). Table 323.20: Master's degrees conferred by postsecondary institutions, by race/ethnicity and sex of student: Selected years, 1976–77 through 2014–15. In U.S. Department of Education, National Center for Education Statistics (Ed.), *Digest of education statistics* (2016 ed.). Retrieved from https://nces.ed.gov/programs/digest/d16/tables/dt16_323.20.asp

Patton, L. D. (2009). My sister's keeper: A qualitative examination of mentoring experiences among African American women in graduate and professional schools. *Journal of Higher Education, 80*(5), 510–537. https://doi.org/10.1353/jhe.0.0062

Patton, L. D., & Harper, S. R. (2003). Mentoring relationships among African American women in graduate and professional schools. *New Directions for Student Services, 2003*(104), 67–78. https://doi.org/10.1002/ss.108

Robinson, S. J. (2013). Spoke tokenism: Black women talking back about graduate school experiences. *Race Ethnicity and Education, 16*(2), 155–181. https://doi.org/10.1080/13613324.2011.645567

Schwartz, R. A., Bower, B. L., Rice, D. C., & Washington, C. M. (2003). "Ain't I a woman, too?" Tracing the experiences of African American women in graduate school. *The Journal of Negro Education, 72*(3), 252–268. http://doi.org/10.2307/3211247

Shavers, M. C., & Moore, J. L., III. (2014). Black female voices: Self-presentation strategies in doctoral programs at predominately White institutions. *Journal of College Student Development, 55*(4), 391–407.

Yosso, T. J. (2005). Whose culture has capital? A critical race theory discussion of community cultural wealth. *Race Ethnicity and Education, 8*(1), 69–91. https://doi.org/10.1080/1361332052000341006

CHAPTER 8

BLACK FEMME YOUTH ORGANIZING FOR TRANSFORMATION

Julia Daniel
University of Colorado, Boulder

Annie Thomas
Project South

BACKGROUND

This study examines Black young femme people's engagement with Power U Center for Social Change (referred to as Power U), a youth organization that campaigns for educational and reproductive justice in Miami-Dade County Public Schools (MDCPS). As an organization that sees connections between punitive discipline policies and gender-based violence in schools, Power U has been working to raise the consciousness of young Black people in Miami, while engaging them in struggles for policy changes and resources to change practices. Throughout the process, the leadership of young Black people is developed such that they are able to speak with decision makers and allies about the challenges they face in schools and what they

Black Girl Civics, pages 125–139

would like to see changed. These experiences deepen their political consciousness as well as their feelings of efficacy to create much needed systemic change in their schools and communities.

Miami Dade County, like many school districts, uses a heavy-handed approach to discipline, with school-based arrests, suspensions, and expulsions disproportionately inflicted on Black youth. Respectability discourse towards Black youth prevails, as schools discipline Black students for infractions related to dress and comportment (Carter & Vavrus, 2018). Black students received 47% of out-of-school suspensions in 2013–2014 but were only 23% of the entire student population (Civil Rights Data Collection, 2013–2014).

While discipline disproportionately harms Black youth, there are many practices in schools that especially harm Black femmes, or people who identify as feminine, female, girls, young women, and transgender female. For example, young Black femme students and LGBTQIA students experience sexual harassment from other students as well as staff, which often goes unaddressed by the school system (Carter & Vavrus, 2018). The lack of comprehensive sexual education in the schools leaves young people to learn about their bodies, their desires, and their sexuality largely from popular culture, each other, family members, and community institutions, at times accessing misinformation and limiting their awareness about their reproductive choices and consent (Fine & McClelland, 2006). Discipline practices focus on monitoring and regulating the comportment, dress, and language used by young Black femme students, leaving them both controlled and punished in particular ways that their masculine counterparts are not (Carter & Vavrus, 2018).

In response, Power U has been organizing youth for restorative justice in the schools since 2008, through direct actions at school board meetings, press conferences, and meetings to garner support from school board members and other allies. This organizing brought awareness to the fact that the budget allocations of the district were perpetuating the schoolhouse-to-jailhouse pipeline. Rather than investing in practices to improve relationships and address issues like restorative justice, the district continued to fund punitive discipline measures and a large school police department.

Both of us as the authors of this chapter have participated in different ways in the development of the strategy, survey, and campaign that we're writing about. Annie Thomas, a 24-year-old Black woman has been playing more of a participant role over the years, as a youth member and then as a staff organizer. Julia Daniel, a 39-year-old White woman was a former youth organizer and current board member. In these roles, we have been active in shaping the work, with Annie being deeply embedded in the day-to-day organizing work as well as the long-term visioning of the organization and Julia playing a supporting role as a graduate student researcher. We include this information about ourselves and our roles in the organization as both a political commitment to explaining our positionalities, and because it is relevant to explaining the methodology of the chapter.

In the fall of 2015, under public pressure from Power U and its allies, Superintendent Carvalho was saying that they were going to end the use of out-of-school suspensions. Rather than implement restorative justice initiatives in the schools; however, MDCPS decided to invest in *success centers* that allegedly were going to be a meaningful alternative to out-of-school suspensions and help students keep up with their school work (Veiga, 2015). To assess the new initiative, Power U decided that a student survey would demonstrate how students are experiencing discipline in their schools and the efficacy of success centers.

Beginning in October 2015, the authors worked with youth members to build this survey, learning data collection skills to gather a broad base of data related to issues they were seeing and the concerns they had about the success centers as well as about the gendered and racialized harassment happening in schools. Over the next 18 months, we developed two surveys that the youth then conducted with over 600 students in select schools. Together, we then examined the results of the survey and conducted collective data analysis to "grade" the schools and the district on various measures. They have written a report based on their data that shares the results of the survey as well as some of the young people's firsthand experiences to support their demands for a shift in the district budget to invest in restorative practices in schools.

Simultaneously, the organization was working with other organizers from the county to develop a Black Girls Matter (BGM) platform and collective agenda that would highlight the particular ways that Black femme young women experience systemic and interpersonal violence in the various institutions in their everyday lives. Participation in this work has driven the survey process as well as the organization to have an intersectional lens (Crenshaw, 1989) in the work we do. Youth's experiences in both of these areas of work help us understand how an organization can use an intersectional lens to approach campaign work, lifting up the leadership of Black femme youth with other students as well. The BGM platform and organizing has worked to center Black femme youth's leadership and ensure that their issues receive attention through various mechanisms such as public forums, restorative circles, and published materials.

Annie and Julia began collecting interviews with youth over the summer of 2017 to assess how they are making sense of the data that they gathered, as well as how this data, coupled with their experiences, challenges dominant ideas about low-income Black youth and Black femme students. We also examine how this shapes their ideas about themselves, how it builds their sense of individual and collective efficacy, and how participation in this organization can shift power dynamics in a school district.

THEORETICAL FRAMEWORK

We use a Black feminist approach for understanding the experiences of the participants as being enabled and constrained by intersecting forms of domination (Collins, 2004; Crenshaw, 1989) including racism, sexism, and homophobia that shape their experience in particular ways. Black feminist thought has taught us that understanding the ways that Black young femme people experience intersecting forms of oppression systems will illustrate how these forms reinforce each other and maintain power relationships (Collins, 2014). The leadership of people who live at these intersections, then becomes especially important as we work to understand how oppressive structures operate, how to challenge power dynamics, and how to create change that doesn't end up privileging one group of people at the expense of another (Young, 2010). We also acknowledge that identity markers such as race and gender are socially constructed and thereby fluid and changing (Cahill, 2007), but have real implications on how bodies are read and treated under racial capitalism (Robinson, 2000).

Centering marginalized people in movements for social change is important because of the insights they can bring about the intersecting nature of different forms of oppression (Crenshaw, 1989), and in order to challenge deficit ideas about low-income people of color, queer people, and women (Ransby, 2018). Social movement theory also informs our understanding of how through collective organizing, people form new senses of individual and collective identity (Polletta & Jasper, 2001) and can build and exercise more agency (Emirbayer & Mische, 1998; Jasper, 2004). By politicizing the issues around which people organize, by linking a local struggle to broader phenomenon, and by building this sense of collective agency, social movement organizing can build new consciousness among oppressed power that is linked to a broader sense of power and a more expansive imagination of what they deserve and feel is possible.

LITERATURE REVIEW

In this section, we review literature on the issues around which Power U Youth are organizing, as well as the strategies that they take up for creating the change they seek.

Black Femme Students

literature suggests that students will be more engaged when teachers respect their communities and ethnic or racial backgrounds and can use pedagogy and curriculum that demonstrates both this familiarity and respect in how they treat students (Gay, 2010; Ladson-Billings, 1995). This is important because it can improve student learning and relationships at the school, and also because it can promote important in-school conversations about justice, potentially building the leadership skills for often marginalized students to participate in questions of democratic governance (Ladson-Billings, 2014; Paris, 2012). Similarly, practices such as restorative justice can repair relationships within schools when harms are done and keep students in the learning environment (Gonzalez, 2012) Despite the evidence of these important pedagogical interventions, however, Miami Dade schools overly invest in exclusionary and punitive practices that tend to diminish trust between students and adults, and perhaps more importantly, negatively impact their sense of being cared for in schools and desire to engage in the classroom (Davis, 2014; Geller, Fagan, Tyler, & Link, 2014; Hagan, Shedd, & Payne, 2005; Kupchik & Ellis, 2008; Lewis, Romi, Katz, & Qui, 2008).

Punitive disciplinary practices are not only ineffective at addressing issues and creating solutions, the interaction of such techniques with implicit bias on the part of adults creates racialized, gendered, and class-based patterns of punishment in which Black youth are disproportionately punished as compared to their White counterparts (Aaron & Ellis, 2008; Gregory, Skiba, & Noguera, 2010; Skiba, Michael, Nardo, & Peterson, 2002). Black femme students experience disciplining practices from adults in the school in particular ways that are both racialized and gendered (Wun, 2014), resulting in being 5.5 times more likely to be suspended than White femme students (National Women's Law Center, 2017). Black femmes, transgender, and gender non-conforming youth deal with sexual harassment and assaults from school staff and disparaging comments about how they dress and present their gender (Carter & Vavrus, 2018), while receiving inadequate sexual education and support (Fine & Ruglis, 2009).

As their identity is disciplined and regulated by school staff and teachers in particular punitive ways (Evans-Winters & Esposito, 2010), they are forced to choose between being good and being "ghetto" (Jones, 2009) and often criminalized for nonconformity and for being seen as overly assertive (Morris, 2012), characteristics that when exhibited in other students are encouraged. Teachers are more likely to perceive Black femme students as disruptive and as less attentive than other female students (Francis, 2012) and tend to discipline them more harshly regardless of their behavior (Wun, 2016). Adults additionally tend to perceive Black femme youth as less innocent; as older; as less in need of nurturing, protection, and support; and as knowing more about sex than White femme youth (Epstein, Blake, & Gonzalez, 2017). As Wun (2016) points out, "By defining the girls as problems, structural forms of violence, including violence from school authorities, are obscured in favor of disciplining and punishing the girls" (p. 6). In this context, the leadership of Black femme students in shaping demands, mobilizing their peers, and shifting the dominant discourse on the issues is key to winning improvements that begin to address both the structural and interpersonal forms of violence they are facing.

Organizing for Power

Literature on community organizing suggests that such practices can help challenge negative ideas about young people of color, both internally within the group and externally in popular conceptions (Cahill, 2007; Kirshner, 2015). Through community organizing, people from disadvantaged backgrounds can build their sense of collective efficacy in ways that can shift power dynamics to win reforms that improve the educational context and enable more reforms in the future (Rogers, Mediratta, & Shah, 2012; Warren, Hong, Rubin, & Uy, 2009). Such efforts can build important leadership and critical thinking skills among previously marginalized people such that they can continue to advance larger campaigns for social change (Warren & Mapp, 2011).

Similarly, participatory action research (PAR) is a form of research that grounds the methodology, questions, and research development in the knowledge of the people normally relegated to being the subjects of study and is driven in large part by their leadership and towards changing conditions (Fals-Borda, 1987; Golob & Giles, 2013). When it's done with a critical eye, it can unearth and challenge negatively held stereotypes and beliefs about people often based on race (Bradbury, 2017; Torre, 2009). Engaging young people in research and organizing work can build leadership, challenge accepted knowledge about issues they experience, and develop youth as resources for community transformation (Checkoway & Richards-Schuster, 2004; Gambone et al., 2006; Su, 2010). With this study, we hope to further the research on how a Black feminist, anti-capitalist approach to organizing can undermine the power relations within which the social justice organizing takes place.

METHODOLOGY

This is an autoethnographic case study that examines how young Black femmes in a community organization experience and challenge intersectional oppression. Both authors were active in shaping and participating in the strategy and practices that we studied, and our experiences are reflected in the findings over four years. Our interviews and observations aim to deepen our understanding of both the issues that young Black femme students confront as well as the tactics that an organization like Power U uses. To that end, we conducted open-ended interviews with participants about their experiences in schools and at Power U, as well as observations at Power U meetings, public forums, and during the survey process.

This study centers on the youth organizers and members of Power U and ally organizations that participated in the BGM. The participants are 7 young Black femme people, three Black masculine youth, and one Black femme adult. Participants were all U.S. born (some with parents from the Caribbean), aged 13–24, from low-income backgrounds who participated in the strategic campaigning, PAR, and BGM work to change district policies around discipline and gender justice in MDCPS. We have used pseudonyms to protect the participants' identities.

FINDINGS

The findings are divided into two separate but related sections. For the sake of explaining them, we have split them into a focus on the BGM work and the PAR that included a survey and analysis process that drew on the BGM framework. We explain a bit more of the processes and include quotes that illustrate what we saw as important findings throughout.

We found that spaces that were specifically designed to support Black femmes helped to create a safe environment to talk about issues that the young people were facing and to connect their issues to structural forms of oppression in their schools and communities. Through public forums, healing circles, and applying an intersectional lens to the work, the organizing efforts of Power U and allies challenge the racialized and gendered nature of oppressions that the young people face. The PAR helped document the systemic nature of these oppressions, demonstrating that they are not individual cases but need to be addressed at a systemic level. The process of developing the survey, conducting it with students, and analyzing the data helped recruit and politicize new youth into the organization, and helped shape demands that were reflective of students' experiences.

Black Girls MIA Public Forum

The idea to create specific spaces for Black femme youth and organizers came years ago when we were talking about how Black femmes are missing from the conversation on school discipline and to make sure we included an intersectional analysis into that conversation. The public constructions of Black femininity in media and other places were driven by stereotypes about Black women being loud and angry, as well as overly sexualized. For example, in our schools we saw that when a Black femme wears a certain piece of clothing, she is more sexualized than when a White student wears the same thing. We wanted to challenge stereotypes and bring attention to school pushouts, particularly around Black femmes, focusing on the over-policing of Black femmes that is not seen by the general public.

To raise awareness, we started the BGM workshop with ally organizations in Miami and in different schools. We developed and presented different scenarios in which Black women face oppression, allowing us to collect information about how Black girls were targeted. Participants acted out scenarios about the issues we were dealing with and then we talked about what they saw in relation to their day-to-day life. People shared stories about dress code issues, getting in trouble for having their shirts or jeans too tight, and being harassed by security guards. One young woman was told by a security guard that she was gay because she "didn't have any good 'd' [dick] in her life." This young woman went to the administration about it, and it remained unaddressed until she brought it to the public in an event we organized.

We then organized a BGM town hall meeting with 7 panels on different issues including mental health, foster care, policing, and immigration. All of the panels focused on how Black femmes experienced that issue in different ways. Some of our youth members spoke, as well as community allies and leaders. The approximately 800 participants in the audience were actively listening to the conversation and wanted to support the work after. This brought the BGM work to the forefront of our work with this coalition, as we saw the importance of these conversations from the audience's interest. We moved from our outreach focus to a community-wide response, centered on the BGM circles.

Using a Reproductive Justice Lens in Organizing

At an organizational level, Power U tries to incorporate a reproductive justice lens to the campaigns, recognizing that the reproductive choices that young people make are informed by many things, including how safe, happy, and healthy their communities and public institutions are. We borrow from Sister Song's definition of reproductive justice as "the human right to maintain personal bodily autonomy, have children, not have children, and parent the children we have in safe and sustainable communities" (Sister Song, 2019). The reproductive justice lens is then attentive to issues of gender and race and challenges the organization to be attentive to such issues internally as well as in choosing issues to work on. This approach challenges the ways that patriarchy can manifest in organizing spaces through developing both young femme and young masculine people's abilities to identify and disrupt oppressive, gendered discourse. The approach also works to ensure that an intersectional lens is applied to the campaigns and programs that the young people take on to address both racial and gendered forms of oppression in the schools, seeing the interlocking nature of these forms of domination.

Restorative Justice and Healing Circles

Annie and other Black femme leaders used restorative justice techniques such as speaking in circles as we built Black femme's leadership and further the conversation of how Black femme students in particular are impacted by school policies and practices. These included healing circles, or grief circles, for all the Black femmes who had died that year due to different forms of violence. We discussed the many ways that the system had failed them and what could have happened instead. It was both healing and empowering for people because it was a space where they could connect with other Black femmes and realize that their issues weren't just individual problems, but that, in fact, these issues are systematic. This helped lift the burden off of the young participants while empowering them to have a voice. In addition, the participants got a chance to build their leadership as we took turns leading the circles. This process led some of the students to join one or more of the organizations after participating, wanting to continue challenging these issues in a systemic way.

Through this, the circle process became integrated into the work of the organizations as well, as they saw the usefulness of the process for planning, addressing issues, and having hard conversations. One of the organizers of the process, Shay, a young Black femme talked about one of the healing circles used at Power U to address some of the challenges they were finding:

> We talk about how what people are going through is unfair and not normal and how it's related to white supremacy and capitalism. Some people get it, especially if they've been directly impacted, but some will be like, um, well, that's so and so's fault…like one young person last week said that they deserve to be treated the way they do because they've been acting up. So, then that's a continuing conversation because then we want to talk about what conditions exist for their friend to be behaving like that in the first place. If those conditions were different would he still be behaving like that.

A lot of times when a femme would join Power U, they would work more with the young moms. They do a variety of things—some of it is learning autonomy of their bodies, talking about their choices in reproductive work, talking with the young women about these issues, and holding circles for healing and group discussion. Some would be working on the restorative justice campaign, learning to be circle keepers. We created spaces in which Black femme students could discuss challenges they were facing and linking them to larger systems that they would also work to transform. As one femme youth, Vivian, stated, "You can share anything without being judged or without people saying negative things."

As youth members are connecting their individual experiences to structural forms of oppression, they're also given the tools to fight oppression, instilling a sense of agency so youth don't become fatalistic about their futures. Understanding that a range of skills are needed to do such work, Power U does political education to deepen our members' analysis of the root causes of issues we challenge. We also train them in hard skills such as outreach and public speaking to make them effective organizers. Members seem to be ready to absorb these skills when they see it can help them to make a difference, as Lily shared:

> Power U teaches me everything that school don't. I feel like I learned a lot because my communication skills are way better, like if was school it's like "yea I can read that word, but can I really understand it?" but at Power U it's like "you can read the word and you can understand it." I feel more motivated to learn at Power U.

Building organizing and leadership skills among the young people increases their power and ability to envision change. This includes meeting with decision makers to talk about what changes they want as well as doing protests when there is resistance from the decision makers. This seems to be an empowering way for young people to be able to express themselves and make their voices heard when they're usually excluded from policy-making conversations. Layla says, "I like protesting—because I like seeing a change and I like seeing everybody so passionate about something. Seeing people so passionate makes me want to do it." The reproductive justice lens informed the development of the PAR work discussed next in that we made sure to include questions specific to Black femme and LGBTQIA students. We continue to have separate spaces for Black femme members and participate in the BGM coalition which includes a number of our ally organizations.

Participatory Action Research

Beginning with a collective understanding of the goals of the survey as aligned with the strategic campaign work of Power U youth, we held a series of workshops to create a survey and implementation plan with the youth members. Julia organized these workshops to build the ability of youth members' to build a broader understanding of what was happening in the schools through eliciting students' opinions. We considered how the public narrative of racialized school violence perpetuated investment in punitive measures and a lack of commitment from the district to implement restorative measures. Recognizing the need to share their counter-story, a way of sharing stories that are not normally included and that challenge the dominant discourse (Delgado, 1989), the youth outlined what they felt like were key areas of "our story" that were important to investigate.

The survey was written with the goal of including Black youths' lived experiences into the public dialogue to shape how the public understands racial equity in Miami schools. Youth understood from their experiences that when they don't feel encouraged, supported, and challenged by adults in their schools, their attendance, behavior, and performance can decline. Together, we piloted the survey and made revisions and additions as we realized some of the phrasing of the questions wasn't clear and we were missing a few important areas. The youths' insights were crucial here, as they often understood if there were misunderstandings, why that happened, and how to improve them. The youth then collected over 600 surveys from high school students who were majority, self-identified as Black with some Latino, White, and other racial identifications as well.

The youth then worked together in small groups, participants collectively analyzed the responses into ideas that reflected the findings and then came back together to share their analysis with the group. At this time, Power U youth made the strategic decision that they wanted to create a report card that specifically graded the schools they were organizing in comparison to a more privileged school, as well as grade the district. They then graded the schools using a rubric that Julia designed, and grounding the grades in the survey results, district discipline data, and MDCPS policies. As they looked at the results of the data, Lena, one of the young women noted that "a lot of kids didn't know about success centers and that's a real problem. The ones that did know about success centers told me that they don't do anything in the success centers, there's no transportation, they don't do work." For many students this treatment felt normal.

Power U challenges what has become normalized through conversations and confronts challenges to participation such as fear of public speaking, and also trains them to be able to practice governing and making decisions. Believing that young people should have a say in policies and practices that affect them, they know they need to teach the members about the structures and rules that govern their schools.

We also collected data on student opinions of sexual education and harassment at their schools and with other grassroots organizations like the Miami Workers Center developed a committee to work for comprehensive sexual education. Felicia, who identifies as lesbian, shares her thoughts on the importance of a sexual education program that includes students being able to learn about their bodies:

I also want more comprehensive sex ed. We have a program but they don't really teach us anything. When I had it, they were like "Oh we're going to teach you about sex and this and that" but it was mostly like "Oh if you're in an abusive relationship just leave him." A topic like about depression they didn't really touch on. My dream sex ed class would be like learning about our bodies and showing us how to do things that we don't know about, that they don't talk to us about, because some of us don't get to talk with our families about this.

This work also focuses on building a more robust understanding and practice of consent among the young people and having that be a key piece of the campaign. Vivian shares that "young adults and parents to help us fight for better and comprehensive sex education because a lot of people don't know what consent is." The BGM work as well as the participatory research have worked in tandem to discover and address issues faced by young Black femme students, recognizing that this will benefit all students.

CONCLUSION

Organizing work can be truly transformative for young people when they feel supported and inspired by staff. While some of the youth who were recruited had a sense that things were wrong, they didn't have a full analysis of why or think they had the power to change them. Power U, like many similar grassroots direct action organizations, teaches perhaps the most essential lesson to young people—that they can fight oppressive conditions and win. As Felicia shared,

I think more about my life than I used to before because yea I was woke, but I wasn't this woke . . . When I say I'm woke I mean I'm woke about what's happening in this world and why it's wrong and how—where before I knew when things were wrong, but now I know how it's wrong and why they're doing it.

As a form of leadership development, organizing that includes political consciousness raising and participation in base-building and strategic actions can engage young people in a powerful way. Using a reproductive justice lens that attends to race and gender and centers the leadership of Black femme students pushes the organization and all the members to be anti-oppressive in their thoughts and actions. While there is always a lot of room for improvement, such models engage youth in ways that not only build their leadership, but make them active learners and creators of change. We find this model promising as an educational opportunity for young Black femme people as well as a way of improving oppressive educational circumstances in intersectional ways.

ACKNOWLEDGMENTS

We would like to acknowledge and thank all the youth and organizers leading this important work with power U and in our ally organizations.

REFERENCES

Bradbury, H. (2017). Community-based participatory research with communities defined by race, ethnicity, and disability: Translating theory to practice. In C. Nicolaidis & D. Raymaker (Eds.), *The SAGE handbook of action research* (pp. 167–178). Thousand Oaks, CA: SAGE.

Cahill, C. (2007). The personal is political: Developing new subjectivities through participatory action research. *Gender, Place & Culture, 14*(3), 267–292. https://doi.org/10.1080/09663690701324904

Carter, N. P., & Vavrus, M. (2018). Black girls matter : An intersectional analysis of young Black women's experiences and resistance to dominating forces in school. In J. Daniel & T. White (Eds.), *Intersectionality of race, ethnicity, class, and gender in teaching and teacher education* (pp. 124–136). Leiden, The Netherlands: Brill. https://doi.org/10.1163/9789004365209

Checkoway, B., & Richards-Schuster, K. (2004). Youth participation in evaluation and research as a way of lifting new voices. *Children Youth and Environments, 14*(2), 84–98.

Civil Rights Data Collection. (2013–14). Office of Civil Rights. Retrieved from https://www2.ed.gov/about/offices/list/ocr/docs/crdc-2013-14.html

Collins, P. H. (2004). *Black sexual politics: African Americans, gender, and the new racism.* New York, NY: Routledge.

Collins, P. H. (2014). Intersectionality's definitional dilemmas. *Annual Review of Sociology, 41*(1), 1–20. https://doi.org/10.1146/annurev-soc-073014-112142

Crenshaw, K. (1989). Demarginalizing the intersection of race and sex: A black feminist critique of antidiscrimination doctrine, feminist theory and antiracist politics. *The University of Chicago Legal Forum, 1989*(1), 139–167. Retrieved from http://heinonlinebackup.com/hol-cgi-bin/get_pdf.cgi?handle=hein.journals/uchclf1989&section=10

Davis, W. A. (2014). *Examining student perceptions : Ethics and misconduct in today's police department* (Master's thesis). The University of Southern Mississippi, Hattiesburg.

Delgado, R. (1989). Storytelling for oppositionists and others: A plea for narrative. *Michigan Law Review, 87*(8), 2411–2441.

Emirbayer, M., & Mische, A. (1998). What is agency? *American Journal of Sociology, 103*(4), 962–1023.

Epstein, R., Blake, J., & Gonzalez, T. (2017). *Girlhood interrupted: The erasure of black girls' childhood.* Washington, DC: Georgetown Law Center on Poverty and Inequality.

Evans-Winters, V. E., & Esposito, J. (2010). Other people's daughters: Critical race feminism and black girls' education. *Educational Foundations, 24*(1–2), 11–25.

Fals-Borda, O. (1987). The application of participatory action-research in Latin America. *International Sociology, 2*(4), 329–347. https://doi.org/10.1177/026858098700200401

Fine, M., & McClelland, S. (2006). Sexuality education and desire: Still missing after all these years. *Harvard Educational Review, 76*(3), 297–338.

Fine, M., & Ruglis, J. (2009). Circuits and consequences of dispossession: The racialized realignment of the public sphere for US youth. *Transforming Anthropology, 17*(1), 20–33.

Francis, D. V. (2012). Sugar and spice and everything nice? Teacher perceptions of Black girls in the classroom. *The Review of Black Political Economy, 39*(3), 311–320.

Gambone, M. A., Yu, H. C., Lewis-Charp, H., Sipe, C. L., & Lacoe, J. (2006). Youth organizing, identity-support, and youth development agencies as avenues for involvement. *Journal of Community Practice, 14*(1–2), 235–253.

Gay, G. (2010). *Culturally responsive pedagogy* (2nd ed.). New York, NY: Teachers College Press.

Geller, A., Fagan, J., Tyler, T., & Link, B. G. (2014). Aggressive policing and the mental health of young urban men. *American Journal of Public Health, 104*(12), 2321–2327. https://doi.org/10.2105/AJPH.2014.302046

Golob, M. I., & Giles, A. R. (2013). Challenging and transforming power relations within community-based participatory research: the promise of a Foucauldian analysis. *Qualitative Research in Sport, Exercise and Health, 5*(3), 356–372. https://doi.org/10.1080/2159676X.2013.846273

Gonzalez, T. (2012, April). Keeping kids in schools: Restorative justice, punitive discipline, and the school to prison pipeline. *Journal of Law & Education, 41*(2), 281–335.

Gregory, A., Skiba, R. J., & Noguera, P. A. (2010). The achievement gap and the discipline gap: Two sides of the same coin? *Educational Researcher, 39*(1), 59–68. https://doi.org/10.3102/0013189X09357621

Hagan, J., Shedd, C., & Payne, M. R. (2005). Race, ethnicity, and youth perceptions of criminal injustice. *American Sociological Review, 70*(3), 381–407. https://doi.org/10.1177/000312240507000302

Jasper, J. M. (2004). A strategic approach to collective action: Looking for agency in social-movement choices (Paulo R. C. Deon, Trans.). *Mobilization, 9*(1), 1–16.

Jones, N. (2009). *Between good and ghetto: African American girls and inner-city violence.* Rutgers, NJ: Rutgers University Press.

Kirshner, B. (2015). *Youth activism in an era of education inequality.* New York, NY: NYU Press.

Kupchik, A., & Ellis, N. (2008). School discipline and security: Fair for all students? *Youth & Society, 39*(302), 549–574. https://doi.org/10.1177/0044118X07301956

Ladson-Billings, G. (1995). Toward a theory of culturally relevant pedagogy, *32*(3), 465–491.

Ladson-Billings, G. (2014). Culturally relevant pedagogy 2.0: A.k.a. the remix. *Harvard Education Review, 84*(1), 74–85.

Lewis, R., Romi, S., Katz, Y. J., & Qui, X. (2008). Students ' reaction to classroom discipline in Australia, Israel, and China. *Teaching and Teacher Education, 24*(3), 715–724. https://doi.org/10.1016/j.tate.2007.05.003

Morris, M. W. (2012). *Race, gender and the "school to prison pipeline": Expanding our discussion to include Black girls.* New York, NY: African American Policy Forum.

National Women's Law Center. (2017). *Let her learn: Stopping school pushout for girls of color.* Retrieved from: https://nwlc.org/wp-content/uploads/2017/04/final_nwlc_Gates_GirlsofColor.pdf

Paris, D. (2012). Culturally sustaining pedagogy: A needed change in stance, terminology, and practice. *Educational Researcher, 41*(3), 93–97. https://doi.org/10.3102/0013189X12441244

Polletta, F., & Jasper, J. M. (2001). Collective identity and social movements. *Annual Review of Sociology, 27*(1), 283–305. https://doi.org/10.1146/annurev.soc.27.1.283

Ransby, B. (2018). *Making all Black lives matter: Reimagining freedom in the twenty-first century.* Oakland: University of California Press.

Robinson, C. J. (2000). *Black marxism: The making of the Black radical tradition* (2nd ed.). Chapel Hill: University of North Carolina Press.

Rogers, J., Mediratta, K., & Shah, S. (2012). Building power, learning democracy: Youth organizing as a site of civic development. *Review of Research in Education, 36*(1), 43–66.

Sister Song. (2019). *Women of color reproductive justice collective.* Retrieved from https://www.sistersong.net/reproductive-justice

Skiba, R. J., Michael, R. S., Nardo, A. C., & Peterson, R. L. (2002). The color of discipline: Sources of racial and gender disproportionality in school punishment, *The Urban Review, 34*(4), 317–342.

Su, C. (2010). Marginalized stakeholders and performative politics: Dueling discourses in education policymaking. *Critical Policy Studies, 4*(4), 362–383.

Torre, M. E. (2009). Participatory action research and critical race theory: Fueling spaces for Nos-otras to research. *The Urban Review, 41*(1), 106–120. https://doi.org/10.1007/s11256-008-0097-7

Viega, C. (2015, September 27) Troubled Miami-Dade students finding success amid suspensions. *Miami Herald.* Retrieved from: https://www.miamiherald.com/news/local/education/article36755190.html

Warren, M. R., Hong, S., Rubin, C. L., & Uy, P. S. (2009). Beyond the bake sale: A community-based relational approach to parent engagement in schools. *Teachers College Record, 111*(9), 2209–2254.

Warren, M. R., & Mapp, K. L. (2011). *A match on dry grass: Community organizing as a catalyst for school reform.* New York, NY: Oxford University Press

Wun, C. (2014). Unaccounted foundations: Black girls, anti-Black racism, and punishment in schools. *Critical Sociology, 42*(4–5), 1–14. https://doi.org/10.1177/0896920514560444

Wun, C. (2016). Angered: Black and non-Black girls of color at the intersections of violence and school discipline in the United States. *Race Ethnicity and Education, 21*(4), 423–437. https://doi.org/10.1080/13613324.2016.1248829

SECTION 3

MEDIA INTERSECTIONS

CHAPTER 9

CLAIMING A SEAT AT THE TABLE

Highlighting the Civic Engagement of Young Black Girls

Cassandra Jean
Howard University

Dana J. McCalla
Howard University

Black girls have become increasingly visible in social activism in the United States and around the world since the turn of the century. They have become central figures in the fight against injustice and inequality in their communities, on social media platforms, and in public forums for issues including gun reform, sexual violence, mental health awareness, and representation in youth literature (Jean-Marie, 2006; Kelly, 2018; Wicker, 2019). Although their identities as young, Black girls have been historically disadvantaged in society, their efforts in pushing the Black voice further through activism have been pivotal in the broader movement for social justice (McIntosh, 2016).

Black Girl Civics, pages 143–157
Copyright © 2020 by Information Age Publishing
All rights of reproduction in any form reserved.

In singer and songwriter Solange's 2016 album *A Seat at the Table*, she used music as a tribute to the strength and struggles of Black people worldwide. Her songs resonated deeply with the Black community, especially among Black women and girls, who could personally relate to her messages (Watson, 2017). In describing the emotions behind the album, Solange stated that "[these feelings] were everyday feelings, everyday confrontations that were staring me in the face" (Watson, 2017). Titles such as "Weary," "F.U.B.U.," "This Moment," and "Mad" all speak to the Black lived experience, directly addressing the experiences of Black women and girls. Each song was rooted in a narrative of Black oppression and the fight towards liberation, bringing light to issues that Blacks often encounter. Messages of strength and empowerment can be heard in her lyrics and interpreted from the song titles. In a time in which civic engagement and political protests have become a resurging phenomenon (Anderson, Toor, Rainie, & Smith, 2018; Sydell, 2017), it is crucial that the voices of marginalized communities who face multiple disadvantages—specifically, oppression on the axes of race, gender, and age—be included in the conversation.

This chapter acknowledges the civic work of four African-American girls: Havana Chapman-Edwards (#TheTinyDiplomat), Naomi Wadler (March for Our Lives), Marley Dias (#1000BlackGirlBooks), and Amariyanna "Mari" Copeny (Little Miss Flint)—girls who are young, Black, and often overlooked in news media. Overall, this chapter aims to (a) explore the societal forces impacting Black girl social consciousness, which influences their involvement in civic action and (b) highlight Black girl civic engagement of the 21st century by juxtaposing the song titles in Solange's (2016) *A Seat At The Table* alongside the trailblazing leadership of the four Black girls. Additionally, this chapter will examine newspaper article coverage of the girls, evaluate the driving forces that push Black girls to engage in social movements, and analyze the impact that their engagement has had on the pursuit of their goals as activists.

To select the girls included in this study, an initial Google search of "Black girls participating in civic engagement" was conducted. From this primary search, a select group of 20 Black girls and women developed. Initially, there was a consideration for Black women because they are commonly referred to as Black girls, specifically with regard to the hashtag movements #BlackGirlMagic and #BlackGirlsRock. However, Black women over the age of 18 were subsequently excluded to emphasize a focus on Black youth. The final list of four girls emerged as the study aimed to highlight Black girls under 18 who had over five article mentions in online news articles and who had participated in social justice or activism-related issues within the last 5 years.

BACKGROUND

Comprehending Black girl civic engagement and activism requires acknowledgment of the historical and contemporary forces of oppression that work against Black girls, including but not limited to objectification, criminalization, and sexual violence. Although a considerable amount of literature exists on issues such as gendered discrimination, negative media portrayals of Black girlhood, inequitable school discipline, and the politics of Black sexuality (Collins, 2004; Crenshaw, 2005; Gordon, 2008; Morris, 2007; Nebbitt & Lombe, 2010; Wun, 2014), the extent to which these societal forces have impacted young Black girls and helped to shape their identities and perspectives is still worthy of discussion. Facing direct exposure to oppression and marginalization in their immediate environments has propelled young, Black girls of the past and present into action and has arguably enhanced their political consciousness (Hyman & Levine, 2008).

We maintain that this enhanced consciousness—relative to male peers and young girls of other races—has prompted them to follow a call to action for their communities that is both necessary and timely. Research posits that Black people are more likely than other racial groups to be vulnerable to unfortunate or fatal circumstances, yet are most often neglected; Black girls, moreover, are too frequently deemed unworthy victims, consequently having their experiences dismissed as well (Sommers, 2017). An awareness of and subjection to these various oppressive circumstances provoke Black girls, specifically, to engage in grassroots organizing and take on activist leadership roles to express dissent with the unequal conditions plaguing their environment (Hyman & Levine, 2008; Sommers, 2017). Their intersectional attributes of being young, Black, and female, along with their life experiences shaped by these attributes, can catalyze involvement in political matters that are oppressing them and the broader community (Hyman & Levine, 2008). As Black women authors who were once young, Black girls, we acknowledge that our understanding of the Black experience and the adversity that inspires civic leadership among Black girls is unequivocally tied to the positions we assume in our writing.

LITERATURE REVIEW

The Lens of Intersectionality

Numerous theories have set out to unpack the myriad challenges that Black youth, specifically Black girls, face (Arthur & Shapiro, 1987;

Herrnstein, Murray, & Jacobs, 1999; Jensen, 1969; Ogbu & Simons, 1998). Some of these theories include critical race theory (Evans-Winters & Esposito, 2010), Black feminism (Collins, 2009; Crenshaw, Gotanda, Peller, & Thomas, 1995), contingency of self-worth theory (Adams, 2010), theory of adultification (Epstein, Blake, & Gonzalez, 2017), and gender schema theory (Buckley & Carter, 2005). Each of these theories speaks to specific aspects of the lived experience of Black girls. Many of them focus on the intersection of gender and race issues in the larger oppressive political and social system, and the self-perceptions that Black girls hold as a result of these oppressive forces. Overarchingly, many studies that examine the Black girl experience have incorporated the theory of intersectionality either to complement other theories used or to serve as the underlying theoretical framework (Blake, Butler, Lewis, & Darensbourg, 2011; Collins, 2009; Cooper, 2015; Crenshaw, 1989).

As an analytical framework, intersectionality refers to the various oppressive systems of power that affect an individual on the axes of gender, race, sexuality, religion, ethnicity, disability, class, and other identities (Collins, 2009; Cooper, 1892; Cooper, 2015; Crenshaw, 1989). Crenshaw's (1989) seminal construction of the intersectionality framework has generated important discourse on this juncture, particularly as it relates to the multiple identities of women of color and the marginalization that results from their lack of inclusion in the discussion on identity politics. She asserts that a single-axis analysis misrepresents the multidimensionality of the Black woman experience (Crenshaw, 1989). It is worthy to note that intersectionality not only functions to examine the marginalization of particular groups but also "highlights how the intersection of identities can leave particular groups oppressed" (Harrison, 2015, p. 1025). For Black women and girls, they have existed at the critical juncture of race, class, and gender oppression for centuries providing them with viewpoints and voices that deserve acknowledgment. This point is especially important because they possess a unique lived experience and therefore a distinctive consciousness that is capable of impacting change, a key point heard throughout Solange's album.

Although there is a notion that "the colored girl is not known and hence not believed in," many Black girls have used their identities as a platform to expose the systems that diminish their voices—especially entities within the state apparatus—and to increase the visibility of Black girls' stories in society (Collins, 2009, p. 3). An intersectional lens assists in explaining the experiences of Black female youth, a group whose triple identities have often left them triply marginalized and who, therefore, can benefit from a targeted intersectional analysis.

Civic Engagement

For the purposes of this chapter, civic engagement, social justice, and activism encompasses the involvement in and awareness of political systems and institutions, social responsibility and prosocial behavior, and future civic participation, including voting and volunteerism (Hope & Jagers, 2014). Evidence produced by Hope and Jagers' (2014) study suggests that perceived institutional discrimination and the acknowledgement of systemic inequity are strongly associated with civic engagement among Black youth. Each girl highlighted in this chapter has engaged in various forms of community activism, each of which are highlighted in this operationalized definition.

Accounts of Black women and girls as agents of resistance against oppression are historically vast. Claudette Colvin, Ruby Bridges, and Diane Nash were three young women from the civil rights era who gave U.S. civil rights activism a Black girl face. Their participation in the rejection of social and political structures of the time have left indelible marks in history. Similarly, the more recent contributions of Black girls have proven to be impactful in contemporary times (Jean-Marie, 2006; Wicker, 2019). Consider the founders of the #BlackLivesMatter movement: Alicia Garza, Opal Tometi, and Patrisse Cullors—three Black women who recognized the fatal threat of anti-Black racism and anti-LGBTQIA discrimination in American society and therefore created "an ideological and political intervention" as "an affirmation of Black folks' contributions to this society, [their] humanity, and [their] resilience in the face of deadly oppression" (Hobson, 2014). In an age in which social movements are publicly regaining momentum, Black women and girls have continued to answer the call to leadership through their diverse approaches in activism, including through music. King (1988) asserts that "for as long as black women have known our various discriminations, we have also resisted those oppressions. Our day-to-day survival, as well as our organized political actions, have demonstrated the tenacity of our struggle against subordination" (King, 1988, p. 43). Female resistance against various forces of oppression is not a new phenomenon, but it continues to be deserving of recognition in the literature.

Studies have suggested that Blacks are influenced to question core American ideals such as justice because of their historical and societal knowledge of racial prejudice and discrimination (Hope & Jagers, 2014). In alignment with the theory of Black girl civics, these young girls take on roles of political actors, asserting their civic identities in a society that has consistently negatively characterized them. As previously mentioned, their intersectional attributes, as well as the life experiences shaped by these attributes, can catalyze involvement in political matters that are oppressing them and the broader community (Hyman & Levine, 2008).

Although some scholars believe that there is a "civic achievement gap" among Black youth, research posits that Black youth have opted to use nontraditional methods of civic engagement including participatory culture through online social forums, activism through music, providing familial financial assistance, advocating for resources in schools, and even simply following news and current events (Cammarota, 2008; Ginwright, 2010; Mirra & Garcia, 2017). These nontraditional forms of social and political participation not only stem from a lack of faith in traditional methods of activism but also from a historical lack of access to them (Ginwright, 2010). For Black girls, in particular, civic engagement involves a purposeful resistance and protection against dominant structures of White supremacy and patriarchy. Their leadership, therefore, brings new facets to the established notions of civic engagement.

METHODOLOGY

In exploring Black girl civic engagement, this chapter looked at 64 online news articles and journals, which highlighted the four girls and the work that they have done within the last 5 years. The online news articles and journals were the general focus as they were used to highlight the exposure that Black girls received compared to their White counterparts. Search engines used included LexisNexis, Ebsco, Google Scholar, and Academic Search Premier. Through a random sampling of online publications, the sources selected contained excerpts of speeches, direct interviews from the girls, or a full news spread dedicated to them individually. Words used to research these girls include Naomi Wadler, March for Our Lives; Havana Chapman-Edwards, #TheTinyDiplomat; Marley Davis, #1000BlackGirl-Books; and Amariyanna Copeny, Little Miss Flint. Based on our working definition of civic engagement, this study focused on Black girls, ages 18 and under, who were involved in social movements, community affairs, or civic engagement between 2014 and 2019. The girls selected had to have at least five articles highlighting their participation in civics. Those chosen for this study have also made national news within the last 5 years thereby bringing attention to themselves and their causes. The reports on these girls included excerpts of their speeches, direct interviews, newspaper spreads about them, or general highlights regarding their achievements. Excluded were individuals outside of the age range or outside of the chosen range of years. Girls who were not Black, based on phenotypic identification, or who have not received the same level of media coverage were not selected. Selection of girls whose activism fit the song titles also led to the exclusion of others from this study to align with the theme of Solange's album. Lastly, books, paper articles or publications, blogs, and opinion pieces were omitted from this study.

BLACK GIRL ACTIVISTS: NAOMI, HAVANA, MARLEY, AND MARI

Track 3—"Interlude: This Moment"

"If you don't understand us and understand what we've been through, then you probably wouldn't understand what this moment is about."

Naomi Wadler is a young activist from Alexandria, VA whose call to civic engagement was inspired by the fatal shooting that transpired at Marjory Stoneman Douglas High School in Parkland, FL on February 14, 2018. Wanting to get involved in the wave of activism that followed the tragic incident, Naomi and a classmate organized an 18-minute walkout at their elementary school to honor the lives of the 17 Parkland victims as well as that of a young 17-year-old Black girl, Courtlin Arrington, who was shot to death a few weeks later in Alabama. Since that time, Naomi has spoken out against gun violence, using a public platform to shed light on the lack of attention given to Black girls and Black women who are statistically more vulnerable to death by gun violence than any other racial group (Murphy, Xu, Kochanek, Curtin, & Arias, 2017).

On March 24, 2018, Naomi and several young student activists from around the country came together in Washington, DC for the March for Our Lives protest demanding strictly regulated gun control laws. In her speech, she directly addressed the violence plaguing Black communities across the United States and challenged the notion that people with darker skin are considered less valuable than their White counterparts. One of her most poignant lines read,

> I am here to acknowledge and represent the African American girls whose stories don't make the front page of every national newspaper, whose stories don't lead on the evening news...I represent the African-American women who are victims of gun violence, who are simply statistics instead of vibrant, beautiful girls full of potential. (Nirappil, 2018)

While Naomi is well under the age of 18, she recognizes the centuries of unmitigated violence that has damaged the Black and Brown community (Ginwright, 2010) and has used this knowledge to engage in civic affairs (Beckett, 2018). She was quoted saying, "My speech might not have caused a giant impact on society, but I do hope all the Black girls and women realize there's a growing value for them" (Nirappil, 2018).

Track 1—"Rise"

"Walk in your ways, so you won't crumble."

Inspired by Naomi Wadler, Emma Gonzales, and her mother, Havana Chapman-Edwards, was the only protestor at her elementary school to participate in the nation-wide walkout following the Parkland shooting in 2018. As a 7-year-old during that time, Havana rejected the idea that her young age discredited her participation in civic engagement and yearned to amplify the voices of those plagued by gun violence, much like Naomi. Havana's mother stated that Havana engages in public activities because she "[wants] to represent for African and African-American girls who are victims of gun violence, as well as her cousin, Tony, who was a victim of gun violence" (Gontcharova, 2018).

Havana, at a young age, understood the damaging impact that gun violence had on her community and asserted that her age was not a reason to shy away from protesting against it. Havana stated that "just because I'm only seven doesn't mean I can't help change the laws. There are adults who keep saying that kids don't know what we're [talking] about but we know we are never too little to make a difference" (Simon & Hayes, 2018, n.p.). Currently, Havana partakes in civic activities by engaging in climate change awareness events, participating in "die-ins" as a form of silent protest, promoting literacy and representation, and working with young girls in Ghana. Offering advice to other youth, Havana claims that "you don't have to be a grownup or be famous to change the world. Sometimes you just have to choose kind[ness] to change the world" (Rearick, 2018, n.p.).

Track 13—"F.U.B.U." (for Us by Us)

"One for us."

Marley Dias has become a role model for young Black girls of this generation. A self-identified TBN, or "total book nerd," Marley is the creator of the #1000BlackGirlBooks initiative, a movement developed to diversify the reading lists of young kids across the nation. Marley was moved to start this initiative after being inspired by a book gifted to her by her aunt, which featured a Black girl as its main character. When asked by her mother about the one thing she would want to change in her life, Marley realized that she was frustrated by the lack of representation of girls of color in the "classics" she was required to read in school and decided to turn that frustration into innovation. In 2015, at the hopeful age of 11, Marley embarked on her journey into social activism by launching a campaign to collect and donate one thousand books with Black girl protagonists to libraries across the United

States. As scholars have argued, Black girls subvert power relations of race and gender by challenging, and even defying the "counterpublic of the everyday popular sphere," and this is something that Marley set out to do (Lindsey, 2013, p. 30; Gaunt, 2006).

Her efforts to uplift Black children and increase the representation of Black girls in books have not gone unnoticed, including being featured in several newspaper publications, including Forbes. Now a published author, her work has caught the attention of many politically engaged celebrities and activists who support her fight to transform the face of young adult literature. Marley's 2018 book—*Marley Dias Gets It Done—And So Can You!*—discusses her vision for a new world, "a world where black girls [are] free to be complicated, honest, human; to have adventures and emotions unique just to them. A world where black girls' stories mattered" (Dias, 2018, as cited in Stevens, 2018, n.p.). Marley's commitment to social activism and representation in literature will have a tremendous positive impact on the lives of young, Black girls and will open their eyes to a more diverse and dynamic experience of learning through books. This desire to counteract the lack of representation of Black girls in literature was a way in which Marley demanded a space for Black girls to self-define their worth and challenge rigid norms, which stand to diminish the rhetoric of Black girl empowerment (Lindsey, 2013).

Track 2—Weary

"I'm weary of the ways of the world, be weary of the ways of the world."

Since 2016, at the age of eight, Amariyanna "Mari" Copeny, best known as Little Miss Flint, has been an active representative and activist in her community in Flint, Michigan. Currently, Mari uses her platform to vocalize the griefs and struggles of what's going on in her community, mainly the water crisis, which has led to thousands of children diagnosed with lead poisoning. Mari has taken her woes to multiple government officials, even exposing her community's strife to both former President Barack Obama and current President Donald Trump. Gifted the name "Little Miss Flint," Mari has been the driving force and political figure advocating on behalf of the children in Flint, which is a predominantly low-income Black area. She has annually reminded people through social media that the people of Flint are still without clean water and continues to be a face and significant power for the movement towards fair living conditions despite her young age. *The New York Times*, the newspaper that frequently mentions Mari, has spoken about her perseverance and the initiative she took to write a letter to former President Barack Obama about the conditions plaguing her community (Dickerson, Hassan, & Correal, 2017). With seven articles written about her, articles highlighted her initiative to garner the attention of major political figures, with her impact going beyond state officials, to exemplify the need for assistance in her town.

FINDINGS AND DISCUSSION

In conducting this analysis, we found that three of the four selected girls have had their stories covered in both *The New York Times*, located in New York City, and the *Washington Post*, located in Washington, DC—two Democratic-leaning, predominantly liberal publications in progressive cities in the United States. These news outlets are more likely to highlight people of color and other news topics that are otherwise overlooked by others. Marley Davis was featured in two stories in the *New York Times*, and one each in NPR, *Chicago Tribune*, CBS News, and *Essence* magazine. Mari was mentioned in 14 publications overall in the *New York Times*, *The Guardian* (London), *USA News*, *Time Magazine*, and *Essence* magazines. Naomi was covered in a total of 36 articles between the *New York Times*, *The Guardian* (London), and the *Washington Post*. Havana, the youngest of the four and the one with the most media exposure, had a total of 126 article mentions including outlets such as CNN, ABC News, and *Time Magazine*, and was the only girl with a spread in Fox News, a conservative-leaning news organization.

Although Marley, Mari, Naomi and Havana were featured across various media publications, we noticed a disparity in the coverage of their activism when compared to their non-Black counterparts. For example, the four students who served as leaders in the March for Our Lives campaign, Cameron Kasky, Jaclyn Corin, David Hogg, Emma Gonzalez, and Alex Wind, were featured in over 900 articles highlighting their activism and demands for gun control reforms. Emma Gonzalez, a young activist of Cuban descent, and the only person of color in the bunch, had over 920 articles solely focused on her. *The New York Times* mentioned her 69 times, while the *Washington Times* gave her 47 mentions and the *Tampa Bay Times* gave 48. Although Naomi Wadler was able to speak during the march and made some profound remarks, Emma Gonzalez received more media coverage than all of the girls in this chapter combined. Emma Gonzales is a young woman of color and a Parkland shooting survivor, and she justifiably received a generous amount of media exposure. It is fair, however, to argue that young Black girls, especially the girls chosen for this study, can also be considered survivors of their particular circumstances and survivors of the conditions of being a Black girl in American society and abroad.

The articles that spoke about the four girls discussed in this chapter did not elaborate on their greater achievements or contributions to civic engagement but rather, focused on a specific or smaller public act, often uplifting other individuals involved. Compared to the Parkland students, who had numerous articles dedicated to their life stories leading to the point of the march, these girls were only awarded brief mentions for their efforts. Articles on Mari primarily focused on her being an 8-year-old who wrote a letter to President Obama about the Flint water crisis, while all other achievements and community organizing that she participated in were not attached to her name. Although spoken about in the context of their contributions to their respective causes, spreads on Naomi, Havana, and Marley, were rarely as substantial as the ones written on their White counterparts.

A clear and common observation made is that Black girls are not receiving the same amount of coverage in news publications and media that other young girls of color, White youth, or young men of color are receiving. Black girls' narratives and scopes of influence are seldom covered in major news outlets. This lack of attention is a significant gap in the media. Scholars on Black girl civic engagement should take advantage of this void and highlight the critical contributions that Black girls can provide.

CONCLUSION

Young Black girls are a group whose multiple realities warrant a more developed body of critical and theoretical research (Evans-Winters & Esposito, 2010; Harrison, 2015). According to Hope and Jagers (2014), issues of racial oppression inform the ways that Black youth interpret their social, political, and economic conditions. Racial discrimination has existed on both interpersonal and institutional, systemic levels, influencing person-to-person relationships and shaping societal norms. Historically, Black girls have had to endure multiple challenges; they have been victims of sexual violence, exploitative labor, negative media portrayals, and so much more because of this discrimination (Collins, 2009; Nebbitt & Lombe, 2010; Speno & Aubrey, 2017). Research reveals that "adolescents not only recognize such institutional race-based discrimination, but [that] these perceptions of institutional discrimination are related to lower life satisfaction and self-esteem" (Hope & Jager, 2014, p. 461). The capacity of these external forces to negatively impact young adolescents and shape their self-perceptions is not to be understated. However, the ability of these forces to inspire activism and social change should not be understated either.

History shows us that Black girls and women have served as strong activists disrupting the dominant culture and narratives regarding Black girlhood and womanhood (McArthur, 2016). In a media-saturated society in which musical and visual content are forms of media that shape the ideologies and perspectives of the larger culture, Solange's *A Seat at the Table* has been profoundly impactful in affirming this disruption. The album not only asserts the importance of recognizing Black girls and their intersecting identities on the axes of gender, race, and age but also pushes for Black girls to be portrayed in a more positive light, matching the media exposure received by their White counterparts (Harrison, 2015; Hulko, 2009). Research has shown that challenging the dominant discourse that has continuously marginalized, objectified, and silenced Black girls will change the culture surrounding how Black girls view themselves as well as the perceptions held by the larger society (Harrison, 2015; McArthur, 2016).

Given the historical tendency of news media to portray Black girls in a less-than-positive way, we maintain that there is tremendous power in the growing number of Black girls championing social causes that affect them both broadly and acutely (Sommers, 2017). Aligning with the sentiments expressed in Solange's *A Seat at the Table*—feelings of weariness, anger, frustration, and potential liberation—Naomi, Havana, Marley, and Mari have exhibited the complex experiences of Black women and girls around the world and have used their voices to resist an unjust status quo. They, along with a multitude of Black girls' marginalized voices deserve to be heard, and their stories deserve to be told. It is through their leadership and trailblazing involvements in civic engagement that one can be optimistic about the future of social justice and reserve their right to claim a seat at the table.

REFERENCES

Adams, P. E. (2010). Understanding the different realities, experience, and use of self-esteem between Black and White adolescent girls. *Journal of Black Psychology, 36*(3), 255–276.

Anderson, M., Toor, S., Rainie, L., & Smith, A. (2018). Activism in the Social Media Age. *Pew Research Center.* Retrieved from https://www.pewinternet.org/2018/07/11/activism-in-the-social-media-age/

Arthur, J., & Shapiro, A. (1987). The truly disadvantaged. In W. J. Wilson (Ed.), *Color–class–identity* (pp. 109–122). New York, NY: Routledge.

Beckett, L. (2018). *Never again: How 11 year old Naomi Wadler became a rallying voice of Black protest.* Retreived from https://www.theguardian.com/us-news/2018/mar/31/naomi-wadler-the-11-year-old-helpi ng-lead-a-protest-movement

Blake, J. J., Butler, B. R., Lewis, C. W., & Darensbourg, A. (2011). Unmasking the inequitable discipline experiences of urban Black girls: Implications for urban educational stakeholders. *The Urban Review, 43*(1), 90–106.

Buckley, T. R., & Carter, R. T. (2005). Black adolescent girls: Do gender roles and racial identity impact their self-esteem? *Sex Roles, 53*(9–10), 647–661.

Cammarota, J. (2008). The cultural organizing of youth ethnographers: Formalizing a Praxis-based pedagogy. *Anthropology & Education Quarterly, 39*(1), 45–58.

Crenshaw, K. (1989). Demarginalizing the intersection of race and sex: A Black feminist critique of antidiscrimination doctrine, feminist theory and antiracist politics. *University of Chicago Legal Forum, 1989*(1), Article 8.

Crenshaw, K. (2005). Mapping the margins: Intersectionality, identity politics, and violence against women of color (1994). In R. K. Bergen, J. L. Edleson, & C. M. Renzetti (Eds.), *Violence against women: Classic papers* (p. 282–313). Auckland, New Zealand: Pearson Education.

Crenshaw, K., Gotanda, N., Peller, G., & Thomas, K. (1995). *Critical race theory: The key writings that formed the movement.* New York, NY: The New Press.

Collins, P. H. (2009). *Black feminist thought: Knowledge, consciousness, and the politics of empowerment.* New York, NY: Routledge.

Collins, P. H. (2004). *Black sexual politics: African Americans, gender, and the new racism.* New York, NY: Routledge.

Cooper, A. J. (1892). *A voice from the south: By a Black woman of the south.* Xenia, OH: The Aldine Printing House.

Cooper, B. (2015). Intersectionality. *The Oxford Handbook of Feminist Theory.* https:// DOI.org/10.1093/oxfordhb/9780199328581.013.20

Dickerson, C., Hassan, A., & Correal, A. (2017, January 14). A president who inspired big dreams, and big smiles, in a young generation. *The New York Times.* Retrieved from https://www.nytimes.com/2017/01/14/us/politics/kids-legacy -obama.html

Epstein, R., Blake, J., & Gonzalez, T. (2017, June 27). *Girlhood interrupted: The erasure of Black girls' childhood.* http://dx.doi.org/10.2139/ssrn.3000695

Evans-Winters, V. E., & Esposito, J. (2010). Other people's daughters: Critical race feminism and Black girls' education. *Educational Foundations, 24*(1–2), 11–24.

Gaunt, K.D. (2006). *The games Black girls play: Learning the ropes from double-dutch to hip-hop.* New York, NY: Routledge.

Ginwright, S. A. (2010). Peace out to revolution! Activism among African American youth: An argument for radical healing. *Young, 18*(1), 77–96.

Gontcharova, N. (201.). A 7-year-old activist tells us why she speaks out against gun violence. Retrieved from https://www.refinery29.com/en-us/2018/06/201622/ havana-chapman-edwards-7-year-old-activist-pulse-shooting

Gordon, M. K. (2008). Media contributions to African American girls' focus on beauty and appearance: Exploring the consequences of sexual objectification. *Psychology of Women Quarterly, 32*(3), 245–256.

Harrison, L. (2015). Redefining intersectionality theory through the lens of African American young adolescent girls' racialized experiences. *Youth & Society, 49*(8), 1023–1039.

Herrnstein, R., Murray, C., & Jacobs, L. (1999). The bell curve: Intelligence & class structure in American life. *Philosophy of the Social Sciences, 29*(1), 121–145. Retrieved from http://search.proquest.com/docview/215028415/

Hobson, J. (2014). A herstory of the #BlackLivesMatter movement. In A. Garza (Ed.), *Are all the women still white?: Rethinking race, expanding feminisms* (pp. 23–28). Albany: SUNY Press.

Hope, E. C., & Jagers, R. J. (2014). The role of sociopolitical attitudes and civic education in the civic engagement of Black youth. *Journal of Research on Adolescence, 24*(3), 460–470.

Hulko, W. (2009). The time- and context-contingent nature of intersectionality and interlocking oppressions. *Journal of Women and Social Work, 24*(1), 44–55.

Hyman, J. B., & Levine, P. (2008). *Civic engagement and the disadvantaged: Challenges, opportunities and recommendations* (Working Paper #63). Center for Information & Research on Civic Learning & Engagement, Tufts University, Medford, MA.

Jean-Marie, G. (2006). Welcoming the unwelcomed: A social justice imperative of African-American female leaders at Historically Black Colleges and Universities. *Educational Foundations, 20*(1–2), 85–104.

Jensen, A. (1969). *How much can we boost IQ and scholastic achievement?* Cambridge, MA: Harvard Educational Review.

King, D. K. (1988). Multiple jeopardy, multiple consciousness: The context of a Black feminist ideology. In *Race, gender and class* (pp. 36–57). New York, NY: Routledge.

Kelly, L. L. (2018). A snapchat story: How Black girls develop strategies for critical resistance in school. *Learning, Media and Technology, 43*(4), 374–389.

Knowles, S. (2016). "A Seat at The Table". Saint Records and Columbia Records.

Lindsey, T. (2013). "One time for my girls": African-American girlhood, empowerment, and popular visual culture. *Journal of African American Studies, 17*, 22–34.

McArthur, S. A. (2016). Black girls and critical media literacy for social activism. *English Education, 48*(4), 362–379.

McIntosh, A. (2016, September 30). *These young Black entrepreneurs will inspire you to win at life.* Retrieved from https://www.buzzfeed.com/abigailmcintosh/these-young-black-female-entrepreneurs-will-inspire-you-to-w

Mirra, N., & Garcia, A. (2017). Civic participation reimagined: Youth interrogation and innovation in the multimodal public sphere. *Review of Research in Education, 41*(1), 136–158.

Morris, E. W. (2007). "Ladies" or "loudies"? Perceptions and experiences of Black girls in classrooms. *Youth & Society, 38*(4), 490–515.

Murphy, S., Xu, J., Kochanek, K., Curtin, S., & Arias, E. (2017, November). Deaths: Final data for 2015. *National Vital Statistics Report, 66*(6), 1–75.

Nebbitt, V. E., & Lombe, M. (2010). Urban African American adolescents and adultification. *Families in Society, 91*(3), 234–240.

Nirappil, F. (2018). *The story behind 11-year-old Naomi Wadler and her March for Our Lives speech.* Retrieved from https://www.washingtonpost.com/local/education/the-story-behind-11-year-old-naomi-wadler-and-her-march-for-our-lives-speech/2018/03/25/3a6dccdc-3058-11e8-8abc-22a366b72f2d_story.html

Ogbu, J. U., & Simons, H. D. (1998). Voluntary and involuntary minorities: A cultural-ecological theory of school performance with some implications for education. *Anthropology Education Quarterly, 29*(2), 155–188. https://doi.org/10.1525/aeq.1998.29.2.155

Simon, C., & Hayes, C. (2018). Two years after the Orlando shooting, young activists hold a die-in on the Capitol lawn. Retrieved from https://www.usatoday.com/story/news/2018/06/12/two-years-after-orlando-young-activists-protest-gun-violence-capitol/695132002/

Sommers, Z. (2017). Missing white woman syndrome: An empirical analysis of race and gender disparities in online news coverage of missing persons. *The Journal of Criminal Law & Criminology, 106*(2), 275–314.

Speno, A. G., & Aubrey, J. S. (2017). Sexualization, youthification, and adultification: A content analysis of images of girls and women in popular magazines. *Journalism & Mass Communication Quarterly, 95*(3), 625–646.

Stevens, S. (2018, January). Marley Dias, the brains behind #1000BlackGirlBooks, is touring with a book of her own. *The Chicago Tribune.* Retrieved from https://www.chicagotribune.com/columns/heidi-stevens/ct-life-stevens-tuesday-marley-dias-book-appearances-0130-story.html

Sydell, L. (2017). On both the left and right, Trump is driving new political engagement. *NPR.* Retrieved from https://www.npr.org/2017/03/03/518261347/on-both-left-and-right-trump-is-driving-new-political-engagement

Watson, E. (2017). Solange Knowles shows us all what can happen when a woman finds her purpose. *Glamour.* Retrieved from https://www.glamour.com/story/women-of-the-year-2017-solange-knowles

Wicker, J. (2019, February). 5 young Black activists making history right now. *Teen Vogue.* Retrieved from https://www.teenvogue.com/story/5-young-black-activists-making-history-right-now

Wun, C. (2014). Unaccounted foundations: Black girls, anti-Black racism, and punishment in schools. *Critical Sociology, 42*(4–5), 737–750.

CHAPTER 10

THE CLAPBACK

Black Girls Responding to Injustice Through National Civic Engagement

Cierra Kaler-Jones
University of Maryland–College Park

Autumn Griffin
University of Maryland–College Park

Stephanie Lindo
University of Maryland–College Park

Historically, media coverage of Black girls[1] and women has privileged disparaging stereotypes that suggest they are unworthy of protection, willing participants in their own oppression, and disruptive forces of Black communities (Morris, 2016). Such wide dissemination of anti-Black, anti-women narratives—rarely written or told by Black women and girls themselves—erase and distort the participation of Black girls in seminal movements in United States history and in current events (Collins, 2002). For example, Kenidra Woods, an 18-year-old activist, launched the first *Hope for Humanity:*

Black Girl Civics, pages 159–173
Copyright © 2020 by Information Age Publishing
All rights of reproduction in any form reserved.

National Rally for Peace in St. Louis, Missouri to bring together individuals who have experienced gun violence. During her speech, she addressed how Black teens have long been vocal in the fight for gun control, but are rarely seen in mainstream media coverage about it (Crumpton, 2018).

One example of the criminalization of Black girl activists is the treatment of Patrisse Khan-Cullors, one of the founders of the #BlackLivesMatter (BLM) movement, who was labeled a "terrorist" by national television host Bill O'Reilly for her outspoken activism against police brutality in the Black community. O'Reilly's actions facilitated the widespread usage of the term "terrorist" to describe Khan-Cullors, and the co-founders of BLM, Opal Tometi, and Alicia Garza, making it acceptable for others to use the term to condemn their activism and organizing. In her memoir *When They Call You a Terrorist,* Khan-Cullors detailed how O'Reilly's remarks led to life-threatening responses as well as a petition sent to the White House claiming that the Black Lives Matter movement made the three co-founders threats to U.S. society (Khan-Cullors & bandele, 2018). Because of her efforts towards social justice for all, Cullors and her work were criminalized.

Recent shifts in access to publications, via changes in digital communication, have allowed for the inclusion of much more nuanced stories about Black girls' civic engagement. Such online outlets are spaces for Black women and girls to take control of their own narratives and write in affirming and uplifting ways about themselves and their sisters (i.e., other Black girls; McArthur, 2016). By examining these news media sites and focusing on digital platforms that have Black women editors-in-chief, we highlight how these burgeoning digital platforms allow Black girls a space to *clapback* or write against narratives that seek to mislabel and misrepresent them and their work. In this chapter, we aim to answer: (a) "How do stories about the civic engagement of Black girls published on alternative digital news outlets disrupt White supremacist and sexist narratives about Black girls?" and (b) "What literary and journalistic strategies do Black women and girl authors of alternative digital news stories employ to disrupt negative narratives about Black girls' civic engagement?"

MEDIA PORTRAYALS OF BLACK WOMANHOOD AND GIRLHOOD

The experiences of many Black girls point to a generally negative disposition Americans have towards Black femininity. For example, when Rachel Jeantel, a friend of Trayvon Martin, spoke about his wrongful death in court and the media, she was mocked for her use of English and her perceived lack of intelligence (Cobb, 2013). Despite her ability to speak three languages, media outlets demeaned her, questioning both her character and intellect. Although she was portrayed negatively, Jeantel continued to speak and protect the legacy of her friend.

People often describe Black girls as assertive, outspoken, and asking too many questions. These attributes are often viewed positively when talking about men, but when describing Black girls they become negative descriptors (Morris, 2007). This racial and gendered bias is created by privileging White middle-class norms of femininity which are often marked by reserved behaviors such as meekness and modesty (Blake, Butler, Lewis, & Darensbourg, 2011).

In the report, *Girlhood Interrupted: The Erasure of Black Girls' Childhood,* Epstein, Blake, and González (2017) revealed that young Black girls are often perceived as being more adult-like than their White peers. Epstein and colleagues (2017) call this phenomenon the *adultification of Black girls,* whereas other scholars have deemed this the *dehumanization of Black women and girls* (Arditti, 2014). By minimizing the very human needs of Black girls, people who imagine them in this way diminish their humanity.

As evidence, we return to our previous example of Khan-Cullors. Because she has chosen to take up the mantle of speaking truth to power, those who subscribe to the dominant White narrative have chosen to belittle and dehumanize her by labeling her a "terrorist" leaving her vulnerable to verbal attacks. Similarly, when Bree Newsome, a Black woman in South Carolina, climbed a flagpole to remove the confederate flag in an act of defiance, police threatened to electrocute the pole, which would have left Bree lifeless at its foundation. Because they did not see her life as valuable, the solution was to let her fall to her death. Because Black women and girls are thought to be in less need of protection and care, those with power often act on those perceptions through policing and control of their civic engagement practices. Thus, Black girls are denied the freedom to express their humanity and their right to petition without fear of retaliation.

THEORETICAL FRAMEWORK

Drawing on stories that counter dominant stereotypical narratives opens up a new way of understanding the power structures and imbalances in society. Privileged groups' ways of learning, constructing knowledge, and developing language about the world reaffirm the status quo, as some groups reassert anti-Black narratives as the "American way" (Crichlow, Goodwin, Shakes, & Swartz, 1990). Extending the work of Brown (2013) and the counter-storytelling tenet of critical race theory (CRT; Solorzano & Yosso, 2002), this chapter uses the lenses of Black girlhood and CRT to highlight positive and creative narratives about Black girls' civic engagement practices in 21st-century movements through a critical examination of online news media sources.

Black girlhood, as a framework (Brown, 2013), highlights how Black girls add critical perspectives of human experience, produce and validate knowledge that disrupts dominant deficit-based narratives, and use experience as a source of strength. Further, Brown (2013) argues that when Black girls examine their lived experiences, they come up with radically unique ideas about those experiences. By focusing on news media articles written by Black women and girls about Black women and girls, this chapter contributes to an emerging tradition in education by centering Black women and girls' voices in traditionally male-dominated and White-dominated spaces, such as the media.

METHODS AND DATA COLLECTION

The three authors of this chapter identify as Black millennial women pursuing graduate degrees (two doctorates and one masters) in K–12 education. Our research interests all center the experiences of Black students, specifically Black girl students, to make educational institutions safe and supportive environments for Black girls to grow, develop, and thrive. We operate under the belief that educational and other institutions (i.e., government, news, media) function as bodies of Eurocentrism and patriarchy and owe a great deal of educational debt (Ladson-Billings, 2006) to Black students.

We conducted a critical discourse analysis (Fairclough, 1995) to center Black girls' civic engagement in 21st-century social justice movements. Critical discourse analysis aims to "uncover, reveal, or disclose what is implicit, hidden, or otherwise not immediately obvious" with regards to power relations and underlying ideologies that play a role in influencing and reproducing the status quo (Van Dijk, 1995, p. 18). Further, critical discourse analysis examines control as it pertains to "action and cognition" or how the status quo privileges one group's influence or ways of knowing over another group's (Van Dijk, 1995). Because Black women and girls are sharing stories and making their voices heard in mediums traditionally used to oppress them, we chose critical discourse analysis to guide our study.

We analyzed 21 media stories across seven digital publications, including four pop media sources (*Elle Magazine, Teen Vogue, Blavity, Essence*), and three news outlets (*The Root, Huffington Post, and Google News*). We also used social networking sites, such as Facebook and Twitter to better understand how Black girls express their opinions about current events in their own words.

We chose these publications because all, with the exception of *Elle Magazine,* currently have editors-in-chief who are Black women. *Elle Magazine* was selected because Marley Dias, the Black girl founder of the hashtag

#1000BlackGirlBooks, is the editor of a 'zine created exclusively for *Elle*, entitled *Marley Mag*. We use both *Marley Mag* and *Elle Magazine* in this study.

To answer the first research question, we used the *Google News* search to compare and contrast mainstream news outlets (i.e., *New York Times*, CNN) with the alternative news media sources. Although this is not the focus of the study, it is important to give a frame of reference for understanding how Black girl activists and journalists are disrupting negative narratives.

We chose Twitter and Facebook because according to survey data collected by the Pew Research Center (2018), Black people and women use these two social media networking sites at higher rates than their White and male counterparts. Together, these three types of online sources of information highlight (a) how Black girl activists are described in Black-focused and women-focused digital news outlets, (b) how Black girl activists are described in non-mainstream news outlets, and (c) how Black girl activists counter negative narratives, or *clapback*, by utilizing online spaces to tell their own stories.

We conducted a formal search for terms including *Black girl activism, Black girl civic engagement,* and *Black girl.* We searched *Elle Magazine, Teen Vogue, Blavity, Essence, The Root, Huffington Post,* and Google News websites. Across all seven outlets, there were over eight million articles that mentioned Black girls. From these searches, we selected articles based on three selection criteria.

First, the individual or group in the article had to be explicitly described as a Black girl or woman using Ruth Nicole Brown's (2009) definition of Black girlhood.[2] We eliminated any and all articles that did not meet this criterion and narrowed the number of articles to approximately 1,000. The second criterion was that the article had to have been published within the last 10 years (from 2008–2018) to allow us to critically analyze how Black girl activists are being portrayed in current media and social movements. Paring down data according to this criterion left us with approximately 700 articles. Third, we chose articles that were both written by Black girls and highlighted them from an asset-based perspective. We define asset-based as recognizing and acknowledging the importance of the knowledge, experience, and civic engagement practices of Black girls that contribute to the deconstruction of pervasive patriarchal and Eurocentric norms and values (Kretzmann, 2010).

This selection criteria decreased our number of articles to approximately 70. That a criterion of an asset-based lens decreased the number of articles from 700 to 70 substantiates our claim that narratives about Black girls are often deficit-based or not written by Black girls or women themselves. For the purpose of in-depth analysis of articles in this study, we selected three of the most recent articles from each publication resulting in 21 articles.

We drew on our definition of clapback, Black girlhood perspectives, and the counter-storytelling tenet of CRT to help create themes and codes.

Utilizing Fairclough's (1995) dimensions of critical discourse analysis, the authors looked critically at article text and images (Dimension 1), the writer's use of indirect and direct quotes (Dimension 2), and the social analysis or explanations (Dimension 3).

For Dimension 1, we looked specifically at how the Black girl in the article was addressed (i.e., whether or not her name was used, how many times, and where—in the headline, the lead, or the body text). We decided that the use of a name rather than a demographic descriptor gives visibility, humanity, and individuality to the subject of the article. For Dimension 2, we explored whether the author used direct quotes or paraphrased the words of the Black girl activist, because including direct quotes indicates that the author let the Black girl activist speak for herself, rather than interpreting her story. For Dimension 3, we searched for positive nouns, adjectives, and verbs to describe the Black girl activist throughout the article. Our analysis focused on stories that did not characterize Black girl activists as a monolith (see Table 10.1). From these dimensions or themes, we created the codes:

TABLE 10.1   Fairclough's Dimensions of Critical Discourse Analysis Themes

Text Analysis (Dimension 1)	Processing Analysis (Dimension 2)	Social Analysis (Dimension 3)
(Description)—Nouns Headline | Lead | Body text	(Interpretation)—Quotes Direct Quotes | Indirect Quotes	(Explanation)— Deficit/Asset-Based Narrative Themes
• Writer did not use the name/s of Black girl activist, but rather other nouns (i.e., Black, woman, girl, Statue of Liberty climber) in the headline. • Writer used the name of the Black girl activist in the lead. • Writer used the name of the Black girl activist in the body of the text. • Writer used the name of the Black girl activist in two or more parts (headline, line, body text) of the article. • Writer used a positive adjective to describe Black girl activist in headline (i.e., "brave").	• Writer included Black girl activists' direct quotes. • Writer did not include Black girl activists' direct quote (paraphrase).	• Writer included positive nouns/verbs to describe Black girl activist ("shine," "standing tall") • Writer included negative nouns/verbs ("the episode," "unexpected spectacle") • Writer included a description of the Black girl activist that moved beyond stereotypical assumptions about Black women ("strength and sadness," i.e., "upset," "scared," "difficult" also coupled with "it was important," "optimism" within at most three sentences (Nunn, 2018).

visibility, name, inspiration/optimism, sadness/pain, humanity, and *countering negative narrative.*

FINDINGS

Our analysis led to three themes. First, social media and alternative media provide an online space for Black girls to assert their visibility in a format where they can clapback against those who try to delegitimize and attack their work. Second, social and alternative media allow Black girls to move their narrative beyond a one-dimensional scope by showcasing both their "strength and sadness" (Nunn, 2018). Lastly, Black girl journalists used three tactics to disrupt negative narratives about Black girls in their writings: (a) including positive, affirming language, (b) using direct quotes from Black girl activists, and (c) showcasing visual images that exemplified a more nuanced portrayal of Black girls and their activist practices.

Reasserting Black Girl Visibility as a Form of Clapback

Despite threat and pushback from society, Black girls use online spaces to bring national attention to the discrepancies in whose voices are silenced and whose are celebrated in activism. For example, Naomi Wadler's speech at the 2018 March for Our Lives in Washington, DC, discussed how there are many Black girls who are and have been the victims of gun violence but were not highlighted as part of the #NeverAgain movement.

Symone Sanders, a Black woman political strategist, referenced Wadler's speech in a tweet:

> Naomi Wadler is currently standing in the gap for all of the Black girls and Black women who are victims of gun violence. All the Black girls and Black women who don't get a hashtag and who don't become front page news. Thank you, Naomi.

The aforementioned tweet received over 3,280 retweets and 12,824 likes. Such attention increased the reach of Sanders' idea about the importance of the visibility of Black girls (Sanders, 2018).

Chanice Lee, the young Black girl author of *Young Revolutionary: A Teen's Guide to Activism,* took to Facebook and her blog *The Melanin Diary* to express her frustration with the lack of national support for low-income communities of color experiencing high rates of gun violence. She posed, "So, I thought to myself: If the shooting happened in my low-income, Black neighborhood, would the residents of the predominantly White, wealthy neighborhoods show up for Black Teens? . . . Probably not, unfortunately" (Lee, 2018, para. 4). Importantly, Lee uses her platform to analyze the lack of attention communities of color receive and places her question at the center of the discourse.

Furthermore, two articles written by Black girls in *Elle Magazine* use Naomi Wadler's name directly in the title, including "Naomi Wadler Continues to Fight for Black Girls" and "Naomi Wadler Is the 11-Year-Old Activist You Need to Know" (Dias, 2018; Epstein, 2018). By featuring her name, she is no longer invisible but a headline. Marley Dias (2018), the author of the second piece, is the 13-year-old activist who started the hashtag #1000Black-GirlBooks. Dias's (2018) article provided an opportunity for two young Black girls to be in conversation about their unique perspectives on what it is like to be activists at the intersection of race, gender, and age. Black girl journalists take control of their own narrative, defying the historical stereotypes we discussed in the previous sections, by writing and reporting on their own stories.

Additionally, the authors of both pieces used words and phrases like "electrified the crowd," "chance to shine," and "stood and demanded that people see and appreciate the lives of Black girls," which portray Wadler as powerful. Such a word choice denotes a quality of brightness and visibility, connotations that stand in stark contrast to both the erasure of Black women's voices and contributions in historical movements and constructions of Black femininity characterized by darkness, negativity, or pathology (Epstein, 2018; Dias, 2018).

A common thread amongst more mainstream digital outlets, such as CNN and *NY Times,* is that they do not name girls in the title; some articles even failed to mention their names at all. Journalists used descriptors such as "woman" and "girl," erasing their identities from the headlines. For example, a *NY Times* article describing Therese Patrice Okoumou, an activist who climbed the Statue of Liberty on July 4th, 2018 to protest immigrant family separation at the United States–Mexican border, used the headline "Statue of Liberty Climber Upends Holiday for Thousands." In the article, a representative for the National Park Service called Okoumou's form of protest a "stunt" that "ruined the plans for many that tried to visit the island" and never addressed her valiant intention (Rojas, 2018, para. 15).

In contrast, an article published by *Essence Magazine* included a headline that read, "Black Woman Who Climbed Statue of Liberty Says She Was Inspired by Michelle Obama," followed by Okoumou's own words that she "went as high as she could," in reference to former First Lady Michelle Obama's quote, "When they go low, we go high" (Rogo, 2018, para. 3). Importantly, the Black woman author (Rogo) of this article uses her agency to assert the visibility of not one, but two Black women—Okoumou and former First Lady, Michelle Obama.

Additionally, the article mentioned that Okomou wore a black t-shirt with the words, "white supremacy is terrorism" across the chest, which the *NY Times* article failed to mention (Rojas, 2018). Alternative media is being used as a space where Black girls, both activists and journalists, are showcasing the visibility that is often stripped from them as a racist practice to relegate them to inferior status.

Online Activism to Disrupt Negative Stereotypes About Black Girls

Black girls allow both their strength and their sadness to be exhibited in alternative media, which disrupts White supremacist narratives that relegate Black girls to the status of Mammy, Jezebel, and Sapphire. Drawing on Nia Michelle Nunn's (2018) super-girl model, alternative media presents a new understanding of how Black girls balance both the strength of "self-defined feminine power" as well as the sadness of having to protect themselves from harsh discriminatory practices. From a historical context, Black girls and women are perceived as solely "innately emotionally strong and unbreakable," which has denied them the ability to express a wide range of human emotions (Evans-Winters & Girls for Gender Equity, 2017, p. 419; Beauboeuf-Lafontant, 2009). It is because of these long-held beliefs about Black girl identity that Black girls are often portrayed as one-dimensional or as not expressing their emotions, which further dehumanizes them.

Allowing audiences to witness how Black girls continue to persist and act on injustice despite adversity brings national and international consideration to the complexities of Black girlhood. For instance, *Teen Vogue* quoted Nupol Kiazolu of #BlackLivesMatter Greater New York who said, "I was spit on, called the n-word, tear-gassed, and hit in my back full force by a grown man" (Kirst, 2018, para. 3). She not only expresses fear and terror, but also follows up by detailing how those pivotal movements made her realize the extent of the work that still needed to be done: "That was the scariest day of my life, and I think about it every day, but it made me realize all the work there is to do" (Kirst, 2018, para. 3). Despite the physical threat and fear Kiazolu felt, she persisted.

Another example is that of Bree Newsome, who in 2015 scaled a 30-foot flagpole to remove the Confederate flag at the state Capitol in South Carolina (Harris-Perry, 2015). In an *Elle Magazine* interview, Newsome noted, "The physical battle to climb up there and get that flag was like the struggle to dismantle systemic racism. Nothing about it is easy." She continued, "We have to keep moving" (Harris-Perry, 2015, para. 10). Although the courageous act was strenuous, Newsome discussed how important it is to keep moving and explains how her optimism for a more just society motivated her to remove the flag. The aforementioned examples show how Black girls are not highlighted in alternative media sources as adhering to historical stereotypical depictions of Black girls (i.e., Mammy, Jezebel, & Sapphire), but rather as both claiming their power and expressing their emotions in their activism.

Disrupting Negative Visual Images

The inclusion of images or video footage of activists themselves increases the visibility of Black girl activists in widely consumed online spaces. Mari Copeny, dubbed "Little Miss Flint" for her outspoken activism throughout the ongoing Flint, Michigan water crisis, was depicted in a story in *Essence Magazine* with her hands on her hips, smiling, almost in a superwoman-esque pose, and showing strength. The article mentions how Copeny understands the importance of representation because she raised money to take other students to see the film *Black Panther*, a work that subverts dominant, historically rooted portrayals of Black people as victims and instead frames them as powerful superheroes, genius scientists, formidable warriors, and courageous leaders (Scott, 2018).

An article in *Essence Magazine* shows a picture of Johnetta Elzie, one of the foremost activists during the 2014 Ferguson and 2015 Baltimore protests, in a bright red dress and jacket, almost mid-dance pose, and looking straight into the camera. Her pose coupled with her straight-on look expresses power and passion (Viera, 2016). The article prefaces the interview with Elzie with the sentence: "Because revolutionaries speak their own truths best, here's how Netta creates her own Black Girl Magic" (Viera, 2016, para. 3). Her physical stature and the color red, which pops against the blank, grey background, suggests courage to "speak her own truth best," (Viera, 2016, para. 3) as Viera details.

Another story published on *Teen Vogue* depicts Patrisse Khan-Cullors in an angelic white dress, with her hand on her heart, looking up, and smiling, as if she is being praised. Although mainstream media outlets characterized Khan-Cullors as a "terrorist" and "criminal," the *Teen Vogue* article shows a different illustration—one that shows humanity and beauty in a Black woman (Blades, 2017).

DISCUSSION

In this chapter, we highlighted three major findings in our research: (a) Black girls use digital media outlets to reassert their visibility as a form of clapback, (b) Black girls use digital media outlets to showcase both their strength and sadness, and (c) Black girl journalists use positive, affirming language and images that exemplified nuanced portrayals of them to disrupt negative narratives about Black girls. As stated by Ruth Nicole Brown (2009), Black girls are often "the people least guaranteed to be centered as valuable in collective work and social movements that they could very well lead and organize" (p. 1). As such, the work these girls have done to insert themselves into national discourse and begin to dismantle disparaging stereotypes is revolutionary.

Critical discourse analysis through the lens of Black girlhood as a theoretical framework is an underutilized combination in understanding how power and privilege is perpetuated through language in media sources. Research suggests that individuals use internet resources to develop their racial identities and the internet has been discussed as an important space for constructing Black identity (Brock, 2009). Our findings suggest that alternative online outlets, especially articles about Black girls written by Black women and girls, are used to write and rewrite Black girl identity.

We also learned that Black girls use online outlets, such as blogs and social media posts, as a space for counter-narrative by commenting on social injustice and Black identity in their communities, country, and the world. This finding is consistent with suggestions from previous research, which shows that online writing, such as blogging, can be a space for highlighting how social issues affect Black communities (Pole, 2005).

This study highlights the importance of showcasing Black girls' contributions to activism. When juxtaposed with mainstream media sources (*New York Times*, CNN), stereotypes about Black girls and women that contribute to the general public's understanding of current events are being consumed on a daily basis. Deficit-based language, including labeling a Black girl as a "terrorist," an act of civil activism as "civil disobedience," or civic engagement as "nuisance" without discussing the sociopolitical context or oppressive structures and systems that lead to protest, undermines the potential of the political process. Moreover, they use alternative media outlets and social media to speak their own truths to power, to tell their own stories from their perspectives, and bring to light the injustices that are too often overlooked or erased to maintain White supremacist, patriarchal values.

IMPLICATIONS

The findings shed light on the current gaps in the literature and lead us to ask additional questions about how media frames Black girl civic engagement and its effects on policymakers, law enforcement, and educators. First, Black girls use alternative and social media as a form of clapback. While our study puts us in conversation with scholars who have begun to raise questions about *how* Black girls engage online generally (McArthur, 2016), there is a need to consider how educators can utilize digital spaces to let students, particularly Black girls, tell their own stories. How can educators use both mainstream and alternative media sources in the classroom to teach students to critique and rewrite deficit-based news stories and become critical consumers and producers of media? As indicated by our findings, stories written about Black girls by Black girls disrupt negative images. How do we continue to use online tools to teach students about how mainstream images can paint only one, monolithic image of people, but can also be used to challenge those images?

Further, we must also consider implications around media control and production. As stated in our findings, most of the outlets that highlighted the positive civic work of Black girls were edited by Black women. Therefore, we must consider who has the power to tell the stories of Black girls and explore how to continue uplifting Black girls' stories. How can Black girl activists' online stories be included in trainings and professional development for educators, journalists, and executives at news and social media companies? What is the impact of cultural competence training that specifically highlights the asset-based narratives of Black girls? By showing Black girl activists as human, we can move past dehumanizing narratives that restrain Black girls' expressions of civic engagement (Epstein et al., 2017).

Lastly, we find it necessary to consider how we can continue to uplift and amplify Black girl activists' voices in research. In the literature, critical discourse analysis is an underutilized methodology in understanding how Black girls use news and social media. We ask: "How can we utilize qualitative research, like critical discourse analysis, to reframe deficit-based narratives, further interrogate monolithic understandings of Black girl activists' experiences, and encourage members of larger society to be critical consumers of the information we take in?"

CONCLUSION

In this chapter, we challenge negative discourse about Black girls' civic engagement in schools and communities by critically investigating examples not widely reported, discussed, or celebrated in the media or academic literature. We seek to recast deficit-based narratives by shedding light on the imperative activist work in which fearless Black girls are engaging throughout the country. Black girls are using alternative news media sources to clapback, or reassert their visibility in a news media space that erases, constricts, and polices their forms of activism. Black girl journalists are using positive, affirming language to describe Black girl activists and portraying them with visual images that showcase the nuances of Black girlhood to disrupt and complicate White supremacist narratives. We must continue to create spaces for research, policy, and practice to share the stories of Black girls from their own perspectives and to speak their truths for themselves.

NOTES

1. The word *girl* is used loosely throughout this text to connote Black girls, adolescents, and young women. As Ruth Nicole Brown (2009) argued, Black girlhood transcends age and instead is the "representations, memories, and lived experiences of being and becoming a body marked as youthful, Black, and female" (p. 1). The term *Black* is used throughout this chapter to be inclusive of African American girls and African diasporic girls.
2. See Endnote 1

REFERENCES

Arditti, J. A. (2014). Childhood adultification and the paradox of parenting: Perspectives on African American boys in economically-disadvantaged families. In L. M. Burton, D.-M. Winn, H. Stevenson, & M. McKinney (Eds.), *Family problems: Stress, risk, & resilience* (pp. 167–182). New York, NY: Wiley.

Beauboeuf-Lafontant, T. (2009). *Behind the mask of the strong Black woman: Voice and the embodiment of a costly performance.* Philadelphia, PA: Temple University Press.

Blades, L. A. (2017, August 24). Patrisse cullors of black lives matter discusses the movement. *Teen Vogue.* Retrieved from https://www.teenvogue.com/story/patrisse-cullors-of-black-lives-matter-discusses-the-movement

Blake, J., Butler, B., Lewis, C., & Darensbourg, A. (2011). Unmasking the inequitable discipline experiences of urban Black girls: Implications for urban educational stakeholders. *The Urban Review, 43,* 90–106.

Brock, A. (2009). Who do you think you are? Race, representation, and cultural rhetorics in online spaces. *Poroi, 6*(1), 15–35.

Brown, R. N. (2009). *Black girlhood celebration: Toward a hip-hop feminist pedagogy* (Vol. 5). New York, NY: Peter Lang.

Brown, R. N. (2013). *Hear our truths: The creative potential of Black girlhood.* Urbana-Champaign: University of Illinois Press.

Cobb, J. (2013, June 27). Rachel Jeantel on trial. *The New Yorker.* Retrieved from https://www.newyorker.com/news/news-desk/rachel-jeantel-on-trial

Collins, P. H. (2002). *Black feminist thought: Knowledge, consciousness, and the politics of empowerment.* London, England: Routledge.

Crichlow, W., Goodwin, S., Shakes, G., & Swartz, E. (1990). Multicultural ways of knowing: Implications for practice. *Journal of Education, 172*(2), 101–117.

Crumpton, T. (2018, July 2). Teen activist Kenidra Woods organized the hope for humanity project rally in St. Louis. *Teen Vogue.* Retrieved from https://www.teenvogue.com/story/teen-activist-kenidra-woods-organized-hope-for-humanity-project-rally-in-st-louis

Dias, M. (2018, April 9). Naomi wadler is the 11-year-old activist you need to know. *ESSENCE Magazine.* Retrieved from https://www.elle.com/culture/a19721055/naomi-wadler-is-the-11-year-old-activist-you-need-to-know/

Epstein, R., Blake, J., & González, T. (2017). Girlhood interrupted: The erasure of Black girls' childhood. *Georgetown Center on Law and Poverty.* http://dx.doi.org/10.2139/ssrn.3000695

Epstein, R. (2018, June 20). Naomi Wadler continues to fight for Black girls. *Elle Magazine.* Retrieved from https://www.elle.com/culture/a21753656/naomi-wadler-continues-to-fight-for-black-girls/

Evans-Winters, V. E., & with Girls for Gender Equity. (2017). Flipping the script: The dangerous bodies of girls of color. *Cultural Studies ↔ Critical Methodologies, 17*(5), 415–423.

Fairclough, N. (1995). *Critical discourse analysis. The critical study of language.* New York, NY: Longman.

Harris-Perry, M. V. (2015). One year after she took down the Confederate Flag, activist Bree Newsome looks back. *Elle Magazine.* Retrieved from https://www.elle.com/culture/career-politics/news/a37315/bree-newsome-confederate-fla

Khan-Cullors, P., & bandele, A. (2018). *When they call you a terrorist: A black lives matter memoir.* London, England: St. Martin's Press.

Kirst, S. (2018, July 25). Nupol Kiazolu of black lives matter of greater New York explains her journey into activism. *Teen Vogue.* Retrieved from https://www.teenvogue.com/story/nupol-kiazolu-of-black-lives-matter-of-greater-new-york-explains-her-journey-into-activism

Kretzmann, J. P. (2010). Asset-based strategies for building resilient communities. In J. W. Reich, A. Zautra, & J. S. Hall (Eds.), *Handbook of adult resilience* (pp. 484–495). New York, NY: Guilford Press.

Ladson-Billings, G. (2006). From the achievement gap to the education debt: Understanding achievement in US schools. *Educational Researcher, 35*(7), 3–12.

Lee, C. (2018, March 24). Why I chose not to attend the "march for our lives" [Blog Post]. Retrieved from http://www.themelanindiary.com/why-i-chose-not-to-attend-the-march-for-our-lives/

McArthur, S. A. (2016). Black girls and critical media literacy for social activism. *English Education, 48*(4), 362–379.

Morris, E. W. (2007). "Ladies" or "loudies"? Perceptions and experiences of black girls in classrooms. *Youth & Society, 38*(4), 490–515.

Morris, M. (2016). *Pushout: The criminalization of Black girls in schools.* New York, NY: The New Press.

Nunn, N. M. (2018). Super-girl: Strength and sadness in black girlhood. *Gender and Education, 30*(2), 239–258.

Pew Research Center. (2018). *Social media fact sheet. Report.* Retrieved from http://www.pewinternet.org/fact-sheet/social-media/

Pole, A. (2009). Blogging minorities: Black and Hispanic political bloggers and participation in the United States. Paper presented at the ISA annual convention, New York, NY.

Rogo, P. (2018, July 6). Black woman who climbed Statue of Liberty says she was inspired by Michelle Obama. *ESSENCE Magazine.* Retrieved from https://www.essence.com/news/black-woman-statue-liberty-inspired-michelle-obama/

Rojas, R. (2018, July 4). Statue of Liberty climber upends holiday for thousands. *The New York Times*. Retrieved from https://www.nytimes.com/2018/07/04/nyregion/statue-of-liberty-protester-july-4.html

Sanders, S. (2018, March 24). Naomi Wadler is currently standing in the gap for all of the black girls and black women who are victims of gun violence. All the black girls and Black women who don't get a hashtag and who don't become front page news. Thank you Naomi [Tweet]. Retrieved from https://www.sbs.com.au/topics/voices/culture/article/2018/03/26/meet-11-year-old-who-electrified-crowd-march-our-lives

Scott, S. (2018, January 31). Little Miss Flint and family launch a GoFundMe for kids to see 'Black Panther.' *ESSENCE Magazine*. Retrieved from https://www.essence.com/culture/little-miss-flint-family-gofundme-black-panther/

Solórzano, D. G., & Yosso, T. J. (2002). Critical race methodology: Counter-storytelling as an analytical framework for education research. *Qualitative inquiry, 8*(1), 23–44.

Van Dijk, T. A. (1995). Aims of critical discourse analysis. *Japanese Discourse, 1*(1), 17–28.

Viera, B. (2016, January 6). How activist (and ESSENCE cover star) Johnetta 'Netta' Elzie speaks her truth and what it's like fighting for yours. *ESSENCE Magazine*. Retrieved from https://www.essence.com/celebrity/how-activist-and-essence-cover-star-johnetta-netta-elzie-speaks-her-truth-and-what-its/

CHAPTER 11

TEXTING, TWEETING, AND TALKING BACK TO POWER

How Black Girls Leverage Social Media as a Platform for Civic Engagement

Tiera Tanksley
University of Colorado Boulder

The #BlackLivesMatter movement, which rose to prominence following the state-sanctioned murders of several unarmed Black Americans, shed light on the power of social media to serve as a platform for civic engagement and participatory democracy. In mere moments, video footage capturing the tragic murders of Michael Brown, Sandra Bland, and Philando Castile surfaced online. As the graphic images went viral and the nation erupted in political unrest, many Americans turned their attention to social media to express outrage, raise awareness, and organize for collective change. Data from social media analytics show rapid spikes in user traffic following each murder, with the use of hashtags like #SayHerName, #BlackLivesMatter and #ICantBreathe growing exponentially in only a few short hours (Zerehi, 2014). Studies documenting the offline power of online activism

Black Girl Civics, pages 175–194
Copyright © 2020 by Information Age Publishing
175

identify the virality of these hashtags as being key determinants to the movement's viability, sustainability, and political impact on the world beyond the computer screen (Carney, 2016; Freelon, McIlwain, & Clark, 2016a, 2016b, 2018). With some of the highest rates of social media use to date (Lenhart et al., 2015; Rideout, Foehr, & Roberts, 2010), it is not altogether surprising that Black college-age youth, particularly young Black women, were the primary curators of the politicized social media storm that captured the nation's attention following these race-based tragedies.

Though they represent a minoritized group in the United States, Black teens and young adults play a prevalent role in constructing national discourse on racial justice through their politicized social media engagement. When it comes to college-age youth, social media statistics are literally soaring, marking it as one of the primary platforms of information-gathering, entertainment, and personal expression for a sizable portion of today's undergraduates (Duggan, 2017; Duggan & Brenner, 2013; Lenhart et al., 2015; Pew Research Center, 2017; Rideout et al., 2010; Tanksley, 2016). Nearly one-fourth of young adults' daily internet usage is dedicated to social media use (Lenhart et al., 2015). While social media use is high for college-age youth in general, these usage rates differ significantly once race and gender are considered. In 2016, African Americans (68%) were the group to most frequently be on social media throughout the day compared to White and Hispanic youth (Duggan, 2017; Lenhart et al., 2015). Disaggregating these data along lines of gender reveal similar disparities. While college-age women maintain higher rates of social media use (72%) than their male peers (66%), Black women regularly out-consume their Black male peers by at least one hour of popular media intake a day (Pew Research Center, 2017; Tanksley, 2016). Studies such as these indicate that college students, particularly those that are both Black and female, are the most connected and largest consumers of social media in the United States. Thus, in the midst of the Black Lives Matter movement, where innumerable college students flocked to Facebook and Twitter to extract their daily news (Anderson & Hitlin, 2016; Greenwood, Perrin, & Duggan, 2016), social media became a crucial space for political engagement, personal reflection, and student-led discussions about race, social justice, and American politics for young Black women.

Interestingly, as Black girls' social media activism continues to soar, research examining the civic activities of young people continue to position girls and youth of color as being politically disinterested and disenchanted (Hirshorn & Settersen, 2013; Syvertsen et al., 2011; Twenge, Campbell, & Freeman, 2012). Indeed, extensive scholarship has documented longitudinal drops in conventional indicators of youth civic engagement, including voting, volunteering, reading a newspaper, and enrolling in public affairs or political science courses (Delli Carpini, 2000; Hirshorn & Settersen,

2013; Syvertsen et al., 2011; Twenge et al., 2012). Collectively, these studies suggest that young people, particularly those from historically marginalized communities, suffer from a growing dissatisfaction with the current political structure, the political leaders of the day, and their ability to make tangible change through their participation in conventional forms of civic engagement (CIRCLE, 2017; Hajnal & Lee, 2011; Orr & Rogers, 2011). Consequently, their participation in these traditionally defined methods of civic participation continues to diminish.

While it is true that today's youth express distrust, dissatisfaction, and disinterest in narrowly defined indicators of civic engagement, their staunch participation in alternative forms of civic engagement challenges the normative assumption that they have become politically inactive. Black women's statistical overrepresentation in social media use and their hypervisibility at the forefront of online movements for social justice suggests that youth civic engagement hasn't declined so much as it has undergone a digital transformation (Freelon et al., 2018; Garcia-Castañon, Rank, & Barreto, 2011; Kirshner & Ginwright, 2012). Indeed, the ubiquity of Black girl resistance and political action online sheds light on the transformative power of social media to serve as a platform for participatory democracy in the digital era. Nevertheless, there remains a dearth in scholarship analyzing the intersections of youth civic engagement and social media, particularly as it relates to Black girls and young women. Extent literature examines the ways social media engagement influences numerable facets of civic engagement, including the development of social capital (Gil de Zúñiga, Jung, & Valenzuela, 2012), political awareness (Macafee, & De Simone, 2012; Pasek, Kenski, Romer, & Jamieson, 2006), protest behavior (Valenzuela, 2013; Valenzuela, Arriagada, & Scherman, 2014), and civic efficacy (Kushin & Yamamoto, 2010; Sherrod, Torney-Purta, & Flanagan, 2010). Yet, conspicuously absent from this burgeoning body of scholarship are the voices and experiences of the internet's most visible and vocal activists: Black college-age women.

Given the prevalent role that young Black women play in the construction of internet discourse on social injustice and the ubiquity of narratives positioning Black youth as politically disinterested and technologically incapable, it seems an opportune time to examine the contours of social media as a platform for youth resistance and civic engagement in the digital era. By centering the voices and experiences of Black girls and young women, this study attempts to augment the gendered and raced gaps in civic engagement scholarship by posing the following research question: "What explanations do young, Black women give for their disproportionate use of social networking sites as platforms for civic engagement?"

COMPLICATING CONVENTIONAL NARRATIVES
OF BLACK GIRL CIVICS

As defined by Adler and Goggin (2005), civic engagement refers to "the ways in which citizens participate in the life of a community in order to improve conditions for others or to help shape the community's future" (p. 236). Conventionally, civic engagement has been associated with activities such as voting, formal affiliation to a political party, and enrolling in a political science course (Gerodimos, 2010; Hirshorn & Settersen, 2013; Syvertsen et al., 2011). An extensive body of political science scholarship has demonstrated stark declines in these traditional forms of civic engagement over the past 30 years (Putnam, 1996, 2000; Twenge et al., 2012). In general, Americans are far less likely to vote in an election, volunteer in a campaign, contact a public official or sign a petition than any other point in history (CIRCLE, 2019; Gerodimos, 2010). While this stark decline in political involvement has been noted across demographics, it has become particularly acute among historically marginalized youth (CIRCLE, 2019). Research has shown that youth of color are less trusting of their fellow citizens, less interested in public affairs, and less likely to feel a sense of pride associated with American citizenship—all of which are believed to be indicators of civic engagement (Gerodimos, 2010). They are simultaneously less likely to read a newspaper, watch the news, register to vote or participate in politics beyond voting, including attending a community meeting or contacting a public official (Syvertsen et al., 2011). While informative, these conventional examinations of political engagement construct a misleading and deficit-oriented narrative of civic participation for young Black women.

According to critical theorists, the invisibility of Black girl civics is due, in large part, to an implicit understanding of the word "civics" to mean politically oriented actions that occur offline. Tynes, Garcia, Giang, and Coleman (2011) offer a broader definition of civic engagement that considers the rising role of social media as a more accessible civic space for minoritized youth. Rather than solely focusing on offline actions and discourse, they define civic engagement as "a range of activities that are aimed at improving the public sphere both online and offline, including advocacy, participation in youth organizations and groups, protesting for an important cause, community service, writing, information sharing and civic discourse" (p. 5). Such a definition opens the door for more nuanced articulations of civics in the digital age, particularly as it relates to youth that have been systematically excluded from traditional avenues of political participation.

Racial preferences in news gathering platforms has also been attributed to a growing sense of distrust with television news, particularly for members of oppressed racial and ethnic groups (Knight Foundation, 2017). Research shows that an acute awareness of racial bias and discriminatory reporting in mainstream news makes youth of color less likely to trust offline news sources, including television programs and printed newspapers (Freelon et al., 2018; Knight Foundation, 2017). To combat their growing distrust, youth of color use multiple social networks and news websites to triangulate their news information and ensure its accuracy (Bialik & Matsa, 2017). Cumulatively, these studies provide rich, identity-informed context for why youth of color appear to be disengaging from offline, conventionally defined iterations of civics. At the same time, these data help concretize the reality that Black girls' civics aren't necessarily changing so much as they are undergoing a digital transformation. Indeed, what has for generations been identified as "conventional" civics can be more accurately thought of as "offline" or "unplugged" civics (Tynes et al., 2011).

While some facets of youth civics have merely relocated to social media and the internet, others have been remixed or newly invented on the web to better serve the needs of marginalized communities. Left out of mainstream democratic life, Black Americans have always forged alternative and subversive means of civic engagement (Baldwin, Smidt & Calhoun-Brown, 2003; Harris, 1994, 2001). Just as during reconstruction and Jim Crow, when Black Americans used protests, boycotts, and political mobilization via Black churches to circumvent political suppression, so too do today's youth create alternative pathways into democratic life (Harris, 1994, 2001). Social media practices like hashtagging (i.e., using thematic meta-tags to curate social media content) and meme-ing (i.e., altering popular culture items to have a humorous or satirical critique) are increasingly popular ways of speaking back to power online (Brown, Ray, Summers, & Fraistat, 200); Price-Dennis, 2016; Tanksley, 2016, 2019; Williams, 2015). Through the dynamic, user-generated hashtags like #SayHerName, #TimesUp and #Justice4Nia, young Black women were able to bring intersectional issues to the top of search engine results and trending topic lists that would have otherwise been overlooked by mainstream media (Brown et al., 2017; Noble, 2018b). Google bombing—the process of causing websites to rank highly in search engine results for irrelevant or offensive search via heavy linking—has also been used to center minoritized political views (Gillespie, 2017; Kahn & Kellner, 2004). In 2004, Filipina activist used heavy linking to displace racist search results that revealed ads for mail order brides when users search for "Filipina" on Google. All told, youth of color are using internet technology to (re)engage in civic action and discourse that enable them to center their minoritized standoints, challenge dominant narratives, and participate in intergroup dialogue in creative and subversive ways.

RACE, GENDER, AND ONLINE CIVIC ENGAGEMENT

In an attempt to counter popular rhetoric that positions young people as politically disconnected, recent scholarship has emerged chronicling the new forms of civic engagement that have emerged within the context of the digital sphere. Using hashtags related to a political or social issue, changing their profile picture to show support for a cause, and looking up information on local protests or rallies are just a few of the ways people are engaging in civics via social media platforms. According to a 2018 survey by Anderson, Toor, Rainie, and Smith (2018) a majority of Americans believe that social media is *very* or *somewhat* important for accomplishing offline political goals, such as getting powerful politicians to pay attention to issues (60%) and creating sustained movements for change (67%).

While these online iterations of civic engagement are gaining popularity across a wide range of demographics, they are particularly prevalent amongst users that are young, low-income and belong to historically marginalized racial groups (Anderson et al., 2018). For instance, over half of Black social media users identified these platforms as being critical venues for expressing their political views and getting engaged with issues that are important to them. Black social media users were also more likely than White users to view social media as *very* or *somewhat important* to them when it comes to finding others who share their views about an important issue (54%), getting involved with issues that are important to them (52%), and giving them a venue to express their political opinions (53%). In regards to civic agency and visibility, Black users overwhelmingly describe social media as being an invaluable political tool for those who are historically marginalized. Roughly 80% of Black survey participants say that social media "highlight important issues that might not get a lot of attention otherwise" and "help give voice to underrepresented groups" (Anderson et al., 2018). In addition to race, age, and gender are crucial determinants in the choice to leverage social media as a site of civic engagement. Young internet users aged 18–29 are the group most likely to use social media as a venue for political or civic involvement, and girls tend to gravitate towards social media more than boys to raise awareness on or politically engage in a social issue (Carney, 2016; Tanksley, 2016, 2019). Similarly, young Black women under 29 years old are statistically overrepresented as creators and circulators of politically oriented posts, particularly as it relates to Black Lives Matter (Olteanu, Weber, & Gatica-Perez, 2015).

As exhibited by these case studies, social media are perceived by marginalized peoples, particularly young Black women, to be a viable platform for critical race counter-storytelling. Moreover, the connection Black women activists are making between online activism and their ability to transform policies and structures that foster intersectional oppression are crucial and highlight the potential of social media to foster transformational resistance well beyond the computer screen.

The Offline Impacts of Online Activism

While the aforementioned studies highlight the prevailing belief among young, Black women that social media civics is an avenue for offline change, research on the material impacts of online activism concretize the power of digital activism to change lived realities beyond the computer screen (CIRCLE, 2017; Freelon et al., 2016; Gerodimos, 2017; Kim, Russo & Amnå, 2017). Studies show that when youth seek out information and participate in discussions online, there is a noteworthy increase in their participation in offline civic acts, such as raising money for charity, volunteering in a community organization working on a campaign, attending a political speech, or voting (Kahne, Lee, & Feezell, 2012; McLeod, Kosicki, & McLeod, 2009; Mossberger, Tolbert, & McNeal, 2008; Shah, McLeod, & Lee, 2009). A large-scale study of online civic engagement found salient connections between participation in online political discussions and participation in offline political protests across 16 countries (Steinert-Threlkeld, Mocanu, Vespignani, & Fowler, 2015). Of particular importance is the fact that researchers consistently find salient connections between marginalized identities, social media civics, and an increase in offline political mobilization (Enjolras, Steen-Johnsen, & Wollebæk, 2013). Stated differently, the connection between participation in online civic and increases in offline political participation is mediated by race, age, gender and class. Thus, having a minoritized social status significantly increases the likelihood that these online civics will translate into offline actions for young Black women (Enjolras et al., 2013).

Scholars have also drawn important connections between what trends online and what is subsequently covered on prime-time news. In the case of Michael Brown, whose fatal encounter with Ferguson police was photographed and uploaded to Twitter, news of racially provoked police brutality nearly broke the internet, spreading across social media networks in mere seconds. Photographic evidence of Brown's extrajudicial killing, which first appeared on social media at 3:05 CST p.m. on August 9, 2014, was extensively shared and discussed online for almost 4 hours before it was reported on a mainstream news outlet. The graphic murder of Philando Castile, which was live-streamed on Facebook around 9:00 p.m. on July 6th, 2016, was shared over 2.5 million times online before the story was picked up by mainstream news the following day (Freelon et al., 2016). The tendency for news about anti-Black violence to surface online well before it is covered on mainstream television is one reason scholars assert that social media heavily impacts national coverage about race and justice. It has been argued, and well documented, that authentic accounts of anti-Black racism are rarely covered in mainstream news outlets, and when they are discussed they are often used to uphold hegemonic constructions of Black criminality (Noble, 2014). The tendency of social media to "break the internet" with news of racial violence and galvanize national attention inevitably pressures mainstream news outlets to cover stories of underrepresented groups that would otherwise be left untold (Tanksley, 2019).

Not only do online discussion of minoritized political issues put pressure on mainstream news channels to center the experiences of people of color in more accurate and holistic ways, but they also catalyze individual, institutional and systemic change on a global scale (Freelon et al., 2018). In 2014, the militant group Boko Haram kidnapped more than 270 Nigerian schoolgirls from their boarding school. It wasn't until after the hashtag #BringBackOurGirls went viral and garnered support from high status celebrities, activists, and politicians that the issue became international news and institutional action was taken (Ojebode, 2018). The existence of a viral hashtag and global demands for a resolution, the Nigerian government got involved and offered a hefty cash reward for anyone willing to help locate the missing girls (Ojebode, 2018). Likewise, a 2017 hashtag demanding clemency for Cyntoia Brown, a teenager victim of sex trafficking that was serving a life sentence for killing her rapist, went viral. It didn't take long for high profile politicians, activists, and celebrities to give renewed visibility to Brown's case through social media posts that called out the gendered racism beneath the harsh sentence (Cusumano, 2019; Gafas & Burnside, 2019). The viral hashtag, which brought in fundraising money, raised awareness, and ultimately acquired high quality legal resources, was one of the reasons Brown case was revisited and she was ultimately granted clemency (Cusumano, 2019; Gafas & Burnside, 2019).

Indeed, the ubiquity of Black girls' political action online sheds light on the transformative power of social media to serve as a platform for civic engagement in the digital era. Nevertheless, youth civic engagement online has been criticized as being a lazy, noncommittal type of activism popularly known as "slacktivism." Deemed innocuous and trivial by mainstream scholarship, young, Black women's social media engagement is in fact deeply politicized, historically anchored and indicative of their dedication to community uplift and civic engagement. For far too long, Black women and girls have been overlooked, undervalued, and presumed unworthy of scholarly attention (Brown, 2009; Evans-Williams & Esposito, 2010; Noble, 2012; Tanksley, 2019), particularly in the fields of education and political science.. This chapter stands in direct opposition to these anti-Black, anti-girl narratives by asserting that Black girls' politicized social media use provides a gateway into more nuanced examinations of race, gender, and civics in the digital era.

While existing quantitative literature begin to shed light on Black girls' use of social media for various forms of civics engagement, they nevertheless fail to provide narrative explanations for why Black girls choose to participate in online civics as heavily as they do. Black girls have been analyzed, examined, poked, and prodded, but rarely if ever have they been centered as the experts on their own experiences (Brown, 2009). By centering the voices of 17 young Black women, this study seeks to supplement these informative numerical findings with substantive qualitative data grounded in the everyday perspectives, lived experiences, and digital civics of Black girls and young women. With such an overwhelming online presence, particularly as it relates to political organizing, fundraising, and educating online (Tanksley, 2019), Black girls' online civics undoubtedly provides a critical point of entry for scholars looking to conduct more nuanced examinations of participatory democracy in the digital era.

THEORETICAL FRAMEWORK

As explicated by race theorists, examining issues related to women and girls of color requires one to employ the standpoints and analytical lens created by and for said group. Thus, an empowering analysis of the civic engagement practices of Black girls online necessitates a theoretical approach grounded in race-centered, Afro-feminist values. Consequently, this chapter draws upon Black feminist thought (BFT), critical race theory (CRT), and Black feminist technology studies (BFTS) to shed light on the nuances of Black girls' resilience and political resistance in the digital realm.

As a social justice framework, CRT was designed in response to the emergence of colorblind racism in normalized policies, practices, and beliefs. Its purpose, as explicated by CRT scholars, is to deconstruct colorblind ideology at its racist premise in order to transform those structural aspects of society that maintain the subordination of people of color (Bell, 1992, 1995; Solórzano, 1997, 1998). Though rife with benefits, CRT's central focus on race limits its ability to fully examine what it means to be a young Black woman within a society that is markedly racist, misogynistic, and ageist (Abelove, Barale, & Halperin, 1993; Davis, 2011; Davis, 1989). Recognizing the ways these macro structures intersect to create an exacerbated form of subjugation, critical scholars offer Black feminist thought as a theoretical body containing the cultural knowledge, sociopolitical experiences, and historical insight required to fully understand Black women's triply marginalized state (Collins, 1986, 1990). The notion of intersectionality, a definitive tenet of Black feminist thought, acknowledges that race, gender, and class operate as mutually constructing systems of domination that are inextricably linked in the lives of Black women and girls.

While CRT and BFT can make visible the pervasive presence of racism, sexism, ageism and classism in offline spaces, they are not necessarily equipped to fully examine new articulations of White supremacy in the hardwares, softwares, and infrastructures of the internet. Undergirded by CRT and Black feminist thought, the bureoning field of Black feminist technology studies seeks to disrupt dominant narratives characterizing the internet as post-racial, apolitical, and a democratic equalizer for users from all racial backgrounds (McMillan-Cottom, 2016; Noble, 2014, 2018b; Tanksley, 2019). Instead, BFTS acknowledges the power systems embedded within 21st-century information systems and "shifts discourse away from simple arguments about the liberatory possibilities of the internet toward more critical engagements with how the internet is a site of power and control over Black life" (Noble, 2016, p. 2). By linking Black women in the United States to Black women in the third world, this nuanced theoretical frame illuminates the tech industry's reliance upon Black female bodies for the extraction, consumption, and decomposition of 21st-century media products and platforms (Noble, 2018b; Tanksley, 2017). A Black feminist technology studies approach is also intersectional (Noble, 2016) and makes more visible the ways Black women "intersect with, and are intersected by technologies" (Noble, 2016, p. 2).

A Black feminist technology studies approach recognizes that the belief in post-raciality extends far beyond physical society, manifesting regularly within digital and cyber spaces as well (Daniels, 2009a, 2009b; Noble, 2014). Web browsing, Google search, and social media use viewed through the context of a post-racial utopia wherein users navigate an objective, value-free internet that is unhindered by (and perhaps incapable of reproducing) structures of power and oppression (Daniels, 2009a, 2009b; McMillan-Cottom, 2016; Noble, 2012, 2014, 2018b; Tanksley, 2019). This colorblind construction of internet technology, coupled with the prevailing belief in a post-racial America, poses a unique challenge for scholars attempting to document the deleterious effect of algorithmic oppression on the experiences of young Black women (Daniels, 2009a, 2009b; Noble 2012, 2014, 2018b). Ultimately, the reluctance of scholars to acknowledge the pervasive realities of racial subjugation, especially within the confines of beloved, "apolitical" internet spaces, necessitates the use of a Black feminist critical technology framework (Noble, 2016, 2018a, 2018b) to make sense of the ways algorithmic oppression and technological racism shapes how Black girls navigate and survive the digital realm.

METHODS

Seventeen self-identified Black undergraduate women from 11 universities across the United States and Canada were selected to participate in the study. Since Black women make up a historically underrepresented student group in institutions of higher education, it was necessary to use purposeful sampling in order to accumulate a sizable sample. Consequently, recruitment fliers were posted to university-affiliated social media pages that included demographic identifiers in the title that related to the target population (i.e., Black Student Union, Educated Black Women, Black Girl Magic in College, etc.). Keeping in mind that Black women utilize Facebook, Instagram, and Twitter most prevalently (Lenhart et al., 2015), the researcher posted recruitment fliers to these three social media platforms throughout a 6-week period. Prospective participants filled out a brief survey that recorded relevant demographic information such as name of college or university, current year in school, salient identities that influence educational experiences, and frequency of social media engagement. Participants that completed the online questionnaire were contacted via email to participate in one semi-structured interview that lasted approximately 60 minutes.

FINDINGS

A thorough analysis of qualitative interview data and content analysis data confirmed previous literature highlighting Black girls' overrepresentation in social media as critical content creators, leaders of social justice movements, and as digital change agents. Thus, the overarching takeaway from these data is that social media is a ripe platform for political activism for users experiencing intersectional oppression. Within this larger theme were three subthemes regarding Black girls' explanations for using social media as a platform for civic engagement: (a) social media provides a sense of safety and visibility for young Black women; (b) social media serves as a space for collective anguish, healing and solidarity; and (c) social media provides a renewed sense of trust in news and current events.

Social Media as a Space of Political Activism

When asked to discuss the contours of their social media engagement, participants overwhelmingly identified social media activism as one of their primary activities online. Monique, a first-year student at a large West Coast university, states "Most of the topics I post about on Twitter are politically based . . . I would say probably about 50% of them. My Twitter bio is actually 'protect people of color.'" For Jordan, a third year at a public university in southern California, "[Social media] is where I'm really political . . . I follow people who are grad students or people who express more political views that I share." Likewise, Naomi, a fourth year student at a New England college, explains "I think I use [social media] a lot because I want to keep my ear to the ground to the public, to my communities, to see what's going on." According to Ciani, who goes online to talk about issues related to immigrant rights, "Social media is huge for any type of discussion on race, gender, migration, mobility, displacement. It's amazing because the conversations that we have there are so advanced and it's so beautiful."

Participants drew from personal experience to support their assertions that Black women are the primary leaders of #BlackLivesMatter movement online. According to Ashley, "There are a lot of Black people in general on Twitter, but it's Black women who are really pioneering this movement." Jordan echoed these sentiments, stating, "I think Black women are the most representable groups of Black Lives Matter or have the most politically driven arguments or commentary online. That's true for what I see online and my friends who post about this stuff—they're all Black women for the most part." Likewise, Layla added, "There's Black men definitely in the [#BlackLivesMatter] movement, but Black women specifically are the ones bringing the things out and the ones correcting people online."

When asked why they believed Black women were overrepresented as content creators of Black lives matter posts, the women in this study felt that Black women's avid political participation came as a result of double marginalization. Ashley notes that Black women are "a double minority. We're receiving backlash from white people, but also from Black men. So it's more important for us to say something [about racial injustice]." Like Ashley, many participants were acutely aware of the time and resource constraints that faced them as multiply marginalized persons. They not only felt that their multiple marginalization informed their political awareness, but they simultaneously acknowledged that it made participating in offline forms of civics, like watching real-time news on television, nearly impossible. In fact, many of the women in the study felt that they had "too many responsibilities" to consume news media in conventional formats, such as scheduled television briefings. Participants repeatedly noted that the academic, financial, and familial pressures for Black women in college made watching scheduled news segments particularly challenging. Evenly notes,

> The time where I'm at home watching TV and the news is very small. I would miss everything that way. I can't even sit down for an hour and watch a whole segment. I always have something to do, so scrolling on social media is more accessible and convenient.

Ashley echoed these sentiments, stating, "I think [social media is] just quick and accessible for me. To take the time out my day and sit down and watch the TV would almost never happen. But for me, to just click on an app and see [the news] in front of me is faster."

Social Media Activism Provides a Sense of Safety and Visibility

For Natalie, a third year at a private East Coast university, "Social media is where a lot of political debate happens for me more than in real life." Like Natalie, many participants identified social media as a space where they engaged with politics more frequently than in real life. Participants identified a number of reasons for this, a prominent motive being visibility. Jasmine states, "I'm politically active in real life, but I would say I'm more so online because you share that platform with so many people. You have so many followers and you follow so many people. You feel that you have a voice in the [#BlackLivesMatter] movement because that's your account, that's what you have it for: to voice your own opinion on these issues." Ashley explains that "on [social media] I have more of a chance of being seen by other people than just those people who follow me . . . you have a little bit more visibility." Simone echoes these sentiments, stating, "You can have a conversation with 10 people in real life and maybe get your point out, but if you put it on social media you can share it with 200 or 300 thousand people all at once. It's an easier way to get out your ideas." Likewise, Ashley chooses to voice her opinions on Twitter because, "I have more of a chance of being seen by other people than just those people who follow me . . . With Twitter you have a little bit more visibility."

While visibility was an important rationale for their heavy engagement in digital civics, participants also confessed to feeling significantly safer participating in civic actions online. Layla admits to feeling particularly vulnerable at real life protests and political gatherings. She notes, "I definitely feel safer online. When there are rallies, white people can safely walk away. That's not always the case for Black women." Noriah describes a time a Black undergraduate woman critiqued a racist structure at her university. When the local newspaper got ahold of a quote made at a protest, "Then everyone got a hold of that quote and people were calling for her to leave the school. The administration started getting involved and it was like that side of [offline] activism, a misconstrued quote about racial injustice may cost her her education."

Social Media Activism Provides a Sense of Community

For Evelyn, a third year at a large public university on the West Coast, social media provides a sense of support and community that institutional campus culture lacks. She notes:

I think there's a need for social media spaces and resistance spaces online. I feel supported there. When I go to other spaces on campus or in class I feel almost invisible, like I can't talk about anything that's not surface level or class related. I feel like the [white supremacy rally] that happened in Virginia or [the Black Lives Matter protests] in Ferguson, if I was to be in class or the residence hall when those events happened I would have to pretend I'm not upset and not talk about it. On social media, that's not the case.

Camrinne shared similar feelings, noting:

Black Twitter is so great...it feels like a community space you can go and laugh or grieve or just connect with the rest of the Black community. To me I feel like it's a safe space when I'm at [my university] 'cuz I can go to it and just have a feeling of closeness to Blackness that I don't get on campus.

Jordan similarly cites Black Twitter—a subsection of a popular social networking site in which Black users discuss issues of interest to the Black community—as a space of digital solidarity and community. She explains,

With Black Twitter or memes, you have options to re-tweet and that can show that you agree or you're standing in solidarity. And that's powerful because you don't even have to know the person or be in the same country as them to show your support.

In addition to participating in politically oriented conversations and activities online, Danielle also enjoys engaging in counterhegemonic online spaces, like #BlackGirlMagic and #BlackGirlsMatter instagram pages,

because I can't find anywhere else where you get those affirmations. It's nice to see yourself represented in images and wording that is not putting you down, but telling you the great things about yourself and other people like you who are doing great things. It's inspiring to me so that's why I participate in those spaces.

Social Media Provides More Reliable and Racially Informed News

When asked to identify the primary source of their current events information, a majority of participants cited social media platforms including Facebook and Twitter as their most readily used news outlets. Reflecting back on her social media engagement, Ashley explains, "I usually get my news through Twitter," while Evelyn notes, "Every major news thing that happens, I find out about it through social media." Naomi offers a similar explanation, explaining, "I use Facebook a lot because I want to keep my ear to the ground to the public and to my communities to see what's going on." Overall, social media was considered by the study participants to be more reliable than traditional news outlets when it came to issues of race and social justice. Layla explains that she doesn't trust conventional news "because they show us what they want to show us. They only cover what they want you to know." After discussing a moment when a Black celebrity was removed from a news station after discussing racism in a live news briefing, Iyanna explains, "That's why I believe there's an agenda in conventional news. If you're not following the plan, you get cut off."

A general sense of distrust for conventional news was palpable amongst participants, particularly when it came to gathering information about issues of race and racial injustice. Alleyah explains, "I feel like we will never get the full truth in terms of the news, and that's why I prefer social media." Jasmine is acutely aware of the difference in social media news versus conventional news when it comes to race, noting, "When I go on Twitter I see Black women doing incredible things and people being super excited about it. But then you see [mainstrream] articles and stories where news outlets say things like how aggressive Black women can be." The difference in rhetoric is painful for young Black women and Jasmine admits that "it shocks and hurts me that a lot of the hate Black people are combatting is from news outlets." Naomi similarly experienced a sense of distrust and disappointment with conventional news. Her sentiments were more implied than Jasmine's as she explained,

> I spend a considerable amount of time on Facebook because I'm like "I'm not going to watch the news. Instead, I'm going to look at the trending topics today. I'm going to read some articles in HuffPost and I'm going to read my community's commentary."

Naomi's intentional decision to access news via social media denotes a subtle sense of distrust for dominant news narratives. Rather than gather her description of current events from cable networks, she'd rather get it from the racial, political, and academic communities she chooses to follow on Facebook.

CONCLUSION

Despite their statistical overrepresentation in online civic engagement, Black girls remain under-researched in scholarship about the use of social media for democratic participation and youth civic engagement. Though studies are beginning to examine the unique benefits of social media for youth civic engagement, few studies have sought to directly ask Black girls why they choose to engage in digital activism at such unprecedented rates. This study revealed three main reasons for Black girls' strategic use of social media for civic engagement: social media provided them with a sense of safety and visibility that offline political engagement did not always provide; social media served as a more reliable and critically informed source of news on racial justice; and social media fostered critical counter spaces for Black girls' looking for collective healing, support, and solidarity that was either unavailable or inaccessible offline. These data are only the tip of the iceberg when it comes to understanding Black girls' overrepresentation in civic engagement online. While these findings confirm theoretical suspicions that social media offers marginalized communities unique and unprecedented access to participatory democracy, more research must be done to fully understand the experiences of Black girls' digital civics.

REFERENCES

Abelove, H., Barale, M. A., & Halperin, D. M. (1993). The uses of the erotic: The erotic as power. In A. Lorde (Ed.), *The lesbian and gay studies reader* (pp. 339–343). New York, NY: Routledge.

Adler, R. P., & Goggin, J. (2005). What do we mean by "civic engagement"? *Journal of Transformative Education, 3*(3), 236–253.

Anderson, M., & Hitlin, P. (2016). *Social media conversations about race: How social media users see, share and discuss race and the rise of hashtags like #Blacklivesmatter.* Washington, DC: Pew Research Center.

Anderson, M., Toor, S., Rainie, L., Smith, A., Anderson, M., Toor, S., & Smith, A. (2018). *An analysis of #BlackLivesMatter and other twitter hashtags related to political or social issues.* Pew Research Center. http://www. pewinternet. org/2018/07/11/an-analysis-of-blacklivesmatter-and-other-twitter-hashtags-related-to-political-or-social-issues.

Baldwin, L., Smidt, C., & Calhoun-Brown, A. (2003). *New day begun: African American churches and civic culture in post-civil rights America* (Vol. 1). Durham, NC: Duke University Press.

Bell, D. (1992). *Faces at the bottom of the well: The permanence of racism.* New York, NY: Basic Books.

Bell, D. A. (1995). Who's afraid of critical race theory. *University of Illinois Law Review, 1995*(4), 893–910.

Bialik, K., & Matsa, K. E. (2017). *Key trends in social and digital news media.* Washington, DC: Pew Research Center. Retrieved from https://www.pewresearch.org/fact-tank/2017/10/04/key-trends-in-social-and-digital-news-media/

Bonilla, Y., & Rosa, J. (2015). #Ferguson: Digital protest, hashtag ethnography, and the racial politics of social media in the United States. *American Ethnologist, 42*(1), 4–17.

Brown, M., Ray, R., Summers, E., & Fraistat, N. (2017). #SayHerName: A case study of intersectional social media activism. *Ethnic and Racial Studies, 40*(11), 1831–1846.

Brown, R. N. (2009). *Black girlhood celebration: Toward a hip-hop feminist pedagogy*. New York, NY: Peter Lang.

Carney, N. (2016). All lives matter, but so does race: Black lives matter and the evolving role of social media. *Humanity & Society, 40*(2), 180–199.

Collins, P. H. (1986). Learning from the outsider within: The sociological significance of Black feminist thought. *Social Problems, 33*(6), s14≠s32.

Collins, P. H. (1990). Black feminist thought in the matrix of domination. *Black Feminist Thought: Knowledge, Consciousness, and the Politics of Empowerment, 138*, 221–238.

Cusumano, K. (2019). *How Twitter reacted when Cyntoia Brown, a sex trafficking victim convicted of murder, was granted clemency*. Retrieved from https://www.wmagazine .com/story/cyntoia-brown-clemency/

Daniels, J. (2009a). Rethinking cyberfeminism (s): Race, gender, and embodiment. *Women's Studies Quarterly, 37*(1/2), 101–124.

Daniels, J. (2009b). *Cyber racism: White supremacy online and the new attack on civil rights*. Rowman & Littlefield.

Davis, A. Y. (2011). *Women, race, & class*. New York, NY: Vintage.

Davis, P. (1989). Law as microaggression. *The Yale Law Journal, 98*, 1559–1577.

Delli Carpini, M. X. (2000). Gen.com: Youth, civic engagement, and the new information environment. *Political Communication, 17*(4), 341–349.

Duggan, M. (2017). *Experiencing online harassment*. Washington, DC: Pew Research Center. Retrieved from https://www.pewinternet.org/2017/07/11/ experiencing-online-harassment/

Duggan, M., & Brenner, J. (2013). *The demographics of social media users, 2012* (Vol. 14). Washington, DC: Pew Research Center's Internet & American Life Project.

Enjolras, B., Steen-Johnsen, K., & Wollebæk, D. (2013). Social media and mobilization to offline demonstrations: Transcending participatory divides? *New media & society, 15*(6), 890–908.

Evans-Winters, V. E., & Esposito, J. (2010). Other people's daughters: Critical race feminism and Black girls' education. *Educational Foundations, 24*, 11–24.

Freelon, D., Clark, M. Jackson, S. J., & Lopez, L. (2018). *How Black Twitter and other social media communities interact with mainstream news*. Knight Foundation. Retrieved from https://knightfoundation.org/reports/how-black-twitter-and-other-social -media-communities-interact-with-mainstream-news/

Freelon, D., McIlwain, C., & Clark, M. (2016a). Quantifying the power and consequence of social media protest. *New Media and Society, 20*(3), 990–1011.

Freelon, D., McIlwain, C. D., & Clark, M. D. (2016b). Quantifying the power and consequences of social media protest. *New Media & Society*. Advance online publication) https://doi.org/10.1177/1461444816676646

Freelon, D., McIlwain, C., & Clark, M. (2018). Quantifying the power and consequences of social media protest. *New Media & Society, 20*(3), 990–1011.

Gafas, M., & Burnside, T. (2019). *Cyntoia Brown is granted clemency after serving 15 years in prison for killing man who bought her for sex*. Retrieced from https:// www.cnn.com/2019/01/07/us/tennessee-cyntoia-brown-granted-clemency/ index.html

Garcia-Castañon, M., Rank, A. D., & Barreto, M. A. (2011). Plugged in or tuned out? Youth, race, and Internet usage in the 2008 election. *Journal of Political Marketing, 10*(1–2), 115–138.

Gerodimos, R. (2010). *New media, new citizens: The terms and conditions of online youth civic engagement* (Doctoral dissertation). Bournemouth University, Dorset, England.

Gil de Zúñiga, H., Jung, N., & Valenzuela, S. (2012). Social media use for news and individuals' social capital, civic engagement and political participation. *Journal of Computer-Mediated Communication, 17*(3), 319–336.

Gillespie, T. (2017). Algorithmically recognizable: Santorum's Google problem, and Google's Santorum problem. *Information, Communication, & Society, 20*(1), 63–80.

Greenwood, S., Perrin, A., & Duggan, M. (2016). Social media update 2016. Facebook usage and engagement is on the rise, while adoption of other platforms holds steady. *Pew Research Center.* Retrieved from https://www.pewinternet.org/2016/11/11/social-media-update-2016/

Hajnal, Z. L., & Lee, T. (2011). *Why Americans don't join the party: Race, immigration, and the failure (of political parties) to engage the electorate.* Princeton, NJ: Princeton University Press.

Harris, F. C. (1994). Something within: Religion as a mobilizer of African-American political activism. *The Journal of Politics, 56*(1), 42–68.

Harris, F. C. (2001). Black churches and civic traditions: Outreach, activism, and the politics of public funding of faith-based ministries. In A. Walsh (Ed.), *Can charitable choice work?* (pp. 140–156). Hartford, CT: Leonard Greenberg Center for the Study of Religion in Public Life.

Hirshorn, B. A., & Settersten, R. A., Jr. (2013). Civic involvement across the life course: Moving beyond age-based assumptions. *Advances in Life Course Research, 18*(3), 199–211.

Kahn, R., & Kellner, D. (2004). New media and Internet activism: From the "Battle of Seattle" to blogging. *New Media & Society, 6*(1), 87–95.

Kahne, J., Lee, N. J., & Feezell, J. T. (2012). Digital media literacy education and online civic and political participation. *International Journal of Communication, 6,* 1–24.

Kim, Y., Russo, S., & Amnå, E. (2017). The longitudinal relation between online and offline political participation among youth at two different developmental stages. *New Media & Society, 19*(6), 899–917.

Kirshner, B., & Ginwright, S. (2012). Youth organizing as a developmental context for African American and Latino adolescents. *Child Development Perspectives, 6*(3), 288–294.

Knight Foundation. (2017). *How youth navigate the news landscape.* Retrieved from https://knightfoundation.org/reports/how-youth-navigate-the-news-landscape

Kushin, M. J., & Yamamoto, M. (2010). Did social media really matter? College students' use of online media and political decision making in the 2008 election. *Mass Communication and Society, 13*(5), 608–630.

Lenhart, A., Duggan, M., Perrin, A., Stepler, R., Rainie, H., & Parker, K. (2015). *Teens, social media & technology overview 2015.* Pew Research Center, Internet & American Life Project.

Macafee, T., & De Simone, J. J. (2012). Killing the bill online? Pathways to young people's protest engagement via social media. *Cyberpsychology, Behavior, and Social Networking, 15*(11), 579–584.

McLeod, D. M., Kosicki, G. M., & Mcleod, J. M. (2009). Political communication effects. In *Media effects* (pp. 244–267). New York, NY: Routledge.

McMillan-Cottom, T. (2016). Black cyberfeminism: Ways forward for intersectionality and digital sociology. In J. Daniels, K. Gregory, & T. McMillan-Cottom (Eds.), *Digital sociologies*. Bristol, England: Policy Press

Mossberger, K., Tolbert, C. J., & McNeal, R. S. (2007). *Digital citizenship: The Internet, society, and participation*. Cambridge, MA: MIT Press.

Noble, S. (2012). *Searching for Black girls: Old traditions in new media* (Doctoral dissertation). University of Illinois, Urbana-Champaign.

Noble, S. U. (2014). Teaching Trayvon: Race, media, and the politics of spectacle. *The Black Scholar, 44*(1), 12–29.

Noble, S. U. (2016). A future for intersectional Black feminist technology studies. *The Scholar & Feminist Online*. Retrieved from https://sfonline.barnard.edu/traversing-technologies/safiya-umoja-noble-a-future-for-intersectional-black-feminist-technology-studies/0/

Noble, S. U. (2018a). Critical surveillance literacy in social media: Interrogating Black death and dying online. *Black Camera, 9*(2), 147–160.

Noble, S. U. (2018b). *Algorithms of oppression: How search engines reinforce racism*. New York, NY: NYU Press.

Ojebode, A. (2018). *How Bring Back Our Girls went from hashtag to social movement, while rejecting funding from donors*. Retrieved from https://oxfamblogs.org/fp2p/how-bring-back-our-girls-went-from-hashtag-to-social-movement-while-rejecting-funding-from-donors/

Olteanu, A., Weber, I., & Gatica-Perez, D. (2015). Characterizing the demographics behind the #BlackLivesMatter movement. arXiv preprint arXiv:1512.05671. Retrieved from https://arxiv.org/pdf/1512.05671.pdf

Orr, M., & Rogers, J. (2011). *Public engagement for public education: Joining forces to revitalize democracy and equalize schools*. Stanford, CA: Stanford University Press.

Pasek, J., Kenski, K., Romer, D., & Jamieson, K. H. (2006). America's youth and community engagement: How use of mass media is related to civic activity and political awareness in 14- to 22-year-olds. *Communication Research, 33*(3), 115–135.

Pew Research Center. (2017). *Social media use by race*. Retrieved from https://www.pewinternet.org/chart/social-media-use-by-race/

Price-Dennis, D. (2016). Developing curriculum to support Black girls' literacies in digital spaces. *English Education, 48*(4), 337–361.

Putnam, R. D. (1996). The strange disappearance of civic America. *Policy: A Journal of Public Policy and Ideas, 12*(1), 3–15.

Putnam, R. D. (2000). Bowling alone: America's declining social capital. In *Culture and politics* (pp. 223–234). New York, NY: Palgrave Macmillan.

Rideout, V., Foehr, U., & Roberts, D. (2010). Generation M2: Media in the lives of 8- to 18-year-olds. *Pew Research Center*. Retrieved from https://www.kff.org/wp-content/uploads/2013/01/8010.pdf

Shah, D. V., McLeod, J. M., & Lee, N. J. (2009). Communication competence as a foundation for civic competence: Processes of socialization into citizenship. *Political Communication, 26*(1), 102–117.

Sherrod, L. R., Torney-Purta, J., & Flanagan, C. A. (2010). Political agency and empowerment: Pathways for developing a sense of political efficacy in young adults. In E. Beaumont (Ed.), *Handbook of research on civic engagement in youth* (pp. 525–558). Hoboken, NJ: Wiley.

Solorzano, D. G. (1997). Images and words that wound: Critical race theory, racial stereotyping, and teacher education. *Teacher Education Quarterly, 24*(3), 5–19.

Solorzano, D. G. (1998). Critical race theory, race and gender microaggressions, and the experience of Chicana and Chicano scholars. *International Journal of Qualitative Studies in Education, 11*(1), 121–136.

Steinert-Threlkeld, Z. C., Mocanu, D., Vespignani, A., & Fowler, J. (2015). Online social networks and offline protest. *EPJ Data Science, 4*(1), 19.

Syvertsen, A. K., Wray-Lake, L., Flanagan, C. A., Wayne Osgood, D., & Briddell, L. (2011). Thirty-year trends in US adolescents' civic engagement: A story of changing participation and educational differences. *Journal of Research on Adolescence, 21*(3), 586–594.

Tanksley, T. (2016). Race, education and resistance: Black girls in popular Instagram memes. In S. Noble & B. Tynes (Eds.), *Intersectional Internet: Race, sex, class and culture online* (pp. 243–259). New York, NY: Peter Lang.

Tanksley, T. (2017). Black women and digital diasporas: A post-colonial, global Black feminist perspective. Paper presented at the Black Feminism, Womanism and the Politics of Women of Colour in Europe Conference, Binnenpret, Amsterdam.

Tanksley, T. (2019). Race, education and #BlackLivesMatter: How social media activism shapes the educational experiences of Black college-age women. *UCLA*. Retrieved from https://escholarship.org/uc/item/5br7z2n6

The Center for Information & Research on Civic and Engagement. (2017). *Civics for the 21st century*. Retrieved from https://civicyouth.org/civics-for-the-21st-century/

The Center for Information & Research on Civic and Engagement. (2019). *New national youth turnout estimate: 28% of young people voted in 2018*. Retrieved from https://civicyouth.org/new-national-youth-turnout-estimate-28-of-young-people-voted-in-2018/?cat_id=6

Twenge, J. M., Campbell, W. K., & Freeman, E. C. (2012). Generational differences in young adults' life goals, concern for others, and civic orientation, 1966–2009. *Journal of Personality and Social Psychology, 102*(5), 1045–1062.

Tynes, B. M., Garcia, E. L., Giang, M. T., & Coleman, N. E. (2011). The racial landscape of social networking sites: Forging identity, community, and civic engagement. *ISJLP, 7*(1), 71–100.

Valenzuela, S. (2013). Unpacking the use of social media for protest behavior: The roles of information, opinion expression, and activism. *American Behavioral Scientist, 57*(7), 920–942.

Valenzuela, S., Arriagada, A., & Scherman, A. (2014). Facebook, Twitter, and youth engagement: A quasi-experimental study of social media use and protest behavior using propensity score matching. *International Journal of Communication, 8*, 2046–2070.

Zerehi, S. (2014, August 19). Michael Brown's shooting in Ferguson lost on social media. *CBCnews*. Retrieved from https://www.cbc.ca/news/technology/michael-brown-s-shooting-in-ferguson-lost-on-social-media-1.2740014

ABOUT THE EDITORS

Ginnie Logan is an education practitioner-activist-researcher who is completing her PhD in Learning Sciences and Human Development at the University of Colorado-Boulder. Her research interests center on facilitating and creating emancipatory educational design through educational activism and public scholarship. Specifically, Ginnie utilizes critical race, feminist, and humananizing theoretical and methodological lenses to design learning environments and tools that redress harm, minimize opportunity gaps, and transfer power to the people. Through her scholarship, Ginnie is committed to developing models of praxis that result in emancipatory outcomes for Black girls, other minoritized youth, and practitioners committed to transformative education. Ginnie serves as the Executive Director of a non-profit organization called Big Hair, Bigger Dreams, a girls leadership organization designed around the experiences of Black girls. Formally, Ginnie was a middle school assistant principal, a teacher talent pipeline consultant to school districts nationwide, and high school teacher. She comes from a long tradition of African American women educators who leveraged education as a tool for change.

Janiece Mackey is a PhD candidate at the University of Denver in Higher Education with emphases in Public Policy and Curriculum and Instruction. Due to being one of a few Black folks within academic, political, and professional spaces, she created an organization entitled Young Aspiring Americans for Social and Political Activism (YAASPA) to provide a conduit for youth of color to become civically engaged in community and career. Due to her converging interests in education and policy, she has served as an adjunct

Black Girl Civics, pages 195–196
Copyright © 2020 by Information Age Publishing
All rights of reproduction in any form reserved.   **195**

faculty in Ethnic Studies and Political Science. She desires to deepen, further develop, and expand "healing praxis" for youth and professionals within the public service sector. Thus, Janiece's work and scholarship focuses on the nexus of racial identity development, civic engagement, and education.

ABOUT THE CONTRIBUTORS

Celicia Bell is a PhD candidate at the Florida State University (FSU) in curriculum and instruction with a major in English education. She has a bachelor's degree in English with a concentration in creative writing and a master's degree in English education, both from FSU. Her research interests include the professional preparation of English educators, in and out of school literacies of adolescents and young adults and positive cultural identity formation, and development of ways for nonprofit, community-based programs to better support public schools with after-school and mentoring programs. Celicia's 21-year professional career in the private sector and state government includes experience as a public affairs and public relations coordinator, technical editor and writer, educational policy analyst, community college adjunct English instructor, and project manager.

Jasmine Clayton is currently pursuing a Juris master's degree with a specialization in criminal law and justice at the Florida State University (FSU). She has a bachelor's degree in psychology and criminology (double major) from FSU. She has studied abroad in Valencia, Spain and worked as an undergraduate research assistant and a summer intern at a psychiatric hospital. Jasmine plans to earn a PhD in clinical psychology and work as a licensed psychologist, primarily engaging in forensic assessment and consultation. Her research interests lie within the intersection of psychology and the law. Jasmine wants to advocate for marginalized populations within the criminal justice system. She also writes creative fiction and hopes to add to the reading selection possibilities for minoritized readers.

Black Girl Civics, pages 197–201
Copyright © 2020 by Information Age Publishing
All rights of reproduction in any form reserved.

Sabrina J. Curtis is a doctoral student in the Graduate School of Education and Human Development at The George Washington University. She has research interests in culturally relevant curriculum, critical pedagogy, and African(a) gender theories. Sabrina uses Afrocentric and Black feminist epistemologies to explore the cultural and educational experiences of Black women and girls, and she is interested in developing humanities and literary-based approaches to examining gender equity in teaching for social justice. Before starting her PhD in education and inequality, Sabrina served as a lecturer in English, worked in government and on political campaigns, and cofounded a nonprofit organization whose mission is to connect youth in severely underserved communities with access to quality mentorship and exposure to a range of academic and career opportunities.

Julia Daniel is a PhD candidate in educational foundations, policy and practice at the University of Colorado Boulder. She is committed to community organizing, having done movement-building work for 15 years in Florida around issues of racial, gender, and economic justice. Her research interests include community schools, grassroots organizing, and social movement theory. She holds an BA in sociology from New College of Florida and an MA in urban education policy from Brown University.

Autumn Griffin is a third year student in teaching and learning, policy and leadership at the University of Maryland—College Park. Her research interests center on issues of multiple and digital literacies as they pertain to Black students. In particular, Autumn employs Black feminist and critical race theories to explore the literacies of Black girls both in and out of classrooms and hopes to use her research to influence policy related to literacy, race, and gender. Autumn hopes to amplify the voices of Black girls through her scholarship. Before returning to graduate school, Autumn was a teacher and teacher trainer. She has since served in multiple roles in education.

Jeanelle K. Hope is an Oakland, CA native and assistant professor of comparative race and ethnic studies at Texas Christian University. As a scholar-activist, her research and community-engaged work focuses on Afro-Asian solidarity, Black radicalism, Black girlhood, and the history of Blacks in the West.

Charlotte Jacobs is an adjunct assistant professor at the University of Pennsylvania Graduate School of Education. Her research interests focus on issues of identity development and gender in education concerning adolescent girls of color, teacher education and diversity, and youth participatory action research. Currently, Charlotte is the codirector of the Independent School Teaching Residency program at Penn GSE. Additionally, blending her work with independent schools and youth participatory action research, Charlotte is the research director of the Student Participatory Action Research Collaborative at the Center for the Study of Boys' and Girls' Lives (SPARC-CSBGL).

Island native, **Cassandra Jean** is a PhD student at Howard University in the Department of Sociology and Criminology, concentrating in social inequality, criminology, and research methodology. She has a background in public policy and administration, international relations, and criminal justice. Cassandra's research interests focus on the sociology of poverty and its relationship to federal environmental and housing policies, the sociology of suffering and its correlation to the economy and politics, and social and global stratification. With experience working alongside organizations like the National Park Service, the National Weather Service, and AARP, Cassandra intends to analyze avenues that can generate equitable environments for minorities and underserved populations, while understanding their decision-making, coping mechanisms, and social positions in society.

Kel Hughes Jones earned an EdD in metropolitan education from the University of Michigan–Dearborn in 2019. Her dissertation, "Black Narcissus: The Role of the Suburban Othermother," is a qualitative study of seven Black female educators employed in majority-White suburban school districts, and their experiences as othermothers. While at the university, she was a Center for the Education of Women Margaret Dow Towsley Scholar, a King-Chavez-Parks Future Faculty Fellow, and an Honors Scholar for the College of Education, Health, and Human Services. Her research interests include the ethic of care, othermothering, teacher recruitment and retention, and Black feminism and womanism in education.

Cierra Kaler-Jones is a doctoral student in minority and urban education in the Department of Teaching and Learning, Policy and Leadership at the University of Maryland——College Park. Her work examines how Black girls use arts-based practices, such as movement and music, as forms of expression, resistance, and identity development. At the center of her work is the examination of how, despite negative stereotypes, deficit-based perspectives, and the impact of structural and systemic racism and sexism, Black girls still experience and express childhood joy. As a dance teacher and choreographer, Cierra develops and delivers culturally affirming visual and performing arts curriculum as a strategy to teach Black girls about self-esteem, leadership, and social justice.

Stephanie Lindo is a University of Maryland alumni with her master's degree in minority and urban education. Her research interests are the lived intersectional experience of Black girls within the school to confinement pathways. Stephanie works strategically, efficiently, and thoroughly to influence and change environments to uphold more efficient and inclusive practices. She works to empower educators with the skills they need to prepare all of their students for success despite their race, ethnicity, social class, age, or primary language.

Dr. Tracie A. Lowe is a postdoctoral fellow at the University of Texas at Austin for IUPRA. Her research focuses on the experiences of Black students in higher education with a particular focus on Black women graduate students. Additionally, her research interests include issues of diversity, equity, and inclusion in higher education. Tracie holds a doctorate in educational leadership and policy from the University of Texas at Austin; a master's degree in educational administration and a bachelor's degree in interdisciplinary studies both from Texas A&M University.

Dana McCalla is a Long Island native and master's student in the Department of Sociology and Criminology at Howard University concentrating in social inequality, social stratification, and immigrant assimilation studies. With a background in cultural anthropology, Dana has a wide variety of research interests in the social sciences including ethnic identity formation, identity politics, women in social movements, and cultural globalization. She has had numerous experiences working in and on behalf of underserved communities through teaching, volunteering, and community leadership within organizations such as Teach for America, Urban Leaders Fellowship, and the National Park Service. Dana endeavors to expand the visibility of literature written by and about women of color in the field of sociology.

Alaina Neal-Jackson is a postdoctoral fellow in the School of Education at the University of Michigan, Ann Arbor. Her work is centered on race and gender in schools as per a larger interest in the health and welfare of Black students particularly, but not singularly, in underserved contexts. More specifically, drawing upon sociological frames and critical race and gender theories Dr. Neal-Jackson examines how schools, as social institutions, structure Black girls and women's experiences and opportunities, and in what ways this structuring reproduces social inequalities along raced, gendered, and classed lines.

Dr. Tiera Chantè Tanksley earned her PhD from the Graduate School of Education and Information Studies within UCLA's Urban Schooling program. Broadly, her research examines the intersectional impacts of race, gender, class, and age on the experiences of Black girls in media, technology, and education. Grounded in Black feminist technology studies and critical race theory, her robust research agenda sheds light on the ways Black girls intersect with and are intersected by media and technology systems as they attempt to navigate K–16 educational institutions. Designed in response to #BlackLivesMatter and the growing presence of racialized violence online, Dr. Tanksley's dissertation research examines the socio-academic consequences of witnessing viral Black death for the internet's most vocal and visible users: Black women and girls. Her newest strand of research examines the ways Girls of Color leverage computer science technologies, including virtual reality software, e-textiles, and robotics, to engage in political resistance within and beyond the school setting. Overall, Dr. Tanksley's scholarship responds to calls for more intersectional analyses of digital technology that can recognize the lived experiences, modes of resistance, and technological contributions of Black girls and women around the globe.

Annie Thomas is a Miami native and has been an active freedom fighter in her community since she was 12 years old. As a youth member of Power U Center and the Miami Workers Center, she has helped register 3,000 people to vote and raise community awareness, fought the School to Prison Pipeline, and advanced Restorative Justice. She also played a central role in the takeover of the Florida State Capital by the Dream Defenders following the acquittal of George Zimmerman. She guided organizing and political education workshops, helped develop language for Trayvon's Law, and along with other leaders met with Governor Rick Scott. She hopes to organize young people for public housing and is currently the Southern Regional organizer for Project South in Atlanta, GA.

Vajra M. Watson is a White woman from Berkeley, CA. She is the founder of Sacramento Area Youth Speaks (SAYS) and the UC Davis director of research and policy for equity. Her scholarship focuses on addressing and dismantling White supremacy as a daily practice inside classrooms (micro-level) as well as at the institutional level (macro-structural). She purposefully aims to use research in service of social change.